Berkeley's Principles and Dialogues

Cambridge Philosophical Texts in Context offers a new way of understanding and teaching the canonical texts in the history of philosophy. The purpose of the series is to allow students to comprehend the context in which these texts emerged by providing the primary materials that are their source and immediate intellectual background. These contextual texts are often neglected because they are obscure, unavailable in English, or both. Now this background source material will be available in convenient editions with helpful explanatory introductions and annotations. The series will thus enable teachers to enrich their teaching of the history of philosophy in ways hitherto impossible.

This volume sets Berkeley's philosophy in its historical context by providing selections from works that deeply influenced Berkeley as he formed his main doctrines; works that illuminate the philosophical climate in which those doctrines were formed; and works that display Berkeley's subsequent philosophical influence. The first category is represented by selections from Descartes, Malebranche, Bayle, and Locke; the second category includes extracts from such thinkers as Regius, Lanion, Arnauld, Lee, and Norris; while reactions to Berkeley, both positive and negative, are drawn from a wide range of thinkers – Leibniz, Baxter, Hume, Diderot, Voltaire, Reid, Kant, Herder, and Mill.

Cambridge Philosophical Texts in Context

General Editors:

John Cottingham (University of Reading)
Daniel Garber (University of Chicago)

Other books in series:

Descartes' *Meditations*, edited by Roger Ariew, John Cottingham, and Tom Sorell

Forthcoming:

Kant's *Groundwork of the Metaphysics of Morals*, edited by
J. B. Schneewind
Hume's *A Treatise of Human Nature*, edited by Kate Abramson

Berkeley's *Principles and Dialogues*

BACKGROUND SOURCE MATERIALS

Edited by
C. J. McCracken
Michigan State University
I. C. Tipton
University of Wales Swansea

CAMBRIDGE
UNIVERSITY PRESS

PUBLISHED BY THE PRESS SYNDICATE OF THE UNIVERSITY OF CAMBRIDGE
The Pitt Building, Trumpington Street, Cambridge, United Kingdom

CAMBRIDGE UNIVERSITY PRESS
The Edinburgh Building, Cambridge CB2 2RU, UK   http: //www.cup.cam.ac.uk
40 West 20th Street, New York, NY 10011-4211, USA   http: //www.cup.org
10 Stamford Road, Oakleigh, Melbourne 3166, Australia
Ruiz de Alarcón 13, 28014 Madrid, Spain

© Cambridge University Press 2000

First published 2000

Printed in the United States of America

Typeface Janson Text 10.25/13 pt.   *System* DeskTopPro$_{/UX}$ [BV]

A catalog record for this book is available from the British Library.

Library of Congress Cataloging-in-Publication Data

Berkeley's Principles and Dialogues : backgrond source materials / edited by C.J.
McCracken, I.C. Tipton.
    p. cm. – (Cambridge philosophical texts in context)
    Includes bibliographical references and index,
    ISBN 0-521-49681-0 (hbk) – ISBN 0-521-49806-6 (pbk.)
    1. Berkeley, George, 1685–1753. Treatise concerning the principles of human
knowledge. 2. Berkeley, George, 1685–1753. Three dialogues between Hylas and
Philonous. 3. Knowledge, Theory of. 4. Idealism. 5. Soul. I. McCracken, Charles J.
(Charles James), 1933–   II. Tipton, I. C. III. Series.

B1334 .B47 2000
192 – dc21   99-059435

ISBN 0 521 49681 0 hardback
ISBN 0 521 49806 6 paperback

Contents

Preface

The selections in this volume have been chosen because they either illuminate the background from which Berkeley's philosophical views emerged or illustrate the reactions those views provoked, particularly in the eighteenth century. The explanatory commentaries that accompany the selections aim to show their relation to Berkeley's views. We have modernized the spelling and punctuation of the selections from Henry Lee, John Norris, Arthur Collier, Andrew Baxter, and Samuel Johnson; those from Locke, Hume, Reid, and Mill follow various editions of their works. In the case of selections from works not originally in English, the translations we have used are noted; translations not attributed to others are our own.

For permission to reprint certain materials, we are grateful to the following: Thomas M. Lennon and Paul J. Olscamp, for extracts from Malebranche's *Search after Truth*; Edwin Mellen Press, for extracts from Arnauld's *On True and False Ideas*; Simon and Schuster, for an extract from Arnauld's *The Art of Thinking*; the editor of *Hermathena*, for extracts from Berkeley's letters to Le Clerc; Oxford University Press, for extracts from Hume's *A Treatise of Human Nature* and *An Enquiry concerning Human Understanding*; Peter Gay, for an extract from Voltaire's *Philosophical Dictionary*; and Hackett Publishing Company, Inc., for extracts from Bayle's *Historical and Critical Dictionary* and Kant's *Prolegomena to Any Future Metaphysics*.

For quotations from Berkeley, we have used *The Works of George Berkeley, Bishop of Cloyne*, edited by A. A. Luce and T. E. Jessop (Edinburgh: Thomas Nelson, 1948–57), nine volumes. References to *Works*, followed by the volume number, are to this edition. The following abbreviations have also been used:

Principles, or *PHK*, for *A Treatise concerning the Principles of Human Knowledge*;

Dialogues, or *Three Dialogues*, for *Three Dialogues between Hylas and Philonous*;

PC for Berkeley's notebooks, the *Philosophical Commentaries*.

Quotations from the *Philosophical Commentaries* preserve Berkeley's idiosyncratic punctuation, capitalization, etc.

The responsibility for such flaws as there may be in our translations, commentaries, or notes is of course entirely ours. However, there would have been more had it not been for generous help and advice we received from others. We therefore gratefully acknowledge advice or assistance we received from, among others, Anne and Bruce Freed, Rolf George, Douglas Jesseph, Michael Koppisch, Manfred Kuehn, Thomas Lennon, John Rauk, David Raynor, and Claudia Schmidt. We are particularly indebted to Katherine McCracken, who read the successive drafts of the manuscript and who made many valuable editorial suggestions. She and Diana Tipton have been supportive at every stage.

Introduction

The selections in Part One of this book have been chosen either because they are from works that had some influence on George Berkeley during the period he was forming the views he presented in his *Principles of Human Knowledge* (1710) and *Three Dialogues between Hylas and Philonous* (1713), or because they illustrate the philosophical climate in which his views developed. The selections in Part Two, with one exception, exemplify the reception, positive and negative, given to those views during the eighteenth century – a reception that helped shape some of the ways of viewing Berkeley's philosophy that are still prevalent. As the selections are accompanied by individual commentaries, this introduction aims only to give an overview of the book.

Like every philosopher, Berkeley arrived at his views in a particular intellectual context. The assumptions he made, the problems he grappled with, and the doctrines he developed cannot be fully understood unless that context is taken into account. Many of his central doctrines – that we cannot form abstract ideas, that matter does not exist, that spirits are the only true causes, that God immediately produces our sensations – have a history that antedates Berkeley, and in Part One we have presented selections that are part of that history. Among the most extensive are those from Descartes' *Meditations*, Malebranche's *Search after Truth*, and Locke's *Essay concerning Human Understanding*, works we know, from his notebooks, Berkeley had studied when working out his chief doctrines, and from Bayle's *Dictionary*, which is widely thought to have had a strong impact on Berkeley, though he mentions Bayle only twice in his notebooks. The selections from Antoine Arnauld, Henry Lee, and John Norris are from works we think it likely Berkeley either had read or had some knowledge of. We also include selections from works by Henricus Regius, Pierre de Lanion, and Jean Brunet. While it is unlikely that Berkeley had read these works, they illustrate some phases in the seventeenth-century debate about whether, or how, we can know that there is an external world. The last selections in Part One are from Arthur Collier's *Clavis Universalis*, in which Collier defends a view strikingly close to Berkeley's. Collier belongs in Part One because, although he did not publish his views until 1713, three years after Berkeley's *Principles*, he appears to have arrived at them quite independently of, and indeed before, Berkeley.

Selections in this book are arranged by author, not by topic, but the same topic is often taken up by several authors. The following are probably the most important topics in Part One.

   1. The existence of the external or material world. A recurring theme in Part One is whether, or how, we can know that the material world exists.[1] The question will first be met in Descartes, who made it a central problem but who claimed to prove that bodies exist. A number of his successors were not convinced by his proof. Thus Regius and Malebranche grant that it is highly probable that there are bodies but deny that, apart from revelation, we can establish beyond doubt that there are, while Lanion questions whether philosophy can show it even *probable* that bodies exist. In Arnauld we find a new defense of the Cartesian proof of the existence of bodies. Bayle, however, plumbing the depths of skepticism, argues that Cartesianism has itself undermined belief in the existence of bodies, a belief that he tries to undermine even further. Locke claims that our senses themselves make the existence of bodies known to us, but Norris argues that neither the senses nor reason nor revelation can establish their existence with certainty. Finally, Collier, strongly influenced by Malebranche and Norris, concludes – apparently independently of Berkeley – that there is no external world. For Collier, "all matter, body, extension, &c. exists *in*, or in dependence on, mind."

   2. Abstract ideas. Berkeley held that belief in abstract ideas was a central source of philosophical error in his predecessors, and in several selections we meet some of their views about this topic. Malebranche, although himself committed to what, for Berkeley, were illegitimate abstractions, will be found decrying certain "disordered abstractions" of the mind that he traces back to the idea of "being in general". This idea, according to Malebranche, is indeed always present to our minds – yet, precisely because of this, philosophers have been able, he thinks, to suppose that they are talking sensibly even if the words they use stand for no particular things at all. An example he gives is the Schoolmen's talk of *matter* as something from which they imagine *every* property, even extension, might be "stripped away". In Arnauld we meet an account of abstraction close to one that Berkeley himself will later regard as acceptable – namely, abstraction as selective attention. We also include substantial extracts from Locke on abstract ideas, for Berkeley's attack focused on that account, and criticisms of Locke's account offered by Henry Lee in a work published eight years before the *Principles*. Some of Lee's objections are similar to Berkeley's, and we think that they may have influenced Berkeley.

3. Primary and secondary qualities. Berkeley was highly critical of this distinction, which is the topic of several selections in Part One. Descartes, in particular, contrasts our supposedly clear understanding of what came to be known as the "primary" qualities with our obscure understanding of the "secondary"; while Locke, offering what is generally regarded as the classic defense of the distinction, urges that our ideas of the primary qualities *resemble* qualities in the objects, but that our ideas of qualities such as colors, sounds, and odors do not. Even before Berkeley, however, the distinction was under pressure. Malebranche had embraced it, but had held that our senses mislead us about *both* kinds of quality, for how both primary and secondary qualities appear varies from perceiver to perceiver; and Bayle had found in this consideration grounds for denying that *any* qualities exist independently of perceivers. This was an argument that Berkeley would take up and use.

4. Ideas. The concept of "idea" is of central importance for Berkeley, as it had been for several thinkers he had studied, including Descartes, Malebranche, and Locke. A. A. Luce, a leading Berkeley scholar, held that Berkeley started out with a Lockean notion of "idea", but that from his study of Malebranche he "learned to idealize the thing and to spiritualize the idea."[2] Selections from Malebranche and Locke illustrate their uses of "idea", while, in other selections, Arnauld criticizes Malebranche's use of "idea" and Henry Lee criticizes Locke's use of that term.

5. The nature of the mind. This topic was widely debated in the seventeenth century. Theories of the mind ranged from Descartes' doctrine that the mind is an incorporeal substance to Hobbes's view that the notion of an incorporeal substance is unintelligible and that the mind is really just certain motions in the body, with Locke occupying an intermediate position according to which we cannot determine, with certainty, whether the mind is an immaterial substance or whether God has "given to some systems of matter, fitly disposed, a power to perceive and think."[3] Berkeley took a definite position here, agreeing with Descartes, against Locke, both that we can *know* that the human mind is an incorporeal substance and that it always thinks. On the other hand, like Malebranche, Berkeley held that we have no "idea" of the mind. At one stage, this had even led him to suppose that the mind is unknowable (*PC* 576a, 701), although he soon decided that it can be known, but not by way of idea. Selections from Descartes and Malebranche provide some of the background to Berkeley's doctrine of the mind.

Other topics met with in Part One include Malebranche's Occasionalism (a doctrine Berkeley in part agreed with, for, like Malebranche, he rejected *corporeal* causes, yet in part disagreed with, for he held that *finite* spirits as well as God are true causes), and Locke's observations on the "*idea* of the *substance* of matter." To Berkeley's mind, if material substances are never the true cause of anything, God would have had no *reason* to create them "since God might have done every thing as well without them" (*PHK* §53); while Locke's recognition that "of *substance*, we have no *idea* of what it is" clearly played a role in encouraging Berkeley to drop the notion of "material substance" altogether.

The selections in Part Two have been chosen because they represent notable reactions to Berkeley's philosophy. All but the last come from the eighteenth century. The earliest are opinions communicated to Berkeley in private correspondence soon after the *Principles* first appeared. They are followed by early reviews of the *Principles* and *Dialogues*. There are selections from a wide range of eighteenth-century figures, some of them well known in their day but now largely forgotten, like Andrew Baxter, Pierre-Louis Maupertuis, and Samuel Johnson of Connecticut, others – Hume and Reid, Voltaire and Diderot, Kant and Herder – among the foremost philosophers of that century.

In Part Two we see Berkeley's reputation in the making and meet various ways of viewing him. Many in his own day regarded him as a follower of Malebranche, who – with a consistency that Malebranche lacked – drew the immaterialist conclusion from Malebranche's own principles. Some took him to be an "egoist", that is, a solipsist – or at least someone whose doctrine leads inexorably to egoism. He was also sometimes viewed as a skeptic pretending to oppose skepticism, or else as one who embraced a position that entailed skepticism but who failed to see that it did. Although, with the passage of time, it became rare to classify Berkeley as a Malebranchean, an egoist, or a skeptic, some of the thinking behind these ways of viewing him has found more recent defenders. For example, the importance of Malebranche's influence on Berkeley has been widely recognized in recent decades, as scholars have become increasingly unhappy with the notion that philosophers of the seventeenth and eighteenth centuries can be neatly divided into "Rationalists" and "Empiricists". And the notion that Berkeley's principles *should* have led him to solipsism, or at least to the view that he was alone in the universe with God, has also met with some more recent support.

One early way of classifying Berkeley that was to become virtually canonical was as the quintessential idealist who reduces everything to the mind. In 1724, the influential German philosopher Christian Wolff cited Berkeley as one of the two chief "idealists" (the other was Arthur Collier), and others subsequently also applied this label to him, most notably Kant, who pronounced Berkeley's position "dogmatic idealism", which Kant was eager to distinguish from his own "critical idealism". There were very few in the eighteenth century, apart from Herder, who thought that there was any sense in which Berkeley could be called a "realist". By contrast, some twentieth-century scholars *have* argued that Berkeley was really a kind of commonsense realist.[4]

One thing readers may be surprised to find is that, while a number in the eighteenth century associated Berkeley's position with Malebranche's, no one in our selections except Thomas Reid suggests that Berkeley is the intellectual heir of Locke. Today, every student of the history of philosophy is familiar with the view that there was a sort of linear development involving three great "British Empiricists", leading from Locke through Berkeley to Hume. That view had scarcely more than begun to emerge even late in the eighteenth century. Locke, Berkeley, and Hume did not call themselves "empiricists", and they were not so described by their contemporaries. Nor does Berkeley ever explicitly mention Locke, even as an opponent, in the *Principles* or the *Dialogues*, except in the Introduction to the former for his account of abstract ideas. It should be remembered, too, that admiration for Locke was enormous at a time when Berkeley was usually regarded as an exponent of an absurd position. It is therefore perhaps hardly surprising that the view that Berkeley was working out the implications of Locke's "way of ideas" was one that surfaced rather late. Perhaps the first to enunciate it was Reid, who observed that "Mr Locke had taught us that all the immediate objects of human knowledge are ideas in the mind. Bishop Berkeley, proceeding upon this foundation, demonstrated, very easily, that there is no material world." Hume in turn, according to Reid, "adopts the theory of ideas in its full extent; and, in consequence, shews that there is neither matter nor mind in the universe." It was only in a later period, however, that the notion became quite common that Berkeley was essentially the middle man in a Locke–Berkeley–Hume triumvirate, although early in the nineteenth century Hegel suggested something of this view. In his influential lectures on the history of philosophy (first given at Jena in 1805), Hegel claimed that the "subjective idealism" of Berkeley "has before it the standpoint of Locke, and it proceeds directly from him. For we saw that to Locke the source of truth is experience, or Being as perceived." Hegel went on to describe Hume's skepticism as arising out of the views of Locke and Berkeley, with the result that "Hume really completed the system of Locke."[5] (As already noted, the now familiar view of the history of British philosophy, which this perhaps suggests, has lately had many critics, and, arguably, it never had the universal and unqualified approbation of serious scholars.)[6]

In Berkeley's own time, much of the reaction to the *Principles* and *Dialogues* was hostile, and relatively few took the arguments in them at all seriously. A quite common attitude was that his views were too preposterous to merit refutation. However, there were some who, while firmly rejecting Berkeley's views, did at least undertake to argue against them. For example, an early reviewer of the *Dialogues* sought to answer Berkeley's attempt to prove the mind–dependence of the primary qualities by objecting that one cannot infer, for instance, that solidity is mind–dependent from the fact that how hard something feels varies from perceiver to perceiver. Solidity, the reviewer urges, is not hardness, but that property in one body that prevents another from occupying the same space. Andrew Baxter, who offered the first sustained critique of the *Principles*, although sometimes misinterpreting Berkeley, also makes serious points. Thus Baxter argues, for example, that Berkeley unjustifiably conflates sensations with the *objects* of perception, that he has no more reason for supposing that the only perceivable things are things actually perceived than one would have for supposing that the only combustible things are things actually on fire, and that he has deprived himself of grounds for believing in the existence of other minds.

Berkeley was to be taken more seriously in Scotland than he was elsewhere in Britain, and three Scots – Baxter, Hume, and Reid – are represented in our volume. Hume praised Berkeley's account of general ideas as "one of the greatest and most valuable discoveries" of the day; further, his judgment on the force of Berkeley's allegedly skeptical arguments – they provide "the best lessons of scepticism, which are to be found either among the ancient or modern philosophers" – amounts, in its way, to praise, given that Hume was clearly some sort of skeptic himself. Thomas Reid, for his part, writing *after* Hume, looks at Berkeley from a very different perspective. Because Reid thinks Berkeley's denial of a material world is unanswerable *if* it is supposed – as, according to Reid, Berkeley's predecessors *had* indeed supposed – that the objects of human knowledge are "ideas", and because he thinks this common assumption is false, Reid is able to combine a clear respect for Berkeley's significance as a philosopher with an almost complete rejection of his views.

It would thus be quite wrong to suppose that all eighteenth-century reactions to Berkeley were disdainful. Probably only the colonial American Samuel Johnson can be called a disciple of Berkeley, but the French philosopher Pierre-Louis Maupertuis noted that some of his own views were close to those "a celebrated man, Mr. Berkeley," had taken pains to establish "in a considerable work, *Dialogues between Hylas and Philonous*", while some others – Boullier and Bonnet among French speakers, Hamann and Herder among the Germans – held Berkeley in some measure of esteem, although they rejected his doctrines. Even Kant, who was eager to distance his "critical idealism" from Berkeley's "visionary idealism", concedes that, if the choice had to be made between that and "transcendental realism", one could not "blame the good Berkeley for degrading bodies to mere illusion." Much earlier, Leibniz had written in his copy of the *Principles* that "much in this is right", although that judgment he at once heavily qualified.

The final extract in Part Two dates from much later than the others. It comes from an 1871 review of the first complete edition of Berkeley's works, written by John Stuart Mill – the foremost defender of empiricism in *nineteenth*-century Britain. The tone of this review is far different from that of the early reviews of the *Principles* and *Dialogues*, published over a century and a half earlier. Mill, who saw himself as an intellectual heir of Berkeley, even though he rejected the theological doctrines dearest to Berkeley's heart, offers us yet another perspective on him, now as the forerunner of the doctrine known as "phenomenalism". Mill esteemed Berkeley so highly that, even after naming such philosophical giants as Plato, Descartes, and Kant, he proclaimed Berkeley "the one of greatest philosophic genius."

Mill doubtless had an exaggerated view of Berkeley's genius, yet Berkeley is indisputably an important thinker who had a significant influence on subsequent developments in philosophy. The present volume will have served its purpose if it locates Berkeley's philosophy in its historical context, showing some of the roots from which it sprang, and considering some of the reactions that it provoked and that helped shape subsequent perceptions of Berkeley. It has not, of course, been possible to include, in a single volume, all the texts relevant to this story. It has been necessary to omit selections from some of Berkeley's predecessors who might have been included, and it has not been possible to give *every* relevant text even from such thinkers as Descartes, Malebranche, Locke, and Bayle.

It has been equally impossible to include all the noteworthy eighteenth-century responses to Berkeley. We have excluded, for example, James Beattie's attack, which – although stronger on rhetoric than on logic – was widely read, Joseph Priestley's defense of Berkeley against Beattie's and Reid's strictures, and reactions to Berkeley from such notable figures as John Wesley, the Chevalier Andrew Ramsay, A. R. J. Turgot, and Henry Home (Lord Kames).[7] Nor have we attempted to cover every topic addressed in the *Principles* and *Dialogues*. That is particularly true of Berkeley's views about mathematics and physics, for although these subjects are touched on in the *Principles*, Berkeley sets out his views about them more fully elsewhere, especially in *De Motu* and the *Analyst*, and most of the replies to his views about mathematics were aimed at the *Analyst*.[8] Readers interested in seeing other eighteenth-century responses to Berkeley should consult the valuable collection edited by David Berman, and they will find a detailed account of the early reception of Berkeley's philosophy in an excellent monograph by Harry Bracken.[9]

Notes

1. The terms "external world", "natural world", "material world", and "bodies" were all used to pick out the subject of this discussion. Although these terms do not range over exactly the same things ("external world" is sometimes taken to include both bodies and other minds), our knowledge of the existence of material things was at the center of the debate.
2. A. A. Luce, *Berkeley and Malebranche* (Oxford: Oxford University Press, 1934), p. 70.
3. See Locke, *Essay*, Book 4, Chapter 3, §6. The considerable furor that this suggestion caused at the time is documented in John W. Yolton, *Thinking Matter: Materialism in Eighteenth-Century Britain* (Oxford: Basil Blackwell, 1983), ch. 1 and *passim*; cf. Yolton's *Locke and French Materialism* (Oxford: Clarendon Press, 1991).
4. See below, p. 294, note 8.
5. *Hegel's Lectures on the History of Philosophy*, trans. E. S. Haldane and F. H. Simson (London: Routledge & Kegan Paul, 1974), vol. 3, pp. 364, 370–71.

6. For a vigorous attack on the view that Locke, Berkeley, and Hume constitute a unified movement, and in particular one that clearly separates them from the "Continental Rationalists", see Louis E. Loeb, *From Descartes to Hume: Continental Metaphysics and the Development of Modern Philosophy* (Ithaca: Cornell University Press, 1981).

7. Wesley's thoughtful comments on Berkeley's *Dialogues*, which he read while still at Christ Church, Oxford, will be found in a letter to his mother dated 22nd November 1725 – see *The Works of John Wesley*, editor in chief F. Baker (Oxford: Clarendon Press, 1975–), vol. 25, pp. 186–87. Turgot criticized Berkeley in the article "Existence" in the *Encyclopédie* and in two letters of 1750, first published in his *Oeuvres* (Paris 1808), vol. 3, pp. 136–54. Relevant material from Beattie, Priestley, Henry Home, and Ramsay is reprinted in Berman's collection (see note 9).

8. For a list of those replies, see T. E. Jessop, *A Bibliography of George Berkeley*, 2nd ed. (The Hague: Martinus Nijhoff, 1973), pp. 74–75.

9. David Berman, *George Berkeley: Eighteenth-Century Responses* (New York: Garland, 1989), 2 vols.; Harry M. Bracken, *The Early Reception of Berkeley's Immaterialism: 1710–1733*, revised edition (The Hague: Martinus Nijhoff, 1965).

PART ONE

The Background to Berkeley's Philosophy

ONE

René Descartes

The influence of Descartes can be seen in the work of virtually every important philosopher from the middle of the seventeenth to the middle of the eighteenth century. Berkeley was no exception. Descartes' name, it is true, is not mentioned until far into the second of the young Berkeley's philosophical notebooks (the *Philosophical Commentaries*), when in a flurry of entries he recorded some of his reflections about Descartes' *Meditations on First Philosophy* and Hobbes's *Objections* to the *Meditations*.[1] It is also true that Berkeley does not seem to have formed a high opinion of the *Meditations*. In a letter to Molyneux of 1709 he noted two inconsistencies that he had found in it, adding that "it would take up too much Time to observe to You all the like Blunders that appeard to Me when I formerly read that Treatise."[2] Nonetheless, it was Descartes who had focused the attention of subsequent thinkers on the issue of whether we can know that there is a material world, and it was Descartes who had been the leading defender of the doctrine that the mind is an incorporeal substance whose nature consists in thinking, both issues of central importance in the development of Berkeley's metaphysics. Without Descartes, the philosophical climate in which that metaphysics developed would have been very different. It is with Descartes, therefore, that we begin.[3]

1. Descartes on the Existence of Bodies

Berkeley was to deny that there is a material world, but, among modern philosophers, it was Descartes who first made the existence of such a world an issue.[4] Descartes granted that it was not an issue to be taken seriously in ordinary life, but he stressed that it *must* be taken seriously *by the metaphysician* if the sum of human knowledge, including what we now call physics, is to be set on a sure foundation. Consequently, in the following passage, from the first of his *Meditations on First Philosophy* (1641), Descartes engages in a dialogue with himself in which he considers a series of arguments that become increasingly powerful, leading us, in stages, from the thought that the senses sometimes mislead us to the radical conclusion that they provide no firm ground for supposing that there is an external world. For Descartes, this results in a *temporary* acceptance of a skeptical position from which he will eventually escape. However, as we shall see later, many were unimpressed by his answer to the challenge he himself had so forcefully raised.

Whatever I have up till now accepted as most true I have acquired either from the senses or through the senses. But from time to time I have found that the senses deceive, and it is prudent never to trust completely those who have deceived us even once.

Yet although the senses occasionally deceive us with respect to objects which are very small or in the distance, there are many other beliefs about which doubt is quite impossible, even though they are derived from the senses – for example, that I am here, sitting by the fire, wearing a winter dressing-gown, holding this piece of paper in my hands, and so on. Again, how could it be denied that these hands or this whole body are mine? Unless perhaps I were to liken myself to madmen, whose brains are so damaged by the persistent vapours of melancholia that they firmly maintain they are kings when they are paupers, or say they are dressed in purple when they are naked, or that their heads are made of earthenware, or that they are pumpkins, or made of glass. But such people are insane, and I would be thought equally mad if I took anything from them as a model for myself.

A brilliant piece of reasoning! As if I were not a man who sleeps at night, and regularly has all the same experiences while asleep as madmen do when awake – indeed sometimes even more improbable ones. How often, asleep at night, am I convinced of just such familiar events – that I am here in my dressing-gown, sitting by the fire – when in fact I am lying undressed in bed! Yet at the moment my eyes are certainly wide awake when I look at this piece of paper; I shake my head and it is not asleep; as I stretch out and feel my hand I do so deliberately, and I know what I am doing. All this would not happen with such distinctness to someone asleep. Indeed! As if I did not remember other occasions when I have been tricked by exactly similar thoughts while asleep! As I think about this more carefully, I see plainly that there are never any sure signs by means of which being awake can be distinguished from being asleep. The result is that I begin to feel dazed, and this very feeling only reinforces the notion that I may be asleep.

Suppose then that I am dreaming, and that these particulars – that my eyes are open, that I am moving my head and stretching out my hands – are not true. Perhaps, indeed, I do not even have such hands or such a body at all. Nonetheless, it must surely be admitted that the visions which come in sleep are like paintings, which must have been fashioned in the likeness of things that are real, and hence that at least these general kinds of things – eyes, head, hands and the body as a whole – are things which are not imaginary but are real and exist. For even when painters try to create sirens and satyrs with the most extraordinary bodies, they cannot give them natures which are new in all respects; they simply jumble up the limbs of different animals. Or if perhaps they manage to think up something so new that nothing remotely similar has ever been seen before – something which is therefore completely ficti- tious and unreal – at least the colours used in the composition must be real. By similar reasoning, although these general kinds of things – eyes, head, hands and so on – could be imaginary, it must at least be admitted that certain other even simpler and more universal things are real. These are as it were the real colours from which we form all the images of things, whether true or false, that occur in our thought.

This class appears to include corporeal nature in general, and its extension; the shape of extended things; the quantity, or size and number of these things; the place in which they may exist, the time through which they may endure, and so on.

So a reasonable conclusion from this might be that physics, astron- omy, medicine, and all other disciplines which depend on the study of composite things, are doubtful; while arithmetic, geometry and other subjects of this kind, which deal only with the simplest and most general things, regardless of whether they really exist in nature or not, contain something certain and indubitable. For whether I am awake or asleep, two and three added together are five, and a square has no more than four sides. It seems impossible that such transparent truths should incur any suspicion of being false.

And yet firmly rooted in my mind is the long-standing opinion that there is an omnipotent God who made me the kind of creature that I am. How do I know that he has not brought it about that there is no earth, no sky, no extended thing, no shape, no size, no place, while at the same time ensuring that all these things appear to me to exist just as they do now? What is more, since I sometimes believe that others go astray in cases where they think they have the most perfect knowledge, may I not similarly go wrong every time I add two and three or count the sides of a square, or in some even simpler matter, if that is imaginable? But perhaps God would not have allowed me to be deceived in this way, since he is said to be supremely good. But if it were inconsistent with his goodness to have created me such that I am deceived all the time, it would seem equally foreign to his goodness to allow me to be deceived even occasionally; yet this last assertion cannot be made.

Perhaps there may be some who would prefer to deny the existence of so powerful a God rather than believe that everything else is uncertain. Let us not argue with them, but grant them that everything said about God is a fiction. According to their supposition, then, I have arrived at my present state by fate or chance or a continuous chain of events, or by some other means; yet since deception and error seem to be imperfections, the less powerful they make my original cause, the more likely it is that I am so imperfect as to be deceived all the time. I have no answer to these arguments, but am finally compelled to admit that there is not one of my former beliefs about which a doubt may not properly be raised; and this is not a flippant or ill-considered conclusion, but is based on powerful and well thought-out reasons. So in future I must withhold my assent from these former beliefs just as carefully as I would from obvious falsehoods, if I want to discover any certainty.

But it is not enough merely to have noticed this; I must make an effort to remember it. My habitual opinions keep coming back, and, despite my wishes, they capture my belief, which is as it were bound over to them as a result of long occupation and the law of custom. I shall never get out of the habit of confidently assenting to these opinions, so long as I suppose them to be what in fact they are, namely highly probable opinions – opinions which, despite the fact that they are in a sense doubtful, as has just been shown, it is still much more reasonable to believe than to deny. In view of this, I think it will be a good plan to turn my will in completely the opposite direction and deceive myself, by pretending for a time that these former opinions are utterly false and imaginary. I shall do this until the weight of preconceived opinion is counter-balanced and the distorting influence of habit no longer prevents my judgement from perceiving things correctly. In the meantime, I know that no danger or error will result from my plan, and that I cannot possibly go too far in my distrustful attitude. This is because the task now in hand does not involve action but merely the acquisition of knowledge.

I will suppose therefore that not God, who is supremely good and the source of truth, but rather some malicious demon of the utmost power and cunning has employed all his energies in order to deceive me. I shall think that the sky, the air, the earth, colours, shapes, sounds and all external things are merely the delusions of dreams which he has devised to ensnare my judgement.[5] I shall consider myself as not having hands or eyes, or flesh, or blood or senses, but as falsely believing that I have all these things. I shall stubbornly and firmly persist in this meditation; and, even if it is not in my power to know any truth, I shall at least do what is in my power, that is, resolutely guard against assenting to any falsehoods, so that the deceiver, however powerful and cunning he may be, will be unable to impose on me in the slightest degree. But this is an arduous undertaking, and a kind of laziness brings me back to normal life. I am like a prisoner who is enjoying an imaginary freedom while asleep; as he begins to suspect that he is asleep, he dreads being woken up, and goes along with the pleasant illusion as long as he can. In the same way, I happily slide back into my old opinions and dread being shaken out of them, for fear that my peaceful sleep may be followed by hard labour when I wake, and that I shall have to toil not in the light, but amid the inextricable darkness of the problems I have now raised.[6]

In *Meditations* II to V, Descartes undertook to prove the following: that *he* exists as a mind or "thinking thing"; that God – a supremely perfect being – exists; and that *if* bodies exist, they must be extended things. He also claimed to prove that anything we clearly and distinctly perceive must be true. In *Meditation* VI he tries to establish that there is a material world. Here he argues that it is certainly *possible* that external objects exist, for God can create anything we can clearly and distinctly conceive, and (as geometry shows) we can clearly and distinctly conceive things that are ordered in three dimensions. He then argues that it is *probable* that they exist, for the most likely explanation of the fact that our imagination can form images of extended things is that our minds are united to bodies. Finally, however, he argues that it is *certain* that external objects exist, for he has a great propensity to believe that his sensations come from such objects, and God has provided him with no way of discovering this belief to be false. Since God is no deceiver, and will not allow his creatures to err if they use their faculties aright, we

can be sure that material objects exist. The initial skepticism about
the existence of a material world has thus been countered, but, of
course, only as a consequence of proving that there is a non-
deceiving God. The most important passage reads as follows:

Now there is in me a passive faculty of sensory perception, that is, a
faculty for receiving and recognizing the ideas of sensible objects; but I
could not make use of it unless there was also an active faculty, either in
me or in something else, which produced or brought about these ideas.
But this faculty cannot be in me, since clearly it presupposes no intellectual act on my part, and the ideas in question are produced without my
cooperation and often even against my will. So the only alternative is
that it is in another substance distinct from me – a substance which
contains either formally or eminently all the reality which exists objectively in the ideas produced by this faculty (as I have just noted). This
substance is either a body, that is, a corporeal nature, in which case it
will contain formally <and in fact> everything which is to be found
objectively <or representatively> in the ideas; or else it is God, or some
creature more noble than a body, in which case it will contain eminently
whatever is to be found in the ideas. But since God is not a deceiver, it
is quite clear that he does not transmit the ideas to me either directly
from himself, or indirectly, via some creature which contains the objective reality of the ideas not formally but only eminently. For God has
given me no faculty at all for recognizing any such source for these
ideas; on the contrary, he has given me a great propensity to believe that
they are produced by corporeal things. So I do not see how God could
be understood to be anything but a deceiver if the ideas were transmitted
from a source other than corporeal things. It follows that corporeal
things exist. They may not all exist in a way that exactly corresponds
with my sensory grasp of them, for in many cases the grasp of the senses
is very obscure and confused. But at least they possess all the properties
which I clearly and distinctly understand, that is, all those which, viewed
in general terms, are comprised within the subject-matter of pure mathematics.[7]

2. Descartes on the Mind as a Substance

Berkeley's account of minds ("spirits") is sketchy, but he is definite
that minds are substances (*PHK* §89), and – unlike Descartes, for

whom there is also material substance – that there is no substance other than minds (*PHK* §7). Berkeley also holds that the existence of a mind consists in perceiving and willing (*PC* 429–429a), and hence that the mind always thinks (*PHK* §98), and that the mind is naturally immortal (*PHK* §141). In making these claims, Berkeley was taking a definite position about matters much debated by his seventeenth-century predecessors, a position that was close to Descartes'.

The latter-day Scholastics, under Aquinas's influence, held that the mind and body are not two separate substances, but are instead constituents of a single substance: the mind (or soul) being the "form" of the substance, the body its "matter", in Aristotle's sense of "form" and "matter". Against this view, Descartes argued that although the mind and body are united, they are two distinct substances – the mind a thinking substance, the body an extended substance. While Berkeley was wholly to reject Descartes' claim that the body is a material substance, he shared his view that the mind is a spiritual substance and that its essence can be clearly known.

In the following passage, this time from the *Discourse on the Method* (1637), Descartes, beginning from his initial resolve to doubt all his former opinions, is led to the conclusion that he is a thinking substance.

For a long time I had observed . . . that in practical life it is sometimes necessary to act upon opinions which one knows to be quite uncertain just as if they were indubitable. But since I now wished to devote myself solely to the search for truth, I thought it necessary to do the very opposite and reject as if absolutely false everything in which I could imagine the least doubt, in order to see if I was left believing anything that was entirely indubitable. . . . But immediately I noticed that while I was trying thus to think everything false, it was necessary that I, who was thinking this, was something. And observing that this truth '*I am thinking, therefore I exist*' was so firm and sure that all the most extravagant suppositions of the sceptics were incapable of shaking it, I decided that I could accept it without scruple as the first principle of the philosophy I was seeking.

Next I examined attentively what I was. I saw that while I could pretend that I had no body and that there was no world and no place for me to be in, I could not for all that pretend that I did not exist. I saw on the contrary that from the mere fact that I thought of doubting the truth of other things, it followed quite evidently and certainly that I existed; whereas if I had merely ceased thinking, even if everything else I had ever imagined had been true, I should have had no reason to believe that I existed. From this I knew I was a substance whose whole essence or nature is simply to think, and which does not require any place, or depend on any material thing, in order to exist. Accordingly, this 'I' – that is, the soul by which I am what I am – is entirely distinct from the body, and indeed is easier to know than the body, and would not fail to be whatever it is, ever if the body did not exist.[8]

> In *Meditations* II and VI Descartes sets out more fully his argument for the claim that he (that is, his mind) is a substance, and is distinct from the body, but the argument there is more complex, and, although he does conclude in *Meditation* II that "I am . . . in the strict sense only a thing that thinks; that is, I am a mind, or intelligence, or intellect, or reason," it is only in *Meditation* VI, after he has proved the existence of God, that he completes his proof that "I am really distinct from my body." The crucial passage reads:

I know that everything which I clearly and distinctly understand is capable of being created by God so as to correspond exactly with my understanding of it. Hence the fact that I can clearly and distinctly understand one thing apart from another is enough to make me certain that the two things are distinct, since they are capable of being separated, at least by God. The question of what kind of power is required to bring about such a separation does not affect the judgement that the two things are distinct. Thus, simply by knowing that I exist and seeing at the same time that absolutely nothing else belongs to my nature or essence except that I am a thinking thing, I can infer correctly that my essence consists solely in the fact that I am a thinking thing. It is true that I may have (or, to anticipate, that I certainly have) a body that is very closely joined to me. But nevertheless, on the one hand I have a clear and distinct idea of myself, in so far as I am simply a thinking, non-extended thing; and on the other hand I have a distinct idea of body, in so far as this is simply an extended, non-thinking thing. And accordingly, it is certain that I am really distinct from my body, and can exist without it.[9]

> Descartes held that if a substance were to lose its essence, it would cease to exist. Thus, just as a body that ceased to be extended would

cease to be (since extension is the essence of body), so a mind that ceased to think would cease to be (since thought is the essence of mind). This was to provoke from Locke the rejoinder that a mind might very well exist without thinking – indeed in deep sleep it seems to do so. According to Locke, thought or the perception of ideas is "to the soul what motion is to the body: not its essence, but one of its operations."[10] As for the essence of mind, Locke thought we cannot discover what it is; we cannot even be sure that God "has not given to some systems of matter, fitly disposed, a power to perceive and think."[11] Berkeley here sided with Descartes, against Locke. The *esse* of mind is *percipere*, and it cannot exist without thought (*PC* 650–52 and 842, and *PHK* §98).

3. Ideas and Qualities

Descartes held that we are inclined to make a certain error about the properties of bodies: we suppose that our ideas of certain *sensed* qualities, such as those of color, taste, sound, and warmth, reliably inform us of features of the objects that we take to possess them. Instead, according to Descartes, the only qualities that are actually in bodies are various "modes" of extension, such as size, shape, motion, or rest. Thus, Descartes was committed, without using the terms, to the distinction between what Locke, following Robert Boyle, would later call "primary" and "secondary" qualities. The following selections from Descartes' *Principles of Philosophy* illustrate his distinction between these two kinds of qualities. (He here speaks chiefly of color, but his view was the same about other secondary qualities.)

PART ONE, §68. HOW TO DISTINGUISH WHAT WE
CLEARLY KNOW IN SUCH MATTERS FROM WHAT CAN
LEAD US ASTRAY

In order to distinguish what is clear in this connection from what is obscure, we must be very careful to note that pain and colour and so on are clearly and distinctly perceived when they are regarded merely as sensations or thoughts. But when they are judged to be real things existing outside our mind, there is no way of understanding what sort of things they are. If someone says he sees colour in a body or feels pain in a limb, this amounts to saying that he sees or feels something there of which he is wholly ignorant, or, in other words, that he does not know what he is seeing or feeling. Admittedly, if he fails to pay sufficient attention, he may easily convince himself that he has some knowledge of what he sees or feels, because he may suppose that it is something similar to the sensation of colour or pain which he experiences within himself. But if he examines the nature of what is represented by the sensation of colour or pain – what is represented as existing in the coloured body or the painful part – he will realize that he is wholly ignorant of it.

§69. WE KNOW SIZE, SHAPE AND SO FORTH IN A QUITE DIFFERENT WAY FROM THE WAY IN WHICH WE KNOW COLOURS, PAINS AND THE LIKE

This will be especially clear if we consider the wide gap between our knowledge of those features of bodies which we clearly perceive, as stated earlier [in §48], and our knowledge of those features which must be referred to the senses, as I have just pointed out. To the former class belong the size of the bodies we see, their shape, motion, position, duration, number and so on (by 'motion' I mean local motion: philosophers have imagined that there are other kinds of motion distinct from local motion, therefore only making the nature of motion less intelligible to themselves). To the latter class belong the colour in a body, as well as pain, smell, taste and so on. It is true that when we see a body we are just as certain of its existence in virtue of its having a visible colour as we are in virtue of its having a visible shape; but our knowledge of what it is for the body to have a shape is much clearer than our knowledge of what it is for it to be coloured.

§70. THERE ARE TWO WAYS OF MAKING JUDGEMENTS CONCERNING THE THINGS THAT CAN BE PERCEIVED BY THE SENSES: THE FIRST ENABLES US TO AVOID ERROR, WHILE THE SECOND ALLOWS US TO FALL INTO ERROR

It is clear, then, that when we say that we perceive colours in objects, this is really just the same as saying that we perceive something in the objects whose nature we do not know, but which produces in us a certain very clear and vivid sensation which we call the sensation of colour. But the way in which we make our judgement can vary very widely. As long as we merely judge that there is in the objects (that is, in the things, whatever they may turn out to be, which are the source of our sensations) something whose nature we do not know, then we avoid error; indeed, we are actually guarding against error, since the recognition that we are ignorant of something makes us less liable to make any rash judgement about it. But it is quite different when we suppose that we perceive colours in objects. Of course, we do not really know what it is that we are calling a colour; and we cannot find any intelligible resemblance between the colour which we suppose to be in objects and that which we experience in our sensation. But this is something we do not take account of; and, what is more, there are many other features, such as size, shape and number which we clearly perceive to be actually or at least possibly present in objects in a way exactly corresponding to our sensory perception or understanding. And so we easily fall into the error of judging that what is called colour in objects is something exactly like the colour of which we have sensory awareness; and we make the mistake of thinking that we clearly perceive what we do not perceive at all.

PART TWO, §4. THE NATURE OF BODY CONSISTS NOT IN WEIGHT, HARDNESS, COLOUR, OR THE LIKE, BUT SIMPLY IN EXTENSION

If we [rely on the intellect alone, not the senses], we shall perceive that the nature of matter, or body considered in general, consists not in its being something which is hard or heavy or coloured, or which affects the senses in any way, but simply in its being something which is extended in length, breadth and depth. For as regards hardness, our sensation tells us no more than that the parts of a hard body resist the motion of our hands when they come into contact with them. If, whenever our hands moved in a given direction, all the bodies in that area were to move away at the same speed as that of our approaching hands, we should never have any sensation of hardness. And since it is quite unintelligible to suppose that, if bodies did move away in this fashion, they would thereby lose their bodily nature, it follows that this nature cannot consist in hardness. By the same reasoning it can be shown that weight, colour, and all other such qualities that are perceived by the senses as being in corporeal matter, can be removed from it, while matter itself remains intact; it thus follows that its nature does not depend on any of these qualities.[12]

* * *

How much influence the reading of Descartes' works had on the development of Berkeley's metaphysical position is hard to determine, but in a sense the issue is unimportant. Even if Berkeley had not read him at all – and we know that he did read him – it would remain the case that Descartes was largely responsible for setting the philosophical agenda that made Berkeley's own philosophical position possible. High on that agenda was the issue of the very existence of an external, material reality. Although Descartes thought he had resolved it, we shall see that others did not agree.

Notes

1. See *Philosophical Commentaries*, entries 784 to 822, many of which have Descartes' or Hobbes's objections to Descartes in view. Berkeley had already commented on *Cogito ergo sum* at 738, and had mentioned the Cartesians in earlier entries. He had also referred to Descartes in two of his earliest writings, *Description of the Cave of Dunmore* and *De Ludo Algebraico*. He probably read the *Meditations* in a translation published by William Molyneux in 1680, which included Hobbes's objections.

2. *Works* VIII, p. 26. One of the supposed inconsistencies is that Descartes, as Berkeley reads him, says in *Meditation* II that the notion of a particular piece of wax is less clear than that of wax in general, *after* having observed that general conceptions are usually confused. Jean-Marie Beyssade has suggested to us that this charge (cf. *PC* 784) rests on a misreading of Descartes, based on Molyneux's translation. Arguing that the imagination does not reveal the nature of the wax, Descartes notes, "I am speaking of this particular piece of wax; the point is even clearer with regard to wax in general." In Molyneux's translation this becomes: "I speak of this particular wax, for of wax in general the notion is more clear."

3. Our selections are taken from *The Philosophical Writings of Descartes*, vols. 1 and 2, trans. J. Cottingham, R. Stoothoff, and D. Murdoch (Cambridge: Cambridge University Press, 1984–85).

4. Whether *any* philosophers before Descartes raised this question is a subject of debate among historians of philosophy. See M. F. Burnyeat, "Idealism and Greek Philosophy: What Descartes Saw and Berkeley Missed," *Philosophical Review* 91 (1982), pp. 3–40; and Leo Groarke, "Descartes' First Meditation: Something Old, Something New, Something Borrowed," *Journal of the History of Philosophy* 22 (1984), pp. 281–301.

5. With Berkeley the situation is interestingly different. He, in effect, gives to

God the role that Descartes at this point gives to the malicious demon. For Berkeley, it is God who produces sensations or "ideas" in our minds, without there being material objects, though (in Berkeley's view) this does not make God a deceiver. As Edward Craig puts it, it is "somewhat as if Descartes' demon had turned benevolent." *The Mind of God and the Works of Man* (Oxford: Clarendon Press, 1987), p. 35. For another suggestion along these lines see Louis E. Loeb, *Descartes to Hume*, p. 235n. For further discussion see I. C. Tipton, "Descartes' Demon and Berkeley's World" in *Philosophical Investigations* 15 (1992), pp. 111–30.

6. *Philosophical Writings*, vol. 2, pp. 12–15.
7. *Philosophical Writings*, vol. 2, p. 55.
8. *Philosophical Writings*, vol. 1, pp. 126–27.
9. *Philosophical Writings*, vol. 2, p. 54.
10. *An Essay concerning Human Understanding*, Book 2, Chapter 1, §10.
11. *Essay*, Book 4, Chapter 3, §6.
12. *Philosophical Writings*, vol. 1, pp. 217–18, 224.

Henricus Regius

Central to Descartes' proof of the existence of a material world, or "body", was the claim that "if God were himself immediately producing in our mind the idea of such extended matter, or even if he were causing the idea to be produced by something which lacked extension, shape and motion, there would be no way of avoiding the conclusion that he should be regarded as a deceiver."[1] Berkeley was to claim, in effect, that God does what Descartes thought his veracity would prevent him from doing – he immediately produces ideas or sensations in our minds – though in Berkeley's view this does not make him a deceiver. For rather different reasons from Berkeley's, however, some of Descartes' critics had already rejected the claim that if God produced our ideas directly, he would be guilty of deceit. One of the earliest of these was Henricus Regius, a professor at the University of Utrecht. In a broadsheet published in 1647 Regius had argued that, without Scriptural revelation, we could not be completely certain that bodies exist, for "the mind can be affected by imaginary things just as much as by real things."[2] Then, in the 1654 edition of *Philosophia naturalis*, from which the following extract is taken, Regius argued that establishing the existence of a perfect being is insufficient to prove the existence of bodies.[3]

Some there are who argue thus: God exists from his own nature, and it follows from his infinite perfection that he cannot be a deceiver, so it cannot be the case that the things we perceive and make judgments about are not real bodies but only imaginary things.

Certainly to this we can reply: it is possible for God, who has complete and unlimited power over all things, to use deception, first, in a way that is benign and wise, as, for example, physicians and prudent fathers sometimes do, and second, in a way that punishes wrong-doers, something Scripture attests to when it says:

παρέδωκεν αὐτοὺς ὅ θεὸς εἰς ἀδόκιμον νοῦν[4]

that is, "God himself gave them over to perverted sense," or, if you prefer, "to depravity of mind," which also pertains to the senses. If God makes use of deception, that does not prove his imperfection, but rather proves his power, goodness, wisdom, and justice.[5]

But I prefer to say that God would not be a deceiver if he made things appear to men in such a way that, although one could not conclude from their appearance that they necessarily exist, one could conclude from how they appear that it is quite likely that they exist. For it would be true both that such things had that appearance and that one would believe that they appeared thus, from which one would be justified both in gathering that things probably are as they appear to be and in directing one's actions accordingly. All this would be a true effect produced by God – not a deceptive one but one that is consistent with divine veracity and that demonstrates his all-powerfulness in directing men by means of the appearances he produces for them. And if men, in consequence of this, fall, by a rash and improper judgment, into the error of judging that things – e.g., corporeal things – really and necessarily are as they appear to be, certainly it is not God who deceives men, but men who deceive themselves by their own improper judgment and their habit of judging thus. For it would be possible for men to judge only that things seem to be thus, withholding or omitting judgment on their necessary truth, thereby avoiding error and in the meantime guiding their actions by this probable judgment, acting only in accordance with what nature has given us.

Thus, for example, God is not a deceiver when he brings it about that, because the earth is turning on its own axis, the sun – according to appearances and what seems to be the case – rises and sets; yet the upshot is that most people deceive themselves by a false and improper judgment that ascribes to the sun a true and necessary motion, and to the earth, a true, necessary rest. They could, however, omit or withhold the judgment ascribing necessary motion to the sun and necessary rest to the earth and, by attributing only probable motion and rest to them, be able to avoid error. For even if it is not true that the sun revolves daily round the earth, it nonetheless seems to do so, and hence one who limits himself to this judgment cannot be said to err. . . . But without divine revelation there is no apodeictic certainty but only moral certainty, or probable and likely assurance, that things exist outside our mind; but that is all that is needed in carrying out well and regulating all the actions of human life.

It is unlikely Berkeley read Regius, but his complaint was echoed by others, including two writers Berkeley did read, Malebranche and Bayle. The upshot was that Descartes could be seen to have asked a question – How can we be sure that bodies exist? – that, given his own requirements for certainty, he failed to answer. Berkeley's own answer was very different from that of Regius and Malebranche, who appealed to Scriptural revelation, but their contributions helped bring the problem into clearer focus.

Notes

1. *Philosophical Writings*, vol. 1, p. 223.
2. Descartes included the broadsheet "in its latest form" in his "Comments on a Certain Broadsheet," *Philosophical Writings*, vol. 1, pp. 294–96.
3. From H. Regius, *Philosophia naturalis* (Amsterdam, 1654), pp. 348–51.
4. Rom. 1:28.
5. This argument is already found in some of the *Objections* that Descartes appended to the first edition of the *Meditations*. See *Philosophical Writings*, vol. 2, pp. 89–90, 136, 279–80. It was later repeated by Malebranche and Leibniz. See Malebranche, *Oeuvres complètes*, ed. A. Robinet (Paris: Vrin, 1958–84), vol. 6, p. 185; and Leibniz, *Philosophical Papers and Letters*, trans. L. E. Loemker (Dordrecht: Reidel, 1969), pp. 391–92.

THREE

Nicolas Malebranche

How much the young Berkeley was directly influenced by the writings of Descartes is open to debate. But when it comes to Malebranche's *Search after Truth*, it is widely accepted both that Berkeley came on it at an early stage and that it had a profound effect on him.[1] Malebranche is often referred to by name in the *Philosophical Commentaries*, and in a number of other entries Berkeley clearly has him in mind. We also find that early readers of the *Principles* and *Dialogues* identified Berkeley's views with those of Malebranche. Berkeley repeatedly protested this identification, declaring that "upon the whole there are no principles more fundamentally opposite than his and mine."[2] And indeed there were important differences between the two thinkers, both in approach and doctrine. But these should not mislead us. There are many things in the *Search after Truth* that probably gave some focus or direction to Berkeley's thinking as he worked out his own views. Some of the most important of these are exemplified in the following selections.[3]

1. The Existence of Bodies

Descartes held that, for physics to have a solid foundation, bodies must be proved to exist, and he believed that in the Sixth Meditation he had done this. Malebranche, in the first edition (1674–75) of the *Search*, recognized that Descartes' argument had force, but he nonetheless claimed that it is very difficult to prove conclusively that the things we see as external to us do have "a real existence, independent of our mind." Further, he denied that such a proof is indispensable for either geometry or physics.[4] These sciences, he said, are concerned with relations among our "pure" (non-sensuous) *ideas* of extension, relations that, he held, we can have demonstrative knowledge of, whether or not there are bodies. To the third edition (1677–78) of the *Search*, Malebranche appended some lengthy "elucidations" (*éclaircissements*) of things he had said in the main body of that work. One of these ("Elucidation Six") certainly interested Berkeley. In it Malebranche explained in greater detail why it is difficult to prove that bodies exist.

[S]ince men are more sensible than reasonable, and since they listen more readily to the testimony of their senses than to that of inner truth, they have always relied on their eyes to assure themselves of the existence of matter without bothering to consult their reason. This is why they are surprised when told that it is difficult to prove the existence of matter. They think that they have but to open their eyes in order to assure themselves that there are bodies, and if there is some reason to suspect an illusion, they think it suffices to approach the bodies and touch them – after which they have difficulty conceiving that one might yet have reasons for doubting their existence.

But our eyes represent colors to us on the surface of bodies and light in the air and in the sun; our ears make us hear sounds as if spread out through the air and in the resounding bodies; and if we believe what the other senses report, heat will be in fire, sweetness will be in sugar, musk will have an odor, and all the sensible qualities will be in the bodies that seem to exude or diffuse them. Yet it is certain (for the reasons that I have given in the first book of *The Search After Truth*) that all these qualities do not exist outside the soul that perceives them – at least it is not evident that they are in the bodies that surround us. Why should we conclude then, merely on the testimony of the senses that deceive us on all sides, that there really are external bodies, and even that these bodies are like those we see, i.e., like those that are the soul's immediate object, when we look at them with the eyes of the body. Whatever is to be said of this view, it certainly is not without difficulties.

Furthermore, if on the basis of what the senses report we can assure ourselves of the existence of a given body, that body is the one to which the soul is immediately joined. The most lively sensation and the one that seems to have the most necessary relation to some actually existing body is pain. Yet it often happens that those who have lost an arm feel very severe pain in it even long after the loss of the arm. They know very well that they no longer have the arm when they consult their memory or look at their body; but the sensation of pain deceives them. And if, as often happens, we assume them to have entirely forgotten what they were and to have no other senses than that through which they feel the pain in their imaginary arm, surely they could not be persuaded that they do not have an arm in which they feel such tormenting pain.

There have been those who believed they had horns on their head and others who imagined they were made of butter or glass or that their body was not shaped like other men's, that it was like that of a cock, a wolf, or an ox. They were mad, you will say, and I agree; but their soul was able to be mistaken in these things, and hence all other men can fall into similar errors if they judge objects on the testimony of their senses.[5]

> Much of what Malebranche has said thus far would have sounded familiar to readers of Descartes, for he had impugned the senses and relied on *reason* to establish that bodies exist. However, after developing the point, Malebranche turns to consider Descartes' proof, and does not find it wholly persuasive. He grants that it makes it probable that bodies exist, but he denies that it proves their existence with certainty. Like Regius, he argues that certainty in this matter comes only through faith in God's revelation in Scripture that he did indeed create a corporeal world.

For these reasons, or reasons like them, Descartes, who wanted to establish his philosophy on unshakable foundations, thought he could not assume that there are bodies, and that he should not prove that there are on the basis of sensible proofs, even though they would seem very persuasive to the ordinary man. Clearly he knew as well as we do that he had only to open his eyes to see bodies and that we can approach them and touch them to ascertain whether our eyes deceive us in what they report. He knew the mind of man well enough to judge that such proofs had not been rejected. But he sought neither sensible probabilities nor the vain applause of men. He preferred the truth, even though scorned, to the glory of an undeserved reputation, and he preferred to seem ridiculous to insignificant minds with his doubts that to them might seem extravagant than to accept things that he did not judge certain and undeniable.

But although Descartes has given the strongest proofs that reason alone can muster for the existence of bodies, and although it is evident that God is no deceiver and that He would be said really to deceive us if we deceived ourselves by making the use we must of our mind and of our other faculties of which He is the Author – still we can say that the existence of matter is not yet perfectly demonstrated, i.e., with geometric rigor. For in philosophical matters, we must not believe anything till evidence obliges us to do so. We must make as much use of our freedom as possible; our judgments should have no greater extent than our perceptions. Thus, when we perceive bodies, let us judge only that we perceive them and that these perceptible or intelligible bodies actually exist; but why should we judge positively that there is an external material world like the intelligible world we perceive? . . .

Now it must be noted that since only God knows His volitions (which produce all beings) by Himself, we can know only from Him whether there really is a material world external to us like the one we perceive, because the material world is neither perceptible nor intelligible by itself. Thus, in order to be fully convinced that there are bodies, we must have demonstrated for us not only that there is a God and that He is no deceiver, but also that He has assured us that He has really created such a world, which proof I have not found in the works of Descartes.

God speaks to the mind and constrains its belief in only two ways: through evidence and through faith. I agree that faith obliges us to believe that there are bodies; but as for evidence, it seems to me that it is incomplete and that we are not invincibly led to believe there is something other than God and our own mind. It is true that we have a strong propensity to believe that there are bodies surrounding us; I agree here with Descartes. But this propensity, as natural as it is, does not constrain our belief through evidence; it merely inclines us toward belief through impression. Now, our free judgments should follow only light and evidence; and if we let ourselves be led by sense impressions, we shall be mistaken almost always.

Why are we mistaken in the judgments we form concerning sense qualities, the size, figure, and motion of bodies, if not because we follow an impression like the one that leads us to believe there are bodies? Do we not perceive that fire is hot, that snow is white, and that the sun is brilliant with light; do we not perceive sense qualities as well as bodies external to us? Yet it is certain that these sense qualities we perceive external to us are not really external to us (or if you will, nothing is certain on this matter). What reason have we, then, that besides the intelligible bodies we perceive there are still others we look at? What evidence do you have that an impression that is deceptive not only with regard to sense qualities but also with regard to the size, figure, and motion of bodies, is not so with regard to the actual existence of these same bodies? I ask what evidence of this you have, for I agree that you have no lack of probabilities.[6]

> Descartes had granted that our senses mislead us about what came to be known as secondary qualities; he granted too that we may seem to have been led by nature to believe that the very same colors we perceive through our senses are really present in the objects, just as we have a natural inclination to believe that external objects exist. There is, though, according to Descartes, a crucial difference between these two cases: in the first case, but not the second, the God-given faculty of reason allows us to *correct* our initial judgment. Malebranche agrees that there is this important difference, and thus grants that Descartes' argument, which he summarizes, has force. However, it still does not give us demonstrative certainty that bodies exist. Thus:

This argument is perhaps sound enough. Nevertheless, it must be agreed that it should not be taken as a necessary demonstration of the existence of bodies, for God does not invincibly urge us to yield to it. If we consent to it, we do so freely – we are able not to consent to it. If the argument I have just given is sound, we must believe it entirely probable that there are bodies; but we must not rest fully convinced by this single argument. Otherwise, it is we who act and not God in us. It is by a free act, and consequently one liable to error, that we consent and not by an invincible impression; for we believe because we freely will to do so, and not because we perceive with an evidence necessitating us to believe, as in the case of mathematical demonstrations.

Surely only faith can persuade us that there really are bodies. We cannot have an exact demonstration of other than a necessary being's existence. And if you attend closely, you will see that it is not even possible to know with full evidence whether or not God is truly the creator of the material and sensible world. For such evidence is found only in necessary relations, and there is no necessary relation between God and such a world. He was able not to create it, and if He did create it, it is because He willed to do so and willed freely to do so.[7]

> For Malebranche, then, neither sense nor reason proves conclusively the existence of bodies; only faith in the Bible, with its account of the creation, of miracles, and of various other things that assume

the existence of matter, constrains us to accept that bodies do certainly exist. For Berkeley, both these claims were significant. Entries in the *Philosophical Commentaries* show that what Malebranche had said in Elucidation Six captured the young Berkeley's attention. He has it in mind at *PC* 800: "Malbranch in his Illustration differs widely from me He doubts of the existence of Bodies I doubt not in the least of this."[8] And he is clearly thinking about it in other entries (see *PC* 686, 686a, 818). Malebranche's argument that neither sense nor reason can firmly establish the existence of material substances would naturally have been congenial to Berkeley. However, the claim that their existence is guaranteed by Christian doctrine was one that demanded rebuttal. It is not surprising then that, in the *Principles*, Berkeley attacked this claim.[9] For Berkeley, it is not just sense and reason that fail to establish the existence of "objects without the mind"; the appeal to faith fails too.

2. Causation

According to Descartes, not only do bodies exist, they "transmit" sensations to our minds. But as Gassendi soon pointed out to Descartes, "the general difficulty still remains of how the corporeal can communicate with the incorporeal and of what relationship may be established between the two."[10] How can two substances as different as extended matter and unextended mind interact? Berkeley alludes to this difficulty when he argues that even if "we give the materialists their external bodies, they by their own confession are never the nearer knowing how our ideas are produced: since they own themselves unable to comprehend in what manner body can act upon spirit, or how it is possible it should imprint any idea in the mind" (*PHK* §19). Malebranche went even further than this by denying that any finite being – whether a body or a mind – is ever the true cause of *any* of the effects we normally ascribe to it. Natural events are really only *occasions* on which God, the sole true cause, produces effects.[11] For Malebranche, the only real power or force in the universe is God's will.

It is clear that no body, large or small, has the power to move itself. A mountain, a house, a rock, a grain of sand, in short, the tiniest or largest body conceivable does not have the power to move itself. We have only two sorts of ideas, ideas of minds and ideas of bodies; and as we should speak only of what we conceive, we should only reason according to these two kinds of ideas. Thus, since the idea we have of all bodies makes us aware that they cannot move themselves, it must be concluded that it is minds which move them. But when we examine our idea of all finite minds, we do not see any necessary connection between their will and the motion of any body whatsoever. On the contrary, we see that there is none and that there can be none. We must therefore also conclude, if we wish to reason according to our lights, that there is absolutely no mind created that can move a body as a true or principal cause, just as it has been said that no body could move itself.

But when one thinks about the idea of God, i.e., of an infinitely perfect and consequently all-powerful being, one knows there is such a connection between His will and the motion of all bodies, that it is impossible to conceive that He wills a body to be moved and that this body not be moved. We must therefore say that only His will can move bodies if we wish to state things as we conceive them and not as we sense them. The motor force of bodies is therefore not in the bodies that are moved, for this motor force is nothing other than the will of God. Thus, bodies have no action; and when a ball that is moved collides with and moves another, it communicates to it nothing of its own, for it does not itself have the force it communicates to it. Nevertheless, a ball is the natural cause of the motion it communicates. A natural cause is therefore not a real and true but only an occasional cause, which determines the Author of nature to act in such and such a manner in such and such a situation.[12]

Berkeley, too, held that, strictly, there are no causal interactions between bodies. He is thus happy to acknowledge that "the opinion that there are no corporeal causes . . . has been heretofore maintained by some of the Schoolmen, as it is of late by others among the modern philosophers, who though they allow matter to exist, yet will have God alone to be the immediate efficient cause of all things" (*PHK* §53). However, where Malebranche's reason for rejecting corporeal causes was that *matter* is inert, Berkeley's was that *ideas* are passive (*PHK* §§25–32). Berkeley's views about causality differed from Malebranche's in two other important respects. First, he held that those who reject corporeal *causes* should reject corporeal *substances* too, for if the latter produce no effects, God would have no reason to create them, "since God might have done every thing as well without them" (*PHK* §53). Second, he denied that God is the *only* true cause: *finite* spirits are causes of the things they will. "We move our Legs our selves. 'tis we that will their movement. Herein I differ from Malbranch."[13] Berkeley thus embraces a limited occasionalism; Malebranche, as the following extracts show, a thoroughgoing one.

[W]ere one to assume what is in one sense true, that minds have in themselves the power to know truth and to love good, still, if their thoughts and wills produced nothing externally, one could always say that they are capable of nothing. Now it appears to me quite certain that the will of minds is incapable of moving the smallest body in the world; for it is clear that there is no necessary connection between our will to move our arms, for example, and the movement of our arms. It is true that they are moved when we will it, and that thus we are the natural cause of the movement of our arms. But *natural* causes are not true causes; they are only *occasional* causes that act only through the force and efficacy of the will of God, as I have just explained.

For how could we move our arms? To move them, it is necessary to have animal spirits, to send them through certain nerves toward certain muscles in order to inflate and contract them, for it is thus that the arm attached to them is moved; or according to the opinion of some others, it is still not known how that happens. And we see that men who do not know that they have spirits, nerves, and muscles move their arms, and even move them with more skill and ease than those who know anatomy best. Therefore, men will to move their arms, and only God is able and knows how to move them. If a man cannot turn a tower upside down, at least he knows what must be done to do so; but there is no man who knows what must be done to move one of his fingers by means of animal spirits. How, then, could men move their arms? These things seem obvious to me and, it seems to me, to all those willing to think, although they are perhaps incomprehensible to all those willing only to sense.

But not only are men not the true causes of the movements they produce in their bodies, there even seems to be some contradiction (in saying) that they could be. A true cause as I understand it is one such that the mind perceives a necessary connection between it and its effect. Now the mind perceives a necessary connection only between the will of an infinitely perfect being and its effects. Therefore, it is only God who is the true cause and who truly has the power to move bodies.[14]

The same is true of our faculty of thinking. We know through inner sensation that we will to think about something, that we make an effort to do so, and that at the moment of our desire and effort, the idea of that thing is presented to our mind. But we do not know through inner sensation that our will or effort produces our idea. We do not see through reason that this could happen. It is through prejudice that we believe that our attention or desires are the cause of our ideas; this is due to the fact that a hundred times a day we prove that our ideas follow or accompany them. Since God and His operations contain nothing sensible, and since we sense nothing other than our desires preceding the presence of ideas, we think there can be no cause of these ideas other than our desires. But let us take care. We do not see in us any power to produce them; neither reason nor the inner sensation we have of ourselves tells us anything about this.[15]

If both the objects that surround us and (for Malebranche) finite spirits have no causal powers, why do people so universally believe the contrary? Malebranche's answer, which he spells out in the following, is similar to Berkeley's (see *PHK* §32).

[T]he cause of their error is that men never fail to judge that a thing is the cause of a given effect when the two are conjoined, given that the true cause of the effect is unknown to them. This is why everyone concludes that a moving ball which strikes another is the true and principal cause of the motion it communicates to the other, and that the soul's will is the true and principal cause of movement in the arms, and other such prejudices – because it always happens that a ball moves when struck by another, that our arms move almost every time we want them to, and that we do not sensibly perceive what else could be the cause of these movements.[16]

The doctrine that God alone is the true cause is not just sound philosophy, said Malebranche, it is also the teaching of Scripture. According to him, Adam believed that God was the sole true cause until the serpent persuaded him that something other than God could bring about his well-being. Idolatry and the worship of natural objects like the sun were also, he thought, products of belief in corporeal causes. These views probably influenced Berkeley, who connects belief in matter, as well as belief in corporeal causes, with atheism and idolatry, and even with the fall of man.[17] Malebranche writes:

There is therefore only one single true God and one single cause that is truly a cause, and one should not imagine that what precedes an effect is its true cause. God cannot even communicate His power to creatures, if we follow the lights of reason; He cannot make true causes of them, He cannot make them gods. But even if He could, we cannot conceive why He would. Bodies, minds, pure intelligences, all these can do nothing. It is He who made minds, who enlightens and activates them. It is He who created the sky and the earth, and who regulates their motions. In short, it is the Author of our being who executes our wills: *semel jussit, semper paret*. He moves our arms even when we use them against His orders; for He complains through His prophet that we make Him serve our unjust and criminal desires.

All these insignificant pagan divinities and all these particular causes of the philosophers are merely chimeras that the wicked mind tries to establish to undermine worship of the true God in order to occupy the minds and hearts that the Creator has made only for Himself. It is not the philosophy received from Adam that teaches these things; it is that received from the serpent; for since Original Sin, the mind of man is quite pagan. It is this philosophy that, together with the errors of the senses, made men adore the sun, and that today is still the universal cause of the disorder of men's minds and the corruption of men's hearts. Their actions and sometimes even their words ask why we should not love the body, since bodies are capable of gorging us with pleasure. And why do people mock the Israelites who longed for the cabbages and onions of Egypt, since they were actually unhappy being deprived of something that could make them to some extent happy. But the philosophy that is called new, which is represented as a specter to frighten feeble minds, which is scorned and condemned without being understood, the new philosophy, I say (since it is the fashion to call it thus), ruins all the arguments of the skeptics through the establishment of the greatest of its principles, which is in perfect harmony with the first principle of the Christian religion: that we must love and fear only one God, since there is only one God who can make us happy.

For if religion teaches us that there is only one true God, this philosophy shows us that there is only one true cause. If religion teaches us that all the divinities of paganism are merely stones and metals without life or motion, this philosophy also reveals to us that all secondary causes, or all the divinities of philosophy, are merely matter and inefficacious wills. Finally, if religion teaches us that we must not genuflect before false gods, this philosophy also teaches us that our imaginations and minds must not bow before the imaginary greatness and power of causes that are not causes at all; that we must neither love nor fear them; that we must not be concerned with them; that we must think only of God alone, see God in all things, fear and love God in all things.[18]

This insistence on the immediate dependence of things on God must surely have been congenial to Berkeley, who found it "unaccountable" that belief in natural causes "should be received among Christians professing belief in the Holy Scriptures, which constantly ascribe those effects to the immediate hand of God, that heathen philosophers are wont to impute to *Nature*" (*PHK* §150). Berkeley could thus welcome not only Malebranche's claim that it is impossible to prove beyond doubt that a material world exists (the first halting step, as it were, toward the denial that such a world exists) but also Malebranche's concession that the matter he believed exists is wholly inefficacious.

3. The Errors of the Senses

Malebranche devoted Book One of the *Search* to arguing that we do not learn the properties of bodies from our senses. To show this, he first examined extension, size, shape, and motion, then the "sensible qualities" – warmth, taste, odor, sound, and color. Malebranche's view of the sensible qualities is like Descartes': they have no existence independent of our minds. But even in the case of size, shape, and motion our senses mislead us: they never reveal, for example, the "absolute" size or extension of things. One way Malebranche tried to show this was by arguing that none of these qualities appears the same to everyone – a thing's size, for example, looks different to us from how it would look to a mite.

Berkeley studied this material carefully; in his notebooks, for example, a number of references are clearly to the chapter on extension. The following brief extract is from that chapter, where Malebranche argues not that there is no such thing as external extension but that our eyes never see it just as it is. It should be compared with Berkeley's discussion, in the *First Dialogue*, of how extension and figure vary, depending on who is perceiving them.[19]

Through sight we perceive nothing smaller than a mite. Half a mite is nothing if we accept the testimony of vision. As far as vision is concerned, a mite is only a mathematical point. It cannot be divided without being annihilated. Our sight, then, does not represent extension to us as it is in itself, but only as it is in relation to our body; and because half a mite has no significant relation to our body, and can neither preserve nor destroy it, our sight hides it from us entirely.

But if we had eyes constructed like microscopes, or rather, if we were as small as mites, our judgments about the size of bodies would be quite different. For these tiny animals undoubtedly have eyes that can see both what surrounds them and their own body as though much larger, or as composed of a greater number of parts, than we see it, since otherwise they would not receive the impressions necessary for the preservation of their life, and thus the eyes they do have would be entirely useless to them. . . .

From the fact that we have an idea of a thing, it does not follow that the thing exists and still less that it is entirely like our idea of it. From the fact that God provides us with a given sensible idea of size, as when a fathom ruler is before our eyes, it does not follow that the ruler has only that extension represented to us by the idea. For in the first place, not all men have precisely the same sensible idea of the ruler, since not all men's eyes are disposed in the same way. Second, a given person sometimes does not have the same sensible idea of a fathom ruler when he views it with the right eye and then the left, as has already been said. Finally, it often happens that the same person has different ideas of the same objects at different times, according to whether he believes them to be more or less at a distance, as we shall explain elsewhere.[20]

In the *First Dialogue*, Berkeley draws a more far-reaching conclusion from perceptual relativity than does Malebranche, for Berkeley seems to argue, vis-à-vis the distinction between primary and secondary qualities, that relativity in how *any* quality appears to perceivers shows its mind-dependence, whereas in the case of *extension*, for example, Malebranche holds only that our senses do not reveal true or "absolute" size. Berkeley, however, need not be supposed to have missed this point. In *PHK* §§14–15 he grants that this particular argument "doth not so much prove that there is no extension or colour in an outward object, as that we do not know by sense which is the true extension or colour of the object" – which is no more than Malebranche had claimed, at least in the case of extension, figure, and motion. Also, even in the *Dialogues*, Berkeley carefully restricts the argument to "sensible" qualities, including "sensible" extension. When Hylas tries to save the day by introducing a notion of "absolute" extension, the focus of the debate switches and Philonous attacks it as an abstract idea.

4. Ideas

In Book One of the *Search*, Malebranche had argued that we do not perceive, by our senses, the actual qualities of bodies, and that colors, odors, tastes, and all other "sensations" are simply "modifications" of our souls. In the selections below, from Book Three, he argues, more generally, that we do not immediately perceive material things at all. For one thing, he claims, our soul can only perceive what it is immediately united to, and things located at a distance in space from us cannot be immediately united to our souls; for another, there is no "relation" between material things, which are extended, and the soul, which is unextended – how then could one be immediately present to the other? It must instead be, Malebranche thinks, that God immediately unites our souls to himself and thereby discloses to us his archetypal ideas of things. This led Malebranche to one of his most celebrated doctrines, and one that, despite Berkeley's denials, Berkeley was supposed by many of his early readers to embrace. The doctrine was that "we see all things in God."[21]

I think everyone agrees that we do not perceive objects external to us by themselves. We see the sun, the stars, and an infinity of objects external to us; and it is not likely that the soul should leave the body to stroll about the heavens, as it were, in order to behold all these objects. Thus, it does not see them by themselves, and our mind's immediate object when it sees the sun, for example, is not the sun, but something that is intimately joined to our soul, and this is what I call an *idea*. Thus, by the word *idea*, I mean here nothing other than the immediate object, or the object closest to the mind, when it perceives something, i.e., that which affects and modifies the mind with the perception it has of an object.

It should be carefully noted that for the mind to perceive an object, it is absolutely necessary for the idea of that object to be actually present to it – and about this there can be no doubt; but there need not be any external thing like that idea. For it often happens that we perceive things that do not exist, and that even have never existed – thus our mind often has real ideas of things that have never existed. When, for example, a man imagines a golden mountain, it is absolutely necessary that the idea of this mountain really be present to his mind. When a madman or someone asleep or in a high fever sees some animal before his eyes, it is certain that what he sees is not nothing, and that therefore the idea of this animal really does exist, though the golden mountain and the animal have never existed.

Yet given that men are naturally led, as it were, to believe that only corporeal objects exist, they judge of the reality and existence of things other than as they should. For as soon as they perceive an object, they would have it as quite certain that it exists, although it often happens that there is nothing external. In addition, they would have the object be exactly as they see it, which never happens. But as for the idea that necessarily exists, and that cannot be other than as it is seen, they ordinarily judge unreflectingly that it is nothing – as if ideas did not have a great number of properties, as if the idea of a square, for example, were not different from that of a circle or a number, and did not represent completely different things, which can never be the case for nonbeing, since nonbeing has no properties. It is therefore indubitable that ideas have a very real existence. But now let us examine their nature and essence, and let us see what there can be in the soul that might represent all things to it.

Everything the soul perceives belongs to either one of two sorts: either it is in the soul, or outside the soul. The things that are in the soul are its own thoughts, i.e., all its various modifications – for by the words *thought, mode of thinking,* or *modification of the soul,* I generally understand all those things that cannot be in the soul without the soul being aware of them through the inner sensation it has of itself – such as its sensations, imaginings, pure intellections, or simply conceptions, as well as its passions and natural inclinations. Now, our soul has no need of ideas in order to perceive these things in the way it does, because these things are in the soul, or rather because they are but the soul itself existing in this or that way – just as the actual roundness and motion of a body are but that body shaped and moved in this or that way.

But as for things outside the soul, we can perceive them only by means of ideas, given that these things cannot be intimately joined to the soul. Of these, there are two sorts: spiritual and material. . . .

But here I am speaking mainly about material things, which certainly cannot be joined to our soul in the way necessary for it to perceive them, because with them extended and the soul unextended, there is no relation between them. Besides which, our souls do not leave the body to measure the heavens, and as a result, they can see bodies outside only through the ideas representing them. In this everyone must agree.

We assert the absolute necessity, then, of the following: either (a) the ideas we have of bodies and of all other objects we do not perceive by themselves come from these bodies or objects; or (b) our soul has the power of producing these ideas; or (c) God has produced them in us while creating the soul or produces them every time we think about a given object; or (d) the soul has in itself all the perfections it sees in bodies; or else (e) the soul is joined to a completely perfect being that contains all intelligible perfections, or all the ideas of created beings.[22]

Malebranche proceeds to examine, in *Search*, Book III, Part ii, Chapters 2–5, possibilities (a) to (d), and finds reasons for rejecting each of them. He then defends (e) – the doctrine that the ideas we perceive are *not* modifications of our own souls, but exist externally to our souls in the mind of God, and that we perceive them because God immediately unites our souls to himself. Berkeley was very eager that his readers not confuse his own view with the doctrine that we "see corporeal things, not by themselves, but by seeing that which represents them in the essence of God, which doctrine is I must confess to me incomprehensible" (*PHK* §148). And indeed Berkeley's concept of *idea* does differ markedly from that of Malebranche, for whom "ideas" are quite distinct from "sensations". Yet, like Malebranche, Berkeley held that ideas are not "modes" of the mind, but something distinct from it (*PHK* §49), and that the tree we perceive "is truly known and comprehended by (that is, *exists in*) the infinite mind of God."[23] He also agrees with the claim Malebranche makes below that it is God who causes sensations in us. The following passages give three of Malebranche's reasons for maintaining that "we see all things in God."

In the preceding chapters we have examined four different ways in which the soul might see external objects, all of which seem to us very unlikely. There remains only the fifth, which alone seems to conform to reason and to be most appropriate for exhibiting the dependence that minds have on God in all their thoughts.

To understand this fifth way, we must remember what was just said in the preceding chapter – that God must have within Himself the ideas of all the beings He has created (since otherwise He could not have created them), and thus He sees all these beings by considering the perfections He contains to which they are related. We should know, furthermore, that through His presence God is in close union with our minds, such that He might be said to be the place of minds as space is, in a sense, the place of bodies. Given these two things, the mind surely can see what in God represents created beings, since what in God represents created beings is very spiritual, intelligible, and present to the mind. Thus, the mind can see God's works in Him, provided that God wills to reveal to it what in Him represents them. The following are the reasons that seem to prove that He wills this rather than the creation of an infinite number of ideas in each mind.

Not only does it strictly conform to reason, but it is also apparent from the economy found throughout nature that God never does in very complicated fashion what can be done in a very simple and straightforward way. For God never does anything uselessly and without reason. His power and wisdom are not shown by doing lesser things with greater means – this is contrary to reason and indicates a limited intelligence. Rather, they are shown by doing greater things with very simple and straightforward means. Thus, it was with extension alone that He produced everything admirable we see in nature and even what gives life and movement to animals. For those who absolutely insist on substantial forms, faculties, and souls in animals (different from their blood and bodily organs) to perform their functions, at the same time would have it that God lacks intelligence, or that He cannot make all these remarkable things with extension alone. They measure the power and sovereign wisdom of God by the pettiness of their own mind. Thus, since God can reveal everything to minds simply by willing that they see what is in their midst, i.e., what in Him is related to and represents these things, there is no likelihood that He does otherwise, or that He does so by producing as many infinities of infinite numbers of ideas as there are created minds. . . .

The second reason for thinking that we see beings because God wills that what in Him representing them should be revealed to us (and not because there are as many ideas created with us as there are things we can perceive) is that this view places created minds in a position of complete dependence on God – the most complete there can be. For on this view, not only could we see nothing but what He wills that we see, but we could see nothing but what He makes us see. "Non sumus sufficientes cogitare aliquid a nobis, tamquam ex nobis, sed sufficientia nostra ex Deo est." [2 Cor. 3:5] It is God Himself who enlightens philosophers in the knowledge that ungrateful men call natural though they receive it only from heaven. "Deus enim illis manifestavit." [Rom. 1:19] He is truly the mind's light and the father of lights. "Pater luminum" – it is He who teaches men knowledge – "Qui docet hominem scientiam." [James 1:17; Ps. 93:10] In a word, He is the true light that illumines everyone who comes into the world: "Lux vera quae illuminat omnem hominem venientem in hunc mundum." [John 1:9]. . . .

But the strongest argument of all is the mind's way of perceiving anything. It is certain, and everyone knows this from experience, that when we want to think about some particular thing, we first glance over all beings and then apply ourselves to the consideration of the object we wish to think about. Now, it is indubitable that we could desire to see a particular object only if we had already seen it, though in a general and confused fashion. As a result of this, given that we can desire to see all beings, now one, now another, it is certain that all beings are present to our mind; and it seems that all beings can be present to our mind only because God, i.e., He who includes all things in the simplicity of His being, is present to it. . . .

But although I may say that we see material and sensible things in God, it must be carefully noted that I am not saying we have sensations of them in God, but only that it is God who acts in us; for God surely knows sensible things, but He does not sense them. When we perceive something sensible, two things are found in our perception: *sensation* and pure *idea*. The sensation is a modification of our soul, and it is God who causes it in us. He can cause this modification even though He does not have it Himself, because He sees in the idea He has of our soul that it is capable of it. As for the idea found in conjunction with the sensation, it is in God, and we see it because it pleases God to reveal it to us. God joins the sensation to the idea when objects are present so that we may believe them to be present and that we may have all the feelings and passions that we should have in relation to them. . . .

These are some of the reasons that might lead one to believe that minds perceive everything through the intimate presence of Him who comprehends all in the simplicity of His being. Each of us will judge the matter according to the inner conviction he receives after seriously considering it. But I do not think there is any plausibility in any of the other ways of explaining these things, and this last way seems more than plausible. Thus, our souls depend on God in all ways. For just as it is He who makes them feel pain, pleasure, and all the other sensations, through the natural union He has established between them and our bodies, which is but His decree and general will, so it is He who makes them know all that they know through the natural union He has also established between the will of man and the representation of ideas contained in the immensity of the Divine being, which union is also but His general will. As a result of this, only He can enlighten us, by representing everything to us – just as only He can make us happy by making us enjoy all sorts of pleasures.

Let us hold this view, then, that God is the intelligible world or the place of minds, as the material world is the place of bodies; that from His power minds receive their modifications; that in His wisdom they find all their ideas; that through His love they receive their orderly impulses, and because His power and love are but Himself, let us believe with Saint Paul, that He is not far from any of us, and that in Him we live and move and have our being. "Non longe est ab unoquoque nostrum, in ipso enim vivimus, movemus, & sumus." [Acts 17:28][24]

Malebranche is not consistent in his use of "idea". Sometimes he uses it to refer both to "sensations" and to "pure perceptions" (i.e., ideas supposedly devoid of sensory content, such as the geometer's idea of a triangle). Other times, as in Book Three, he calls only the latter "ideas" and sharply distinguishes them from sensations. It is ideas in *this* sense that are, he claims, in God, whereas sensations are in (are "modes" of) our souls.[25]

Because ideas are *distinct* from the soul, the soul does not become extended when it perceives extension. However, since color, odor, taste, and so on, are *modes* of the soul, the soul, according to Malebranche, actually does become red, stinking, and sweet, when it has these sensations. Berkeley, by contrast, drew no such distinction between ideas and sensations, though he, too, held that ideas are not modes of the soul and that the soul does not become figured or extended when it perceives these ideas (*PHK* §49). For Berkeley, of course, ideas do not "represent" material things, for there *are* no material things.

5. Abstract Ideas

When Berkeley seeks to distance himself from Malebranche, one point he makes is that Malebranche "builds on the most abstract general ideas, which I entirely disclaim."[26] At first sight, therefore, it may seem surprising that A. A. Luce can mention Malebranche as one of those who "had attacked vigorously certain types of abstraction, and no doubt . . . influenced Berkeley, and put him on his guard against abuses of abstraction."[27] For certainly Malebranche did build on what, for Berkeley, were illegitimate abstractions. His notion of non-sensuous "intelligible extension" is one example. Even more glaring is his claim that God is "being in general" and is always present to our minds, for that entails that "being in general" – an idea that is for Berkeley "the most abstract and incomprehensible of all other" (*PHK* §17) – is always present to our minds. Yet, while Malebranche holds that knowledge is possible only because "being in general" is always present to us, he does also insist that this idea is one of the chief sources of philosophical error, for it allows us to imagine that even meaningless terms stand for some "being". In this way, Malebranche could argue that, although it is indispensable, "the vague idea of being in general is the cause of all of the mind's disordered abstractions, and of most of the chimeras of ordinary philosophy."[28] Seen in this light, Luce's suggestion that Malebranche may here have influenced Berkeley is quite plausible.

The clear, intimate, and necessary presence of God (i.e., the being without individual restriction, the infinite being, being in general) to the mind of man acts upon it with greater force than the presence of all finite objects. The mind cannot entirely rid itself of this general idea of being, because it cannot subsist outside God. Perhaps you will say that the mind can withdraw from this idea because it can think about particular beings; but you would be mistaken. For when the mind considers some being in particular, it moves not so much away from God as nearer Him (if one of His perfections may be spoken of as representative of this being) by moving away from all the others. Yet it moves away from them in such a way that it never loses sight of them, and it is almost always ready to seek them out and move near them. They are always present to the mind, but the mind perceives them only in an unsolvable confusion due to its own pettiness and the greatness of the idea of being. One might well not think about oneself for some time, but it seems to me one cannot subsist a moment without thinking of being, and at the very time that one takes himself to be thinking of nothing, one is necessarily filled with the vague and general idea of being. But because commonplace things that do not affect us do not forcefully arouse the mind and command its attention, this idea of being, however great, real, positive, and vast it may be, is so familiar to us and affects us so little that we almost believe ourselves not to see it, do not reflect on it, and then judge that it has but little reality and is formed only from the confused collection of all our particular ideas, although, quite to the contrary, it is in it and by it alone that we perceive all beings in particular.

Although this idea that we receive through the immediate union we have with the Word of God, sovereign Reason, never deceives us by itself as do those we receive because of the union we have with our bodies, which represent things to us other than as they are, yet I have no hesitation in saying that we make such ill use of the best of things that the ineradicable presence of this idea is one of the main causes of all the mind's disordered abstractions, and consequently, [it is one of the main causes] of all that abstract and chimerical philosophy that explains all natural effects with the general terms act, potency, causes, effect, substantial forms, faculties, occult qualities, and so on. For it is certain that all these terms and several others arouse in the mind only vague and general ideas, i.e., those ideas that present themselves to the mind with no difficulty or effort on our part, those ideas that are contained in the ineradicable idea of being.[29]

> In this way, Malebranche alleges, the Scholastic philosophers "pretend to explain nature through their general and abstract terms – as if nature were abstract." An example of this is their belief that matter is something *in addition to* its known properties and, in particular, that it is something *presupposed by* extension. For his part, Malebranche accepted Descartes' view that matter just *is* extension, modified by various figures and motions. Those who suppose matter "a being" presupposed by extension have in fact no idea of it at all. Berkeley was to make a somewhat similar point, perhaps inspired by

Malebranche's, against those who suppose that matter is an unknow-able substrate that *supports* extension, figure, and motion. The fol-lowing extract should be compared with *PHK* §§16–17.

In order to prove now that extension is not a mode of a being but is truly a being, it should be noted that we cannot conceive a mode of a being unless at the same time we conceive the being of which it is the mode. We cannot conceive of roundness, for example, unless we con-ceive of extension, because given that a mode of a being is only that being (existing) in a certain way, e.g., the roundness of wax is the wax itself (existing) in a certain way, we clearly cannot conceive the mode without the being. If extension were a mode of being, then, we could not conceive of extension without that being of which extension was the mode. Yet we can quite easily conceive it by itself. Therefore, it is not the mode of any being, and consequently is itself a being. It is thus the essence of matter, since matter is but one being, and is not composed of several beings, as we have just said.

But many philosophers are so accustomed to general ideas and entities of logic that their mind is more occupied with them than with those of physics, which are particular and distinct. This can be seen from the fact that their reasoning about natural things is based only on logical notions, on act, potency, and an infinite number of imaginary entities they do not distinguish from those that are real. Given, then, that these people have a marvelous facility for seeing in their own way whatever they wish, they fancy that their vision is better than others', that they distinctly see that extension presupposes something, and that extension is only a prop-erty of matter from which it might even be stripped away.

Yet, if they are asked to explain this thing in addition to extension that they pretend to see in matter, they do so in ways that indicate that they have no other idea of this thing than being or substance in general. That this is the case is clear when we notice that the idea in question contains no particular attribute belonging to matter. For if extension is taken from matter, all the attributes and properties we distinctly con-ceive as belonging to it are also taken away, even if this thing they imagine to be its essence is left behind; it is clear that neither an earth nor the heavens nor anything we see could be made from it. And, on the contrary, if what they imagine to be the essence of matter is taken away, provided that extension is left behind, all the attributes and properties we distinctly conceive as included in the idea of matter are also left – for with extension alone we can certainly form the heavens, an earth, and the entire world we see as well as an infinity of others. Thus, this something that they suppose in addition to matter, having no attributes we distinctly conceive as belonging to it, and which are clearly contained in the idea we have of it, is, if we are to believe reason, nothing real and cannot even be used to explain natural effects. And what is said of its being the *subject* and *principle* of extension is said gratuitously and without a clear conception of what is being said, i.e., without there being any idea of it other than a general idea from logic, like principle and subject. As a result, a new *subject* and a new *principle* of this subject of extension could in turn be imagined, and so on to infinity, because the mind represents general ideas of subject and principle to itself as it pleases. . . .

Real ideas produce real science, but general or logical ideas never produce anything but a science that is vague, superficial, and sterile. We must, then, carefully consider the distinct, particular ideas of things in order to discover the properties they contain, and study nature in this way rather than losing ourselves in chimeras that exist only in certain philosophers' minds.[30]

6. The Soul

Malebranche distinguished four ways of knowing things, corresponding to four distinct sorts of object. God is the only thing we know "by a direct and immediate perception." Bodies are known through representative ideas that are quite distinct from them. We each know our own soul not "through its idea" but by "consciousness or inner sensation." By contrast, we know the souls of others by "conjecture", for we suppose "that the souls of other men are of the same sort as our own."[31] Berkeley is in at least verbal agreement with Malebranche that we do not have an idea of our mind, but know it by "inward feeling" or "internal consciousness".[32] There are, however, important differences between the two thinkers about self-knowledge. For one thing, Berkeley, like Descartes and in opposition to both Malebranche and Locke, holds that we do know the soul's essence. For another, Berkeley holds that we *cannot* have an "idea" of the soul, for ideas are passive and cannot represent an active being, whereas Malebranche holds only that we *do not* have an idea of the soul; God has an idea of it, he maintains, but he has not disclosed it to us. In this final selection from Malebranche, he defends the thesis that we have no idea of the soul.

I have said in a number of places, and I even think that I have sufficiently proved in the third book of the *Search after Truth*, that we have no *clear idea* of our soul,[33] but only *consciousness* or inner sensation of it, and that thus we know it much less perfectly than we do extension. This seemed to me so evident that I did not think it necessary to argue so at further length. But the authority of Descartes, who clearly says *that the nature of the mind is better known than the nature of any other thing*, has so prejudiced some of his disciples that what I wrote on the topic has served only to make me seem a person of weak character who cannot grasp and hold fast to abstract truths incapable of arousing and maintaining the attention of those who consider them. . . .

Yet the present question is so suited to the mind's capacity that I do not see the need for any great effort to resolve it (which is the reason I did not pause over it). For I think I can say that the ignorance of most men with regard to their own soul, of its distinction from the body, of its spirituality, immortality, and other properties, is enough to show clearly that they have no clear and distinct idea of it.

We are able to say that we have a clear idea of the body because in order to know the modifications it can have, it suffices to consult the idea representing it. We clearly see that it can be round or square, in motion or at rest. We have no difficulty conceiving that a square can be divided into two triangles, two parallelograms, two trapezia. When we are asked whether something does or does not belong to extension, we never hesitate in our response, because as the idea of extension is clear, we see without any difficulty through simple perception what it contains and what it excludes.

But surely we have no idea of our mind which is such that, by consulting it, we can discover the modifications of which the mind is capable. If we had never felt pleasure or pain we could not know whether or not the soul could feel them. If a man had never eaten a melon, or seen red or blue, he would consult this alleged idea of his soul in vain and would never discover distinctly whether or not it was capable of these sensations or modifications. I maintain, furthermore, that even if one is actually feeling pain or seeing color, one cannot discover through simple perception whether these qualities belong to the soul. One imagines that pain is in the body that occasions it, and that color is spread out on the surface of objects, although these objects are distinct from our soul.

In order to determine whether sensible qualities are modes of the mind, we do not consult the alleged idea of the soul – the Cartesians themselves consult, rather, the idea of extension, and they reason as follows. Heat, pain, and color cannot be modifications of extension, for extension can have only various figures and motion. Now there are only two kinds of beings, minds and bodies. Therefore, pain, heat, color, and all other sensible qualities belong to the mind.

Since we have to consult our idea of extension in order to discover whether sensible qualities are modes of our mind, is it not evident that we have no clear idea of the soul? Would we otherwise ever bother with such a roundabout way? When a philosopher wishes to learn whether roundness belongs to extension, does he consult the idea of the soul, or some idea other than that of extension? Does he not see clearly in the idea itself of extension that roundness is a modification of it? And would it not be strange if, in order to learn of it, he reasoned as follows. There are only two kinds of beings, minds and bodies. Roundness is not the mode of a mind. It is therefore the mode of a body.

We discover by simple perception, then, without any reasoning and merely by applying the mind to the idea of extension, that roundness and every other figure is a modification belonging to body, and that pleasure, pain, heat, and all other sensible qualities are not modifications of body. Every question about what does or does not belong to extension can be answered easily, immediately, and boldly, merely by considering the idea representing it. Everyone agrees on this subject, for those who say that matter can think do not believe that it has this faculty because it is extended; they agree that extension, taken precisely as such, cannot think.

But there is no agreement on what should be believed about the soul and its modifications. There are people who think that pain and heat, or at least color, do not belong to the soul. You even make a fool of yourself before certain Cartesians if you say that the soul actually becomes blue, red, or yellow, and that the soul is painted with the colors of the rainbow when looking at it. There are many people who have doubts, and even more who do not believe, that when we smell carrion the soul becomes formally rotten, and that the taste of sugar, or of pepper or salt, is something belonging to the soul. Where, then, is the clear idea of the soul so that the Cartesians might consult it, and so that they might all agree on the question as to where colors, tastes, and odors are to be found?[34]

* * *

There can be no doubt that the young Berkeley rejected some of the most characteristic features of Malebranche's philosophy, but there can also be little doubt that he learned important lessons from Malebranche's denial that the existence of material substance can be proved, from his insistence that God is the immediate cause of our sensations, and from other things illustrated by the above selections. When A. A. Luce said of Berkeley, "Locke taught him, but Malebranche inspired him,"[35] he summed up their relationship well.

Notes

1. A. A. Luce's pioneering work *Berkeley and Malebranche* (Oxford: Oxford University Press, 1934) traced in detail the influence of Malebranche's *Search* on Berkeley, showing its effect on even Berkeley's earliest publication, the *Arithmetica* and *Miscellanea Mathematica*. The relationship between the two thinkers has often been explored since. See, for example, C. J. McCracken, *Malebranche and British Philosophy* (Oxford: Clarendon Press, 1983), ch. 6, and, in relation to Berkeley's *New Theory of Vision*, Margaret Atherton, *Berkeley's Revolution in Vision* (Ithaca: Cornell University Press, 1990), *passim*.
2. *Works* II, p. 214.
3. There is good evidence that Berkeley read Thomas Taylor's translation of the *Search*, probably using the second (1700) edition. We have consulted that translation, but the following selections are taken from *The Search after Truth*, trans. T. M. Lennon and P. J. Olscamp (Columbus: Ohio State University Press, 1980).
4. *Search*, pp. 48, 482–84.
5. *Search*, pp. 569–70.
6. *Search*, pp. 572–73.
7. *Search*, p. 574.
8. Berkeley here uses "Illustration" for "*Éclaircissement*" ("Elucidation"), as did Taylor in his translation of the *Search*. It is one of the examples that Luce cites as evidence that Berkeley read the *Search* in that translation. Luce, *Berkeley and Malebranche*, p. 46.
9. *PHK* §§82–84; cf. *Third Dialogue*, in *Works* II, pp. 250–56.
10. Descartes, *Philosophical Writings*, vol. 2, p. 239.
11. This theory of "occasional causes" or "Occasionalism", which first appeared among Arab philosophers in the middle ages, was defended by a number of Cartesians before Malebranche, among them Arnold Geulincx, Géraud de Cordemoy, and Louis de La Forge. By the time Malebranche published the *Search*, the theory was quite widely held among Cartesians. On the question of whether Descartes himself may have been committed to this position, see Daniel Garber, "How God Causes Motion: Descartes, Divine Sustenance, and Occasionalism," *Journal of Philosophy* 84 (1987), pp. 567–80.
12. *Search*, p. 448.
13. *PC* 548. Some commentators argue that Berkeley cannot finally avoid siding with Malebranche even on the question of whether or not we can move our

own bodies. See, for example, Nicholas Jolley, "Berkeley and Malebranche on Causality and Volition," in *Central Themes in Early Modern Philosophy: Essays Presented to Jonathan Bennett*, ed. J. A. Cover and M. Kulstad (Indianapolis: Hackett, 1990). What Berkeley usually stresses in his published writings is our power to produce ideas of imagination.

14. *Search*, pp. 449–50.
15. *Search*, p. 671.
16. *Search*, p. 224.
17. *PHK* §§92–94 and 150; *PC* 17 and 411.
18. *Search*, pp. 451–52.
19. *Works* II, pp. 188–90.
20. *Search*, pp. 27–29.
21. For Berkeley's denial that he thinks we see all things in God, see *PHK* §148; *Second Dialogue*, in *Works* II, pp. 213–14; and *Alciphron*, IV.14.
22. *Search*, pp. 217–19.
23. *Third Dialogue*, in *Works* II, p. 235 (emphasis Berkeley's).
24. *Search*, pp. 230–32 and 234–35.
25. In Elucidation Ten, Malebranche qualified this doctrine further. What is in God is not a multitude of distinct ideas, but rather "intelligible infinite extension." By uniting our minds to "a part of this intelligible extension," God represents to us particular parts of corporeal extension.
26. *Works* II, p. 214.
27. In Luce's diplomatic edition of the *Philosophical Commentaries* (Edinburgh: Thomas Nelson, 1944), p. 382. The others Luce mentions in this connection are Bacon, whom Berkeley refers to in *PC* 564, and Hobbes.
28. *Search*, p. 241.
29. *Search*, pp. 241–42.
30. *Search*, pp. 244–45, 247.
31. For the four kinds of knowledge, see *Search*, pp. 236–40.
32. See *PHK* §89 (second edition) and *De Motu* §21.
33. Here and throughout this passage Malebranche denies that we have a *clear* idea of the soul, which might seem to suggest that we have a confused one. He elsewhere explains, however, that when he speaks in this way, he is using "idea" for "anything that is the immediate object of the mind," but that in "the most precise and restricted sense" of the term, we do not have an idea of the soul (*Search*, p. 561). Berkeley makes a comparable distinction at *PHK* §140, where, after denying that we have an idea of the soul, he grants that "in a large sense" we may be said to have an idea of the soul, for we understand the meaning of that word.
34. *Search*, pp. 633–35.
35. Luce, *Berkeley and Malebranche*, p. 7.

FOUR

Pierre de Lanion

Four years after Malebranche's *Search* first appeared, Pierre de Lanion, a Breton priest who, like Malebranche, was a member of the Académie des Sciences, published a work entitled *Meditations on Metaphysics*. He there embraced Malebranche's doctrines that we see all things in God and that God is the immediate cause of our sensations, as well as another tenet stressed by Malebranche: that God acts always by the simplest ways.[1] These doctrines led Lanion to a more radical conclusion than any drawn by Malebranche in the *Search*. Not only can we not demonstrate that bodies exist, reason – were it not corrected by faith – would seem to suggest that they do not exist. Since God is "the source and origin of all my ideas," and they would be exactly as they are even if there were no bodies, it would seem that God, who always acts by the simplest means, would have had no reason to create a material world.

In the *Search*, Malebranche had drawn many conclusions from the principle that God always acts in the simplest ways, but not this one, which went well beyond anything Malebranche had yet suggested. However, a few years after Lanion proposed the argument, Malebranche alluded to it in his controversy with Arnauld, remarking that it could be said "that God does nothing useless and that it is useless to create bodies, since bodies do not act on the mind and, strictly speaking, the mind does not see bodies."[2] Still later, Bayle – who admired Lanion and reissued his *Meditations*[3] – used the argument in "Zeno of Elea".[4] Berkeley, so far as we know, never read Lanion, but he would have met the argument in Bayle, and may also have come on it in Locke, who turned the argument against Malebranche by raising the question, "since God does all things by the most compendious ways, what need is there that God should make a sun that we might see its idea in him when he pleased to exhibit it, when this might as well be done without any real sun at all."[5]

Berkeley saw the argument's force and he, too, used it against Malebranche, whose doctrine of seeing all things in God "hath this peculiar to itself; that it makes that material world serve to no purpose. And if it pass for a good argument against other hypotheses in the sciences, that they suppose Nature or the divine wisdom to make something in vain, or do that by tedious round-about methods, which might have been performed in a much more easy and compendious way, what shall we think of that hypothesis which supposes the whole world made in vain?"[6]

In the following selections,[7] Lanion at first goes no further than Malebranche; as things proceed, however, the case against the existence of bodies becomes stronger, and Lanion ends by suggesting that it would be easy to explain why God might give us sensations even if there were no bodies.[8]

SIXTH MEDITATION

I have recognized in the preceding Meditation that, from my clear and distinct idea of extension, I cannot infer that any extended things exist.[9] Indeed, I see clearly that I cannot demonstrate the existence of any of the things that are represented to me by my ideas. The only exception to this is the existence of an infinitely perfect being, for it is obvious that I do not cause my own ideas (since they come unbidden into my mind) and that they are not caused in me by the bodies around me (since I cannot conceive that something round or square, or of any shape whatever, could have in itself the power to make itself intelligible to me and to make itself perceivable by me), so it is necessary to conclude that there is a God, an infinitely wise and powerful being, who is the source and origin of all my ideas. That being the case, can he not produce in me all my ideas, even if the things that they represent to me do not exist? It is true that at first I find this hard to believe, for it seems I could accuse God of deceiving me were he to give me ideas that represented certain things as existing outside me that, in fact, did not exist. But when I consider more carefully that the idea I have of the sun – i.e., the object most immediately present to my mind when I see the sun – differs completely from me (for I am aware that *I* am not the sun that I see), and differs also from the sun that illumines the world (for the object immediately present to my mind must be an intelligible thing, whereas the sun is a material thing), I am obliged to believe that everything I see exists in the form in which I see it, that is to say, in an intelligible form in the substance of God himself. So instead of calling God a deceiver because he gives me ideas of all things, I should accuse myself of the error of judging too hastily that there exists outside me any being other than God.

Still, it does appear that extended things exist outside me, even though I cannot absolutely demonstrate that they do: for everything that nature teaches me, whether by instinct or in some other way, has in it some truth, since by *nature* I understand nothing other than God himself acting on his creatures. Now nature seems to teach me that I am united to a body, i.e., that I am intimately related to a certain extended thing, and that, as it is benefitted or injured, I feel pleasure or pain. This same nature seems also to teach me that many other bodies surround me that I must avoid or pursue if I am to preserve my life. It is therefore quite likely that extension exists outside me in the way my ideas represent it to me.

I have heard it said, it is true, that nature leads some sick people, viz., sufferers from dropsy, to drink, even though doing so is bad for them; so it seems I should not put my trust in everything nature teaches me, for it can sometimes fool me. But since it belongs to the grandeur and wisdom of God to act always by the simplest ways, bringing effects about by the fewest possible decrees, and since, furthermore, in order to preserve my body, God has decreed that, whenever he causes certain motions in my throat, I will desire something to drink, it can sometimes come about that – in carrying out his own decrees and acting in accordance with the laws he himself has established – God will be obliged to produce thirst in me at a time when it is dangerous for me to drink. But I cannot, because of this, accuse him of injustice or deception, for it is not fitting that he, the general and universal cause of things, should act by particular volitions in each particular case.

I should, however, keep in mind that all the sensations that seem to be produced in me by states of extended things serve more to prove to me that there is a God than that there is an extended world. All those sensations are only so many modifications of my own mind, modifications that I am aware belong to me and that I know not by any clear idea but only by inward feeling. Now I do not produce those sensations in myself – if I did, I would give myself only pleasant ones that would make me happy. Nor do they come to me from external objects, for that

would require that those objects have the power to make me happy or
sad, a power I myself lack; instead, they must come from God, the only
being who has the power to cause my happiness. Thus, my sensations
prove to me clearly that God exists, but they prove the existence of
bodies in only a very imperfect way; for, since God, who acts always by
the simplest ways, is the immediate cause of my sensations, I cannot but
think that it would be too long a detour for this infinitely wise being to
create extension, in order to give me sensations, when extension cannot
even produce those sensations. Thus it is not absolutely necessary that
extension exist.

> Lanion next asks whether his mind might not itself be an extended
> thing; if it were, then – since he is certain his mind exists – he could
> be certain extension exists, too. He replies with an argument, mod-
> eled on Descartes', to prove that the mind is not extended. The
> Sixth Meditation ends:

From all I have said, I can now conclude that it is impossible for me
to demonstrate the existence of an extended world and that our nature
is so weak that there are very few things about which we have certain
and evident knowledge.

SEVENTH MEDITATION

I have done all I can to extricate myself from the doubts my first
Meditation cast me into, but the more I try to find a demonstration of
the existence of the extended world, the more I am persuaded that it is
beyond my powers to find one. For when I consider that what I see must
be something intelligible (or, rather, that what I see is only the substance
of God himself, representing to me what I see), and consider further
that God, using only a few decrees, must always act by the shortest and
simplest ways, and consider finally that God himself directly gives me all
my thoughts, all my ideas, and all my sensations, then I find so little
connection between the way it seems to me that God should act and the
long detour he would have to take were he to create extension in order
to make me see things, that I should accuse myself of imprudence in
having formerly judged that anything exists outside me, except for God,
and of obstinacy in now finding it so hard to persuade myself that there
are no bodies, if it were not that faith, which is superior to reason,
requires me to believe that there are.

Consider further that God, being infinitely good and essentially love-able, created me solely to this end: that I should love him, not with a love that is forced from me or that I give from self-interest, but with a love that I give freely and because he deserves it. Thus, when God produces pleasurable sensations in me, it is so that I, by renouncing those pleasures and turning from myself, toward him, can love him with a love that is free. What I mean is that, although God gives me enough motion to carry me towards him who is all good and all being, he nonetheless leaves me the power to remain at rest in sensuous and particular goods; he does this so that I, by making use of the motion he gives me towards himself when I could turn away towards other goods, can prefer him to them and love him freely. In this way, even without supposing that extension exists, it is not hard to explain why God gives me all my sensations.

Notes

1. Malebranche repeatedly invoked this tenet in the *Search* (for an example, see above, p. 44), and he defended it in the Sixteenth Elucidation of the third edition, which had the title "That God Acts always with Order, and by the simplest ways." (This elucidation was omitted from later editions of the *Search* and is not included in the Lennon-Olscamp translation, but is in Taylor's translation (1700 ed.), vol. 2, pp. 180–82.)
2. Malebranche, *Oeuvres complètes*, ed. Robinet, vol. 6, p. 184.
3. In *Recueil de quelques pièces curieuses concernant la philosophie de Monsieur Descartes* (Amsterdam, 1684); in the preface, Bayle called Lanion's book "a précis of the finest metaphysics" that "takes us well beyond Descartes."
4. See below, p. 81.
5. Locke, *An Examination of P. Malebranche's Opinion of Seeing all Things in God* §20.
6. Berkeley, *Works* II, p. 214; see also *PHK* §19.
7. From the Sixth and Seventh of Lanion's *Méditations sur la métaphysique*, published in Paris in 1678, under the pseudonym Guillaume Wander. We have followed Bayle's edition of this work (see note 3).
8. Some scholars have thought that Lanion may have been the thinker, mentioned by the *Mémoires de Trévoux*, who "has gone even further than Mr. Berkley [*sic*]" by suggesting that he may be the only created thing that exists. This seems unlikely, since Lanion grants that faith assures us of the existence of other creatures. On the identity of this thinker, see Chapter VI, note 4.
9. Lanion's Fifth Meditation had argued that, from our clear and distinct idea of extension, we can deduce a priori all the truths of geometry, but that these truths concern only the *essence* of extension considered as an "intelligible" thing and do not imply the *existence* of corporeal extension.

Antoine Arnauld

The life of Antoine Arnauld (1612–1694) spanned the seventeenth century. In his twenties he wrote the penetrating fourth set of *Objections* that Descartes appended to the *Meditations*;[1] in his forties he wrote, with Pierre Nicole, what was to be the most influential logic text of the seventeenth century, *The Art of Thinking* or *Port-Royal Logic* (1662); in his seventies he carried on a notable correspondence with Leibniz about the latter's philosophy;[2] and in the final decade of his life he engaged in a long, voluminous, sometimes acrimonious, but important controversy with Malebranche about the nature of ideas.[3] Much of his life and energy, however, was used up in theological debate, for he was, with Pascal, the leading defender of the besieged theological movement Jansenism, and many of the forty-two fat volumes of his collected works are given over to religious controversy. Voltaire said of Arnauld that "no one was ever born with a more philosophical mind," though he wasted it in sectarian polemics.[4]

Berkeley never mentions Arnauld, but he can hardly have failed to have some knowledge of him, for the *Port-Royal Logic* was famous by the time Berkeley was a student (it had passed through six French editions by the year of Berkeley's birth, and three English versions had appeared by the time he entered Trinity College); and if, as we believe, Berkeley read Bayle's "Zeno of Elea", he would have come to know some details of Arnauld's controversy with Malebranche from Bayle's account of it. In any case, Arnauld made an important contribution to the seventeenth-century discussion of the nature of ideas, and related issues, that formed the background against which Berkeley's own theory of ideas developed. The following selections illustrate Arnauld's theory of what an *idea* is, his arguments for the existence of bodies, and his account of how the mind forms abstractions.

1. Ideas

Malebranche, we have seen, held that bodies cannot be directly present to the mind; instead, *ideas*, which are different from yet directly present to the mind, represent bodies to it.[5] Such a doctrine, argued Arnauld, means that Malebranche has committed himself to distinguishing three things: the mind's *perception* of an object (which is a modification of the mind itself), the *idea*, which is distinct from the mind, and the *object* represented by that idea. But, said Arnauld, this involves some inconsistency on Malebranche's part, and a significant departure from the correct use of "idea".[6]

For at the beginning of *The Search for Truth* [Malebranche] uses the word *idea* in its true sense to stand for the perception of an object, and he recognizes there that the perception of an object is a modification of our mind. . . . But in Book III, he gives an entirely different sense to the word *idea*, taking it to stand for *a representative being*, distinct from perceptions, an entity which he imagines is necessary in order to put objects, which are assumed not to be intelligible through themselves, into a position to be known by our soul. Thus there are three things which must be distinguished, according to him, in the knowledge of that sort of object: the object to be known, which is not intelligible through itself, the representative being which puts it into a position to be known, and the perception of our mind, through which it is actually known.

Malebranche's whole theory that ideas are spiritual entities, existing in God and distinct from the objects they represent, rests on this threefold distinction, says Arnauld; but, he cautions, the distinction is specious. For a *perception* and an *idea of an object* are the same thing, viewed in two different ways: first as a mental state considered in itself, and then as that mental state considered in relation to an object. Once this is grasped, we need not suppose, with Malebranche, that our perception of the sun involves *two* entities, an idea (the intelligible sun) and a body (the corporeal sun). Instead, we need only distinguish two ways in which one and the same sun can be considered: as a thing in the heavens (what Descartes called its *formal reality*) and as a thing present to the mind (what Descartes called its *objective reality*, an expression also used by Arnauld). Arnauld gave five complex proofs, with definitions, axioms, and postulates, to show that there are no ideas *in Malebranche's sense*. Here we give only some of his definitions, but they suffice to illustrate his own view.

DEFINITIONS

1. The substance which thinks, I call soul or mind.
2. To think, to know, to perceive, are the same thing.
3. I also take the *idea* of an object and the perception of an object to be the same thing. . . . [I]t is certain that there are *ideas* in my sense and that these ideas are attributes or modifications of our soul.
4. I say that an object is present to our mind when our mind perceives and knows it. . . . [T]he way in which I say an object is present to the mind when it is known is beyond question. This sort of presence makes us say that a person we love is often present to our mind because we often think of him.
5. I say that a thing is *objectively* in my mind when I conceive of it. When I conceive of the sun, of a square or of a sound, then the sun, the square or that sound is objectively in my mind whether or not it exists outside of my mind.
6. I have said that I take *the perception and the idea* to be the same thing. Nevertheless it must be noted that this thing, although only one, has two relations: one to the soul which it modifies, the other to the thing perceived insofar as it is objectively in the soul; and that the word *perception* indicates more directly the first relation and the word *idea* the second. So *the perception* of a square indicates more directly my soul as perceiving a square and *the idea* of a square indicates more directly the square insofar as it is *objectively* in my mind. . . . [T]hese are not two different entities but one and the same modification of our soul, which includes essentially the two relations, because I cannot have a perception which is not at the same time the perception of my mind, as perceiving, and the perception of some thing, as perceived, and nothing can be objectively in my mind (which is what I call the *idea*) unless my mind perceives it.
7. When I attack *representative beings* as superfluous, I am referring to those which are assumed to be really distinct from ideas taken in the

sense of perceptions. I am careful not to attack every kind of *representative* being or modality, since I hold that it is clear to whoever reflects on what takes place in his own mind, that all our perceptions are modalities which are essentially *representative*.

8. When it is said that our ideas and our perceptions (for I take them to be the same thing) represent to us the things that we conceive, and are the images of them, it is in an entirely different sense than when we say that pictures represent their originals and are images of them, or that words, spoken or written, are images of our thoughts. With regard to ideas, it means that the things that we conceive are *objectively* in our mind and in our thought. But this *way of being objectively in the mind* is so peculiar to mind and to thought, being what in particular constitutes their nature, that we look in vain for anything similar in the realm of what is not mind and thought. . . . [7]

9. When I say that the *idea* is the same thing as the *perception*, I mean by the perception, anything that my mind conceives by the first apprehension that it has of things, by the judgments which it makes about them, or by what it discovers about them in reasoning. Thus although there are infinitely many shapes whose nature I know only by long processes of reasoning, yet when I have carried out the reasoning, I have as true an idea of those figures as I have of a circle or a triangle, which I can conceive straightaway. Although perhaps I am entirely sure that there truly is an earth, a sun and stars outside my mind only by reasoning, the idea which represents to me the earth, the sun and the stars as truly existing outside my mind no less merits the name 'idea' than if I had it without need of reasoning.

10. There is another ambiguity to clear up. *The idea of an object* must not be confused with *the object conceived*, unless one adds, *insofar as it is objectively in the mind*. For to be *conceived, with regard to the sun* which is in the sky, is only an extrinsic denomination, which is only a relation to the perception that I have of it. But this is not what should be understood when one says that *the idea of the sun is the sun itself, insofar as it is objectively in my mind*. What is called *being objectively in the mind* is not only being the object, at which my thought terminates, but it is being in my mind *intelligibly*, in the specific way in which objects are in the mind. . . . [8]

Since the *perception* and the *idea* of an object are the same thing, Arnauld rejects any theory, like Malebranche's, that treats ideas as *entities* different from, but representative of, objects. Locke's theory of ideas has often been read as another example of the doctrine that ideas are a kind of *tertium quid*, standing between the mind and objects, that Arnauld is here rejecting, although John Yolton and some other Locke scholars hold that Locke's theory, correctly understood, is much like Arnauld's.[9] Had Arnauld lived long enough to read Berkeley, he might, indeed, have accused Berkeley of a confusion similar to the one he accused Malebranche of, for although, like Arnauld, Berkeley identifies ideas with perceptions, he also states that ideas are a kind of *being*, and "entirely distinct" from the mind (*PHK* §§2 and 89).[10]

2. The Existence of Bodies

The mind's perceptions of things, says Arnauld, include "what it discovers about them in reasoning" (def. 9). Since he thinks that Descartes has shown how to establish, by reasoning, that there are bodies, he holds that we have perceptions of bodies themselves. Malebranche, we have seen, criticized Descartes' proof of bodies, arguing that God would not be a deceiver if he caused sensations in our minds even though no bodies existed. Arnauld replied by giving eight new proofs, which he maintained amounted to demonstrations, that God would indeed be a deceiver were there no external reality other than God himself. A number of these bear primarily on the question of whether other *people* exist. We give only the first of Arnauld's arguments, but one that is characteristic of his approach.

We can derive a certain argument for the existence of bodies from speech, together with the principle that God is not a deceiver. For since I know myself, I cannot doubt that I think I speak, i.e., join my thoughts to certain sounds which I think are formed by the body to which I assume I am united, in order to make my thoughts understood to other persons similar to myself, whom I assume are around me, and who, it seems to me, do not fail on their part to make understood that they have indeed understood what I wanted to say to them, either by other words that I imagine I hear, or by other signs that I think I see.

But if I did not have a body, and if there were no other men than me, God must have deceived me countless times, by forming in my mind all the thoughts that I have had of so many diverse sounds, as formed by the organs of my body, and by responding to me himself interiorly in so appropriate a way that I could not doubt that it was the persons to whom I thought I spoke who responded to me, and doing so not once or twice, but countless times. He would have done all that immediately by himself, and no one could say that he did so on the occasion of the motions in my body, since it is assumed that I do not have a body.

Therefore, since God is not a deceiver, it must necessarily be the case that I have a body, and that there are other men who are similar to me and who join their thoughts to sounds as I do, in order to make them known to me.[11]

Although Malebranche had held that reason cannot demonstrate that bodies exist, he had insisted that we can be certain that they do, for this has been revealed to us in the Bible. However, he recognized that he might here be accused of reasoning in a circle, for faith seems to presuppose acceptance that there are bodies. "It seems to assume prophets, apostles, Sacred Scripture, miracles ...." He sought to circumvent this charge by arguing that, even if all these things are considered *merely* as appearances, the appearances must be produced in our minds by God, so they will suffice to make God's revelation, including the revelation that he created bodies, known to us.[12] To this, Arnauld, for whom Descartes' reasoning, supported by his own proofs, seemed sufficient to establish the existence of bodies, made a devastating reply.

I do not know whether I am mistaken, Sir, but I do not believe that there has ever been a more vicious circle. For what is at issue is whether, after assuming that there are no bodies and that there is nothing but God and my mind, I can remain in that assumption up to the point of having faith, and depart from it only by means of faith? I hold that it is impossible, and that the argument of the author does not prove it in any way. On that assumption, insofar as I remain in it, I must believe that God alone could have represented to my mind everything that I have read, good or evil, if I very well know I have not composed the books I read. Therefore, he must have represented to me what I imagine I read in the Koran, as well as what I thought I had read in a book called the Bible. Therefore, on the hypothesis that there is nothing but God and my mind,[13] if the argument holds good with regard to the Bible, that *since God is not a deceiver, and since only he could have represented to my mind what I had imagined I had seen in the Bible, I must take that as incontestable*, I do not see why it would not also hold with regard to the Koran. Thus I am sure that I can get out of the difficulty only by using the maxim that God cannot be a deceiver to convince myself of the evident false- hood of the assumption that there are no bodies, but only God and my mind, and not by using it to conclude that the appearances of prophets, apostles, Holy Scripture and miracles could suffice to make us add faith to Scripture, and thus change those appearances into realities even be- fore we recognized the absurdity of that hypothesis.[14]

3. Abstraction

In the Introduction to the *Principles*, Berkeley mounts an attack on abstraction, abstract ideas, and, in particular, abstract general ideas. Notoriously, he takes Locke as his main target, although he also mentions the Schoolmen as "those great masters of abstraction" and sees the doctrine of abstract general ideas as lying at the root of many fundamental errors in philosophy. It is of interest, therefore, to see what Arnauld says about abstraction in Part I of *The Art of Thinking*.

[We have] observed that we can consider a mode without reflecting explicitly on the substance of which this mode is a mode. Such consid- eration of a mode is an instance of knowledge by *abstraction*.

Because of the limited scope of our minds, we are unable to under- stand perfectly even things which are only slightly composite unless we can consider these things part by part or with respect to their different aspects. Knowing things in such a fashion is often called knowing by abstraction.

Things are composite in different ways. Some things are composite in the sense of having integral parts, that is, parts that are actually distinct: Arms and legs are integral parts of the human body; units are integral parts of numbers. It is easy to see how we can consider one integral part of a thing without considering any other of its integral parts. But knowing a thing by a consideration of its integral parts is not what is commonly meant by abstraction. Still, knowledge through con- sideration of integral parts is an important mode of knowledge, for we come to know many complex things only through this mode of know- ing. . . .

A second kind of knowledge by parts occurs when we consider a mode without paying attention to its substance or consider two modes which are joined together in a single substance, regarding each mode separately. Geometers, the object of whose science is the extended, employ this second kind of knowledge through parts. In order to understand the extended better – that is, what has extension in three dimensions – geometers consider first of all what is extended in only one dimension: line. Next, they consider what is extended in only two dimensions: surface. And finally they consider what is extended in three dimensions: solids.

We now see how unfounded is the argument of those skeptics who wish to cast doubt on the certitude of geometry by claiming that geometry assumes the existence of lines and surfaces, neither of which is found in nature. For geometers do not suppose that there are lines without width or surfaces without depth; geometers suppose only that we can consider length without paying attention to breadth. We certainly do this when we measure the distance from one city to another; we report only the length of the road, not its breadth. . . .

A third way of knowing things by parts occurs when we think exclusively of one characteristic of a thing that possesses several characteristics separable only in thought. Suppose I reflect that I think and that, thus, it is I who am thinking. Then in the idea I have of myself who thinks, I can consider a thing that thinks without paying attention to the fact that it is I myself, even though I and the one who thinks are identical. In the same fashion, if I draw an equilateral triangle on a piece of paper and direct my attention to the place where the triangle is drawn and to all the accidental characteristics of the triangle, I shall have an idea of only that particular triangle. But if instead of considering all these particular circumstances, I consider only that what I have drawn is a figure bounded by three equal lines, then my idea will represent all other equilateral triangles. If I go even further, not stopping with this equality of lines, and consider only that what I have drawn is a figure determined by three straight lines, then my idea represents every kind of triangle. And then, if I go still further and consider only that what I have drawn is a plane surface bounded by straight lines, my idea represents all rectilinear figures. Thus, degree by degree I can ascend to an idea of extension itself. We see in these abstractions that each lower degree is some particular determination of the higher degree: The *I* is a determination of him who thinks; equilateral triangle, a determination of triangle; and triangle, of rectilinear figure. The higher degree, being less determinate, stands for more things. Through such abstractions we move from the idea of a particular to a more general idea, then to an even more universal idea, and so on.[15]

Arnauld thus distinguishes three kinds of "knowledge by parts." The first, which Arnauld says is not usually counted as abstraction, is one that Berkeley grants in *PHK*, Introduction §10. The other two stress the role of selective attention in a way that one would think should be acceptable to Berkeley, who concedes "that a man may consider a figure merely as triangular, without attending to the particular qualities of the angles, or relations of the sides. So far he may abstract."[16] Some argue that this is how Locke, too, conceives of abstraction. Be that as it may, there is no suggestion in Arnauld that the ideas thus formed are images, or that if we have the idea of a line, say, as something extended in only one direction, we must suppose that there is some object that can be so described. Rather, "we can consider length without paying attention to breadth," and to do that *is* to have the idea.

Notes

1. In Descartes, *Philosophical Writings*, vol. 2, pp. 138–53.
2. In *The Leibniz-Arnauld Correspondence*, trans. H. T. Mason (Manchester: Manchester University Press, 1967).
3. Arnauld's contributions to the controversy are collected in Arnauld, *Oeuvres* (Paris, 1775–83), vols. 38–40; Malebranche's in Malebranche, *Oeuvres complètes*, ed. A. Robinet (Paris: Vrin, 1958–84), vols. 6–9.
4. Voltaire, *Siècle de Louis XIV*, quoted by E. J. Kremer in his Introduction to his translation of *On True and False Ideas*, p. xi.
5. See pp. 41–43 above.
6. The following selection is from the first and most important of Arnauld's works against Malebranche, *On True and False Ideas*, trans. E. J. Kremer (Lampeter: Edwin Mellen Press, 1990), p. 157.
7. For Arnauld, as for Brentano and some later thinkers, intentionality, or the mind's being directed on an object, is the essence of the mental.
8. *On True and False Ideas*, pp. 19–21.
9. John W. Yolton, *Perceptual Acquaintance from Descartes to Reid* (Oxford: Basil Blackwell, 1984). The correct interpretation of Arnauld's own theory of ideas has long been a matter of dispute, particularly over the question of whether his theory is a version of "direct realism". The *locus classicus* of this debate is A. O. Lovejoy's " 'Representative Ideas' in Malebranche and Arnauld," *Mind* 32 (1923), pp. 449–61, and John Laird's "The 'Legend' of Arnauld's Realism,"

Mind 33 (1924), pp. 176–79. For recent discussions of the issue, see Steven Nadler, *Arnauld and the Cartesian Philosophy of Ideas* (Princeton: Princeton University Press, 1989), Pt. 5; and E. J. Kremer (ed.), *The Great Arnauld and Some of His Philosophical Correspondents* (Toronto: University of Toronto Press, 1994), Pt. 2.

10. For contrasting views of the relation of Arnauld and Berkeley, see Yolton, *Perceptual Acquaintance*, chaps. 7 and 11, and I. C. Tipton, " 'Ideas' in Berkeley and Arnauld," in *History of European Ideas* 7 (1986), pp. 575–84.

11. *On True and False Ideas*, p. 176.

12. Malebranche, *Search after Truth*, p. 575.

13. The French here is "qu'il n'y a que moi & mon esprit." Kremer is surely correct in assuming that "moi" should be "Dieu".

14. *On True and False Ideas*, pp. 180–81.

15. Arnauld, *The Art of Thinking*, trans. J. Dickoff and P. James (Indianapolis: Bobbs-Merrill, 1964), pp. 47–50.

16. *PHK*, Introduction §16 (second edition); cf. *PC* 318, and *First Dialogue, Works* II, p. 193.

SIX

Jean Brunet

In 1686, Jean Brunet[1] published in the *Journal de médecine* a long article entitled "New Conjectures on the Sense Organs, in which a New System of Optics is Proposed." In it he argued that when we draw distinctions between "objects", "images", "passions", and "kinds" (or sorts) of things, we are really only distinguishing different ways in which the mind can represent things to itself. What we cannot do, according to Brunet, is to think that something exists when it is not thought of. Equally, he argued, consciousness, or thought, "requires for its subsistence a particular object that gives it form and definiteness." From such considerations Brunet concluded that "every object has reality only in the mind" and that "thought and its objects really constitute one and the same existence."

This conclusion seems to differ from the position Berkeley would adopt later, for Berkeley was to insist that minds and their objects (ideas) are radically different kinds of things [*PHK* §89]. And Brunet and Berkeley differed on other issues – for example, Brunet held that one can think of pure space in abstraction from sensible qualities such as color and hardness. Moreover, the obscurity of Brunet's writing is in stark contrast to the clarity and argumentative force of Berkeley's. As Lewis Robinson remarked, Brunet "wrote in an odd, heavy, careless style that reminds one – as do his ideas – of some of the subsequent German idealists."[2] Nonetheless, it is noteworthy that, almost a quarter of a century before Berkeley, the argument had been advanced that it would be a contradiction to suppose that an object can exist apart from thought, in a way that seems to anticipate the argument of *PHK* §§22–23 (see also *Works* II, pp. 200–201).

No copy is known to have survived of the work in which Brunet apparently set his views out most fully, *Projet d'une nouvelle méta-physique*, published in Paris in 1703. But a writer of the time, Flachat de Saint-Sauveur, maintained that in it "Mr. Brunet lays down, as a basic principle, that he alone exists in the world; that his thought is the cause of the existence of all creatures; that when, alas for human beings, he ceases to think of them, they are annihilated."[3] Whether this is an accurate portrayal of Brunet's views is questionable, for Flachat de Saint-Sauveur seemed eager to represent those views in as absurd a light as possible: "It is thus in everybody's interest, so long as we exist, for the all-powerful Mr. Brunet to keep on thinking; when he begins to sleep, I am gripped by a mortal dread lest the whole human race – and I, one of its lesser members – return to nothingness." In the selection from Brunet's 1686 article, here translated, Brunet does not suggest that he is the only thing that exists. However, he does contrast his own view with the distinction made in "every philosophical age . . . between the great world and the little world that each individual contains within himself," the second being "like a mirror or copy of the first," and he points out that the only thing one can know is the little world one contains. While he here seems to suppose that there is a plurality of individuals, each containing his own "little world", it is hard to see what grounds he could give for making such a supposition. Perhaps that is why Flachat de Saint-Sauveur read him as a solipsist, though it remains possible that in his lost work he actually defended solipsism.

That Brunet could be taken, in his own time, for a solipsist has led some scholars to suggest that he is the unnamed thinker, mentioned by the *Mémoires de Trévoux*, who "has gone even further than Mr. Berkley [*sic*]" by supposing it probable that he is the only created thing that exists – a reference that later helped link Berkeley's position in some people's minds with solipsism.[4] Moreover, early in the nineteenth century, the article on Brunet in a standard French reference work of the time boasted that, thanks to him, France, not Britain or Germany, produced the first system of idealism, and went on to wonder whether Berkeley may not have found his starting point in Brunet's book.[5] That is highly unlikely. However, we include a selection from Brunet because it illustrates how the seventeenth-century discussion about whether we can know that there is a world independent of our minds could suggest to another thinker an argument not unlike one that Berkeley would deploy.

Our selection is from "Nouvelles conjectures sur les organes des sens, où l'on propose un nouveau Système d'Optique," section six.[6]

When we consider that nothing can take leave of itself or get outside itself, we soon recognize that our mind imagines nothing of substances that differ from it if they are not spiritualized [*inspiritualisées*] for it. That is why in every philosophical age a distinction has been drawn between the great world and the little world that each individual contains within himself – the second world being like a mirror or copy of the first. And since a particular and determinate being in any existing circumstances can neither produce nor change itself, it was necessary to suppose a Supreme Being who orders and moves the creatures composing the world that we feel ourselves part of and that we see fit to believe external to ourselves.

But since one can conceive only what is in oneself, each must seek within himself the reason and cause of the appearances of the imaginary world over which he alone presides. It is of this world, grounded in human nature, that the Peripatetics so admirably said, *intellectus intelligendo fit omnia*, i.e., *thought makes everything*; all its variety can be related to the diversity of our own modifications and, to preserve conviction and evidence in one's reasonings, one can find no starting point simpler, more fecund, deeper, or more necessary than oneself.

For regardless what state one finds oneself in, there are just two things one can take cognizance of: consciousness [per se] and the [particular] expression of this inner awareness. The first is unchanging, universal, representing us as always the same; the second rules and makes determinate the first. There is nothing in a knowing being that it does not sense and illuminate, and since the action of thinking is distinct from that light which produces it, the mind can itself immediately perceive its action of thinking and then, by a second reflection, it can think about its awareness of its thought, while not ceasing to recognize that it cannot go beyond a comprehensive perception of its own sensations.

We further distinguish, in all our thoughts, their form, or what makes them specific, from the presence of that form to the mind. Thus white, red, cold or hot, pain, water, a house, are objects of thought necessarily perceived as having certain qualities, to which is added that of being known by something different, something which does the perceiving – just as the thinking being is not the same as the conviction I have when I recognize that I am thinking, even though it is the subject and inseparable substance of that thinking.

Whatever exists is known; by that I mean that it would be contradictory to attribute a positive existence to something that one was not thinking of. Hence all things are necessarily known. It is quite impossible for a tree or a table, a pain or colors as such, ever themselves to have the property of knowing. But because the simple quality of thinking is a vague notion that has an essential relation to all that is knowable (just as what can be known has an essential relation to what can know), thinking requires for its subsistence a particular object that gives it form and definiteness; and, reciprocally, every object has reality only in the mind. In general, consciousness is present in all instances of thinking, which can only be distinguished from each other because one is a seeing of one thing, another of another thing, one is a sensation of admiration, another of pain, or of a tree – things very different from consciousness, which becomes exterior to itself at the moment that it conceives itself, for every term is at some remove from the principle of its action. If one should attribute to a thing only what it formally represents, then one cannot say strictly that objects are modifications of thought – just as one does not see thought or consciousness in any of the states of a rock, or as a certain color expresses nothing more than that color itself. But since pain or pleasure is nothing unless it is perceived, and since perception is an incomplete being without the pleasure, pain, etc. that individualizes it, thought and its objects really constitute one and the same existence.[7]

Consider, further, that one spreads oneself into all things and that, on a first and simple view of them, one doesn't distinguish oneself from them; that things are present only when one thinks of them; that one can increase or diminish them to infinity depending on whether one applies the mind to them or turns it away from them; and that one can discover nothing whereby one thought can be distinguished from another save the different forms of their objects which, as presented clearly and perceptibly to us, can be represented by nothing but themselves: such considerations suggest that it is the mind that, by its various turns, seems to give to the instances of its knowledge [*à ses connaissances*] all their various determinations. Such determinations are generally called *objects* when they simply appear to us; *images* or *ideas* when we feel ourselves the master of their being present, the mind being able to examine them as it chooses, and when, in thinking of them, we can represent to ourselves other things that are like these images, except not so indistinct, more external, as if subsisting in themselves because they are conceived as independent of the sensation of them that I now arouse in myself (though these things too would have to pass for ideas or images of ideas or of earlier objects to which we would take them to conform except that they are more subject to our present act of thinking). We call *passions* or *affections* objects that determine us internally and that modify us by feelings of pleasure or pain which are motions of the soul that differ in this: in pain we think chiefly of an object we want to flee from, an object that disturbs us, whereas in the case of pleasure our attention is fixed on something that attracts us. . . . Finally, things are taken for *kinds* or *beings of reason* when we do not particularize them in all the circumstances necessary for them to be differentiated from each other – thus, the essence or reality of a house is an indivisible assemblage of stone, wood, plaster, etc.; and everyone feels in possession of the truth when persuaded of the identity of an object with all its attributes, as when one thinks that everything is what it is, or that two and two are two and two.

Considering, then, the things of nature as if there could be nothing apart from me, or as being multiplied into only as many kinds of things as I have kinds of knowledge or distinct sensations, I will not extend the judgments I make about things beyond the limits of my imagination.

Diverse qualities collected together are represented as one simple individual. For when we make even a small subtraction from an idea, or addition to it, it is no longer the same idea. Thus, as indivisible as I take myself to be, my essence could now be changed into several quite distinct kinds of thing, each of which, being viewed as separate from every other one, would still express unity.

Because my thinking always takes place in the present and all my thoughts are occasioned only by present impressions, it seems that there is, with respect to me, no real succession and that everything occurs in the present moment. Are not temporal priority and posteriority just fictions of my mind? Distinguishing objects as past or future is just my way of conceiving them, for those objects are as positive as ones that appear to me the most present, just as remote places are as real as the place I now occupy. . . .

When I take all the objects of my senses as a whole and without distinction, and do not think of all the individual qualities that differentiate them, I perceive one immense, wholly unitary extension, which has neither color, warmth, etc.; this idea is, as it were, the natural property of the substance that senses, that in which all its faculties exercise themselves and are made manifest. It is in this general extension that all sensations are arranged, because they are contained equally in the greatest and smallest parts, and, being capable of increasing or diminishing by degrees to infinity, they form a continuum that is large only because of the number of its distinct atoms lying one outside the other. It is particular sensations that determine the extension of all the things I call *bodies*, which are colored or transparent, hot or cold, round or square.

Various combinations of odor, warmth, color, give us all the emotions and feelings we are capable of having for bodies. One could even formulate some rules whereby we could benefit from all these compositions. But I here divest material things of these sorts of qualities, leaving them only those they have by virtue of being extended. So considered, I think they are really space itself and that the essential differences among them consist only in differences of location and figure.

Notes

1. He is listed as "Claude Brunet" in the catalogues of the British Library and the Bibliothèque Nationale, but a persuasive case has been made by J. R. Armogathe for the claim that his name was "Jean Brunet". See Armogathe's unpublished mémoire de maîtrise, "Une secte fantôme au XVIIIème siècle: les égoïstes," Mémoires de Sorbonne, 1968–70, Library of the Sorbonne, pp. 163–67.

2. Lewis Robinson, "Un Solipsiste au XVIIIe siècle," *L'Année philosophique* 24 (1913), p. 29.

3. Flachat de Saint-Sauveur, *Pièces fugitives d'histoire et de littérature* (Paris, 1704), pp. 356ff. Quoted by Robinson, p. 19.

4. For the *Mémoires de Trévoux* announcement, see p. 178 below. The proposal that Brunet was the unnamed thinker is defended by Robinson, pp. 15–30, and by J. Larguier des Bancels, "Sur un malebranchiste peu connu," *Revue philosophique* 141 (1951), p. 566. See also Robinson's later article, "Le 'cogito' cartésien et l'origine de l'idéalisme moderne," *Revue philosophique* 123 (1937), pp. 315ff. Others, however, have suggested that the unnamed solipsist was Pierre Lanion, or perhaps a mere invention of the Jesuit editors of the *Mémoires de Trévoux*, who, eager to combat Malebranche's philosophy, were prepared to suggest that it led to Berkeley's views and even to solipsism. See Anita Fritz, "Malebranche and the Immaterialism of Berkeley," *Review of Metaphysics* 3 (1949), pp. 74–75; Maxime Chastaing, "L'abbé de Lanion et le problème cartésien de la connaissance d'autrui," *Revue philosophique* 141 (1951), p. 247, note 3; and M. Chastaing, "Berkeley, défenseur du sens commun et théoricien de la connaissance d'autrui," *Revue philosophique* 143 (1953), p. 230, note 4.

5. *Biographie universelle, ancienne et moderne* (Paris, 1812), vol. 6, p. 115.

6. *Journal de médecine* (Paris), Août-Octobre 1686, pp. 209–19.

7. Brunet added the foregoing paragraph in the "Additions & Corrections" at the end of his work, specifying that it was to be inserted at this point in the text.

SEVEN

Pierre Bayle

In 1697, Pierre Bayle published an *Historical and Critical Dictionary* (an enlarged edition appeared in 1702), a work of monumental scholarship that began with Aaron, ended with Zuylichem, and in between passed in review a vast troupe of characters, historical and mythological, some famous, like Jupiter, King David, Epicurus, Hobbes, and Spinoza, some obscure. But the *Dictionary* is more than a tour de force of scholarship; it is a compendium of skeptical arguments, designed, it seems, to undermine *all* theological and philosophical theories and, on the face of it, to point the moral that in theology and all other areas we are dependent on faith. Whether Bayle's true aim was, as he piously claimed, to show that "reason gets us nowhere, and thus we ought to be completely satisfied with the light of faith," or, as his critics alleged, to undermine religion while pretending to defend it, there can be no doubt that he was a great master of the skeptical argument; indeed, he is usually counted the most important skeptical writer of the period between Montaigne and Hume.

When Berkeley wrote the *Principles*, to investigate "the chief causes of error and difficulty in the Sciences, with the grounds of Scepticism, Atheism, and Irreligion," and the *Dialogues*, "in opposition to Sceptics and Atheists," he almost certainly, Richard Popkin has argued, had Bayle at the front of his mind. And A. A. Luce held that, after Locke and Malebranche, Bayle was the most important influence on Berkeley when he was first formulating his own philosophical position. As the young Berkeley worked, Luce conjectured, "copies of Locke's *Essay* and of Taylor's translation of Malebranche's *Recherche* must have been on his study table, with a volume or two of Bayle's Dictionary."[1] This estimation of Bayle's importance for Berkeley's development may seem surprising, for Bayle is mentioned only twice in the *Philosophical Commentaries* (entries 358 and 424 – further, both entries make precisely the same point), and Berkeley's only other reference to him is a fleeting one in the *Theory of Vision Vindicated* (1733). Nonetheless, Luce and Popkin have made a strong case for the importance of Bayle for Berkeley.[2] That importance was by no means limited to what we must suppose was Berkeley's hostile reaction to Bayle's skepticism, nor to what he probably saw as "atheism a little disguised."[3] Bayle had valuable positive lessons to teach a young immaterialist, too. Berkeley can hardly have failed to pay attention when Bayle declared that extension is something "ideal" and that it exists "only in the mind," and he must surely have taken careful note of the arguments Bayle used to support these claims, however great his misgivings may have been about the skepticism Bayle thought his conclusions led to.

There are several articles in Bayle's *Dictionary* that may have influenced Berkeley, but the selections that follow are from the two that were probably the most important for him, those on Pyrrho, founder of ancient skepticism, and Zeno of Elea, famous for his paradoxes about motion and magnitude.[4] We have arranged these selections, not in the order in which they appear in the *Dictionary*, but topically, in three groups, each of which takes up certain points that would have been important for Berkeley.

1. The Subjectivity of Sensible Qualities

The "new philosophers", as Bayle calls them, taught that color, warmth, odor, and the other "sensible qualities", are not really in the bodies we perceive, but are subjective, belonging to the mind's perception of bodies. It was a view that Descartes, Malebranche, and other Cartesians had stressed. To this, Simon Foucher, an important critic of Descartes and Malebranche, had replied that they gave no better reasons for supposing extension to be external to the soul than for supposing color to be; for extension, like color, is a sensation in the soul. Said Foucher:

> Because all our sensations are nothing other than experiences of several ways of being of which our soul is capable, we know truly by the senses only what objects produce in us, from which it

follows that if one admits that we know extension and figures by
the senses as well as light and colors, one must conclude necessarily that this extension and these figures are no less in us than are
that light and those colors.[5]

Bayle uses this argument in the following passage from "Pyrrho".[6]

Cartesianism put the final touches to this, and now no good philosopher any longer doubts that the [ancient] skeptics were right to maintain
that the qualities of bodies that strike our senses are only appearances.
Every one of us can justly say, "I feel heat in the presence of fire," but
not, "I know that fire is, in itself, such as it appears to me." This is the
way the ancient Pyrrhonists spoke. Today the new philosophy speaks
more positively. Heat, smells, colors, and the like, are not in the objects
of our senses. They are modifications of my soul. I know that bodies are
not at all as they appear to me. They would have wished to exempt
extension and motion, but they could not. For if the objects of our
senses appear colored, hot, cold, odoriferous, and yet they are not so,
why can they not appear extended and shaped, in rest and in motion,
though they are not so?[7] Still further, sense objects cannot be the cause
of my sensations. I could therefore feel heat and cold, see colors and
shapes, extension and motion, even though there were no bodies in the
universe. I have therefore no good proof of the existence of bodies.[8] The
only proof that could be given me of this would be based on the conten-
tion that God would be deceiving me if he imprinted in my mind the
ideas that I have of bodies without there actually being any.[9] But this
proof is very weak; it proves too much. Ever since the beginning of the
world, all mankind, except perhaps one out of two hundred millions, has
firmly believed that bodies are colored, and this is an error. I ask, does
God deceive mankind with regard to colors? If he deceives them about
this, what prevents him from so doing with regard to extension? This
second deception would not be less innocent, nor less compatible with
the nature of a supremely perfect being than the first deception is. If he
does not deceive mankind with regard to colors, this is no doubt because
he does not irresistibly force them to say, "These colors exist outside of
my mind," but only, "It seems to me that there are colors there." The
same thing could be said with regard to extension. God does not irresistibly force you to say, "There is some," but only to judge that you are
aware of it and that it seems to you that there is some. A Cartesian has
no more difficulty in suspending judgment on the existence of extension
than a peasant has in forbearing affirming that the sun shines, that snow

is white, and so on. That is why, if we deceive ourselves in affirming the existence of extension, God would not be the cause, since you grant that he is not the cause of the peasant's errors. These are the advantages that the new philosophers would give to the Pyrrhonists . . . .

> Thus far, Bayle, like Foucher, has argued that extension, figure, and motion are as much "appearances" or sensations as color, odor, or taste – a claim that would have been congenial to Berkeley, who wrote, early in the *Principles*, "Light and colours, heat and cold, extension and figures, in a word the things we see and feel, what are they but so many sensations, notions, ideas or impressions on the sense?" (*PHK* §5). In "Zeno of Elea", Bayle advanced another argument – an important one that was often to be repeated by others – for treating all these qualities as equals. The primary qualities vary just as much as the secondary qualities, relative to the condition or position of the perceiver. Hence, if relativity to the perceiver shows the secondary qualities subjective, it must do the same for the primary. It was an argument that Berkeley would use in a brief and qualified form in the *Principles* (§§14–15), and then, in a more fully developed form, in the first of the *Three Dialogues*.

Add to this that all the means of suspending judgment that overthrow the reality of corporeal qualities also overthrow the reality of extension. Since the same bodies are sweet to some men and bitter to others, one is right in inferring that they are neither sweet nor bitter in themselves and absolutely speaking. The "new" philosophers, although they are not skeptics, have so well understood the bases of suspension of judgment with regard to sounds, smells, heat, cold, hardness, softness, heaviness and lightness, tastes, colors, and the like, that they teach that all these qualities are perceptions of our soul and that they do not exist at all in the objects of our senses. Why should we not say the same thing about extension? If an entity that has no color appears to us, however, with a determinate color with respect to its species, shape, and location, why could not an entity that had no extension be visible to us under an appearance of a determinate, shaped, and located extension of a certain type? And notice carefully that the same body appears to us to be small or large, round or square, according to the place from which it is viewed; and let us have no doubts that a body that seems very small to us appears very large to a fly. It is not then by their own real or absolute extension that bodies present themselves to our minds. We can therefore conclude that they are not extended in themselves. Would you dare to reason in this way today, "Since certain bodies appear sweet to one man, sour to another, bitter to a third, and so on, I ought to affirm that in general they are savory, though I do not know what savor belongs to them absolutely and in themselves?" All the "new" philosophers would hoot at you. Why then would you dare to say, "Since certain bodies appear large to one animal, medium to another, and very small to a third, I ought to affirm that in general they are extended, though I do not know their absolute extension?"[10]

2. Arguments of the Occasionalists

Some Cartesian Occasionalists – Géraud de Cordemoy, Malebranche, Lanion, and Michel Angelo Fardella – denied that reason can prove that bodies exist. Bayle had thinkers like these in mind in Remark H of "Zeno of Elea", where he summarizes the arguments of "some Cartesians who publicly maintain, even in the countries that have an Inquisition, that one can only know by revelation that there are bodies."[11] Bayle does not mention Cordemoy or Lanion (though he certainly *knew* Lanion's *Méditations sur la métaphysique* since he had himself re-issued it, in 1684, in his *Recueil de quelques pièces curieuses concernant la philosophie de Monsieur Descartes*, and the first argument he gives in the following passage is a version of the argument from divine economy), but he gives some account of the positions of Malebranche and Fardella, and of the controversy between Malebranche and Arnauld over whether reason can prove that bodies exist.

Like Malebranche, Fardella denied that either reason or the senses can prove beyond doubt that bodies exist, and he seems to have gone even further than Malebranche by casting doubt on whether Scripture can establish it. When Scripture speaks of *bodies*, it is only adapting itself to ordinary ways of speaking and thinking, said Fardella, for "the special aim of Scripture is not to teach men logic or philosophy, but to instruct them in right morals that lead to salvation."[12] Berkeley refers to Fardella in *PC* 79, where he notes that "I do not fall in wth Sceptics Fardella etc, in y^t I make bodies to exist certainly, wch they doubt of." Fardella's work was rare, and Berkeley probably knew it only from Bayle's reference to it.

The 'axioms' that Bayle appeals to at the beginning of this passage are ones that Berkeley also took seriously: see, in particular, *Works* II, p. 214 and *PHK* §19.

There are two philosophical axioms that teach us: the one, that nature does nothing in vain; and the other, that it is useless to do by several methods what may be done by fewer means with the same ease. By these two axioms the Cartesians I am speaking of can maintain that no bodies exist; for whether they exist or not, God is equally able to communicate to us all the thoughts that we have. It is no proof at all that there are bodies to say that our senses assure us of this with the utmost evidence. They deceive us with regard to all of the corporeal qualities, the magnitude, size, and motion of bodies not excepted; and when we believe them about these latter qualities, we are also convinced that there exist outside our souls a great many colors, tastes, and other entities that we call hardness, fluidity, cold, heat, and the like. However it is not true that anything like these exists outside our minds. Why then should we trust our senses with regard to extension? It can very easily be reduced to appearance, just like colors. Father Malebranche, after having set forth all the reasons for doubting that there are bodies in the world, concludes in this way: "In order to be completely certain of the external existence of bodies, it is therefore absolutely necessary to know God who gives us the sensation of them, and to be aware that since he is infinitely perfect, he cannot deceive us. For if the Intelligence that gives us the ideas of all things wished, as it were, to divert himself by making us know bodies as actually existing, even though there actually be none, it is plain that this would not be difficult for him to do." He adds that Descartes has not found any other unshakable foundation than the argument that God would deceive us if there were no bodies. But he claims that this argument cannot pass for a demonstrative one. "To be fully convinced there are bodies," he says, "it is necessary that it be demonstrated to us not only that there is a God, and that God is no deceiver, but also that God has assured us that he has actually created bodies, which I do not find proven in the works of Descartes. God speaks to the mind and obliges it to believe in only two ways, by self-evidence and by faith. I agree that faith obliges us to believe that there are bodies; but with regard to self-evidence, it is certain that it is not complete, and that we are not invincibly led to believe in the existence of anything other than God and our mind." Notice that when he affirms that God does not prompt us invincibly by self-evidence to conclude that there are bodies, he wants to teach us that the error we might hold in this respect should not be imputed to God. This is rejecting Descartes' proof, that is to say, that God would in no way be a deceiver even though no bodies might exist in reality.

A Sicilian named Michaelangelo Fardella published a logic book in Venice in 1696,[13] in which he maintains the same doctrines as Father Malebranche. Here is a summary of that book.[14] "He tries especially to prove that it is quite possible that objects do not conform to the ideas we have of them. He says that he conceives very clearly that the author of nature could dispose our senses in such a way that they represent to us objects as existing that do not exist at all. . . . When it is objected to him that if the evidence of the senses is not infallible, Jesus Christ was making fun of the disciples when, in order to convince them that he had a real body, he said to them, 'Handle me, and see, for a spirit hath not flesh and bones'; he replies that the methods of arguing that the Scripture usually employs are drawn from a logic adapted to the capabilities of the common man rather than a true logic; from which he concludes that Jesus Christ, in order to convince the apostles that he was not a phantom but a real man, made use of the logic best adapted to the capacity of ordinary people, by which people are used to being convinced that things exist. He adds that God is not obliged to teach us infallibly that there are bodies that exist; and if we have more than a moral certainty of this, it is only by faith that we have obtained it."[15]

We omit Bayle's summary of the debate between Arnauld and Malebranche about whether the existence of bodies can be demonstrated. Arnauld is allowed to come out of the debate rather well, with the consequence, Bayle suggests, that Malebranche's case needs to be supplemented by stronger arguments. Bayle thinks that he has provided such arguments in Remark G of "Zeno of Elea" (to which we will turn in Section 3). Remark H ends:

[I]t is useful to know that a Father of the Oratory [Malebranche], as illustrious for his piety as for his philosophical knowledge, maintained that faith alone can truly convince us of the existence of bodies. Neither the Sorbonne, nor any other tribunal, gave him the least trouble on that account. The Italian inquisitors did not disturb Fardella, who maintained the same thing in a printed work. This ought to show my readers that they must not find it strange that I sometimes point out that, concerning the most mysterious matters in the Gospel, reason gets us nowhere, and thus we ought to be completely satisfied with the light of faith.[16]

3. Paradoxes About Extension

There are, according to Bayle, arguments "which oppose the existence of extension and seem much stronger than all the arguments that the Cartesians could set forth."[17] In Remark G of "Zeno of Elea", Bayle sets out these arguments, which aim to show the "contradictions and impossibilities" that arise from supposing that extension – which the Cartesians took to be the essence of matter – exists. This material is of particular interest to us because Bayle vigorously opposes the notion of infinite divisibility ("the hypothesis . . . of almost all professors in all universities for several centuries"), as well as divisibility into mathematical points, just as Berkeley would, but also because Bayle is led from the consideration that no intelligible account whatsoever can be given of the divisibility of extension to the conclusion that we ought to regard extension as only "ideal". Because Remark G is long, and the underlying concern is as much with motion as with extension, we give here only the part dealing with extension, together with the concluding paragraph of the Remark.

There is no extension; therefore there is no motion. The inference is valid; for what has no extension occupies no space; and what occupies no space cannot go from one place to another, nor consequently move. This is not open to question. The only difficulty then is to prove that there is no extension. Here is what Zeno could have put forth. Extension cannot be made up of either mathematical points, atoms, or particles that are divisible to infinity; therefore its existence is impossible. The consequence seems certain since we can conceive of only these three types of composition in extension. It is therefore only a question of proving the antecedent. It will take me only a few words to establish the case with regard to mathematical points; for persons of the slightest depth can comprehend with complete certainty, if they give the matter a little attention, that several nonentities of extension joined together will never make up an extension. Consult the first course of Scholastic philosophy that you come across; and you will find there the most convincing arguments in the world, supported by many geometrical demonstrations, against the existence of these points. Let us speak no more about this, and let us look upon it as impossible or at least inconceivable that the continuum is composed of these points. It is not any less impossible or inconceivable that it be composed of Epicurean atoms, that is to say of extended and indivisible corpuscles; for every extension, no matter how small it may be, has a right and a left side, an upper and a lower side. Therefore it is a collection of distinct bodies. I can deny concerning the right side what I affirm about the left side. These two sides are not in the same place. A body cannot be in two places both at the same time, and consequently every extension that occupies several parts of space contains several bodies. I know, besides, and the atomists do not deny it, that because two atoms are two beings, they are separable from one another. From which I conclude with the utmost certainty that since the right side of an atom is not the same entity as the left side, it is separable from the left. The indivisibility of an atom is thus illusory. If there is any extension then, it must be the case that its parts are divisible to infinity. But, on the other hand, if they cannot be divisible to infinity, we would have to conclude that the existence of extension is impossible, or at the very least, incomprehensible.

Infinite divisibility is the hypothesis that Aristotle embraced, and it is the one of almost all philosophy professors in all universities for several centuries. It is not that they understand it or can answer objections made to it; but that having understood clearly the impossibility of points, be they mathematical or physical, they found this the only course to take. Besides, this hypothesis furnishes great comfort; for when its distinctions have been used up, without having been able to make this theory comprehensible, one can take refuge in the nature itself of the subject and claim that, since our mind is limited, no one ought to find it odd that we cannot resolve what concerns infinity, and that it is the essence of such a continuum that it be surrounded by difficulties that are insurmountable to human beings. Observe that those who espouse the atomic hypothesis do not do so because they understand that an extended body can be simple, but because they conclude that the two other hypotheses are impossible. Let us say the same about those who admit mathematical points. In general, all those who argue concerning the continuum only come to a decision about choosing a hypothesis on the basis of this principle: "If there are only three ways of explaining something, the truth of the third necessarily follows from the falsity of the other two." They do not, therefore, believe that they can be mistaken in choosing the third when they have understood clearly that the other two are impossible. They are not disturbed at all by the insurmountable difficulties of the third. . . .

A Zenoist could say to those who choose one of these three hypotheses, "You do not reason well, you make use of this disjunctive syllogism:

"The continuum is made up of either mathematical points, or physical points, or parts that can be divided ad infinitum:

"But it is not made up of . . . , or of . . .

"Therefore it is made up of . . . .

"The defect in your argument is not in its form but in its matter. You ought to give up your disjunctive syllogism and employ this hypothetical one:

"If extension existed, it would be made up of either mathematical points, or physical points, or parts that are divisible ad infinitum:

"But it is not made up of either mathematical points, or physical points, or parts that are divisible ad infinitum.

"Therefore, it does not exist."

There is no defect in the form of this syllogism. The sophism of insufficient enumeration of parts does not occur in the major premise. The conclusion is then necessary, provided that the minor is true. But we need only weigh the arguments with which these three sects confound one another and compare them with the answers. We need only do this, I say, to perceive the obvious truth of the minor. Each of these three sects, when they only attack, triumphs, ruins, and destroys; but in its turn, it is destroyed and sunk when it is on the defensive. To realize their weakness, it is sufficient to recall that the strongest, that which quibbles best, is the hypothesis of infinite divisibility. The Schoolmen have armed it from head to toe with all the distinctions that their great leisure was able to allow them to invent. But this served only to furnish their disciples with a jargon to use in public disputation, so that their relatives would not have the mortification of seeing them silent. A father or a brother goes home much happier when the student distinguishes between the "categorematical" infinite and the "syncategorematical" infinite, between the "communicating" and the "noncommunicating" parts, "proportional" and "aliquot," than if he had made no response. It was then necessary that the professors invent some jargon. But all the trouble they have gone to will never be capable of obscuring this notion that it is as clear and evident as the sun: "An infinite number of parts of extension, each of which is extended and distinct from all the others, both with regard to its being and to the place that it occupies, cannot be contained in a space one hundred million times smaller than the hundred thousandth part of a grain of barley."[18]

> Bayle continues by dwelling on other difficulties attending the notion of infinitely divisible extension. One is that infinite divisibility cannot allow for contact between the parts of bodies because the point at which they are supposed to touch must itself be infinitely divisible; another is that, given that there *is* contact between the parts, infinite divisibility must require that they not merely touch but actually penetrate one another; yet another rests on certain problems in geometry. We omit most of this material, much of it technical, but not because it would have been of no interest to Berkeley. For example, in the *Philosophical Commentaries*, Berkeley mentions the two problems in geometry referred to by Bayle (see *PC* 259 and 315); and he would surely have been struck by Bayle's observation that these problems arise whether one assumes infinite divisibility *or* the hypothesis of indivisible mathematical points. They therefore, Bayle says, "serve no other use but to show that extension exists only in our understanding." This notion is also found in the following striking passage that would surely not have gone unnoticed by Berkeley.

Since, then, the existence of extension necessarily requires the immediate contact of its parts, and since this immediate contact is impossible in an extension that is divisible to infinity, it is evident that the existence of this extension is impossible, and that this extension thus exists only in the mind. We must acknowledge with respect to bodies what mathematicians acknowledge with respect to lines and surfaces, about which they demonstrate so many lovely things. They frankly admit that a length and breadth, without depth, is something that cannot exist outside our minds. Let us say the same of the three dimensions. They can only exist in our minds. They can only exist *ideally*. The human mind is a certain terrain where a hundred thousand objects of different color, different shape, and different location are brought together; for we can see at once from a hilltop a vast plain dotted with houses, trees, flocks, and the like. But it is far from being the case that all these things are of such a nature as to be able to be disposed in this plain. Not even two of them could find room there. Each requires an infinite space, since it contains an infinity of extended bodies. It would be necessary to leave infinite intervals around each since between each part and every other there is an infinity of bodies. Let it not be said that God can do anything. For if the most devout theologians dare to say that in a straight line twelve inches long, God cannot make it so that the first and third inches be immediately contiguous, I may be allowed to say that he cannot make it so that two parts of extension touch immediately when an infinity of other parts separate them from one another. Let us then say that the contact of the parts of matter is only ideal; it is in our minds that the extremities of several bodies can be brought together.[19]

> Bayle's underlying concern in Remark G is with *motion* – a topic itself of considerable interest to Berkeley – not just extension, but we have included only the material that deals with extension, which Bayle sees as a prerequisite for motion. What has emerged is what Bayle takes to be a very strong case against the reality of extension, and hence against matter and bodies. At the end of the day, however, Bayle does not deny the existence of extension, motion, or bodies. Although his argument has moved towards an unrelentingly skeptical conclusion, he ends Remark G with a disclaimer that is short and perhaps unconvincing, but quite typical of him.

We can suppose that it was thus that our Zeno of Elea combatted motion. I would not wish to say that his arguments convinced him that nothing moves. He could have had another conviction even though he believed that no one refuted his arguments or eluded their force. If I were to judge about him by myself, I would affirm that he believed, just as others do, in the motion of extension; for even though I myself feel completely incapable of resolving all the difficulties that have just been presented, and it seems to me that the philosophical answers that can be made to them are far from solid, nevertheless I do not fail to follow the common opinion. I am even convinced that the exposition of these arguments can be of great service to religion, and I say here about the difficulties concerning motion that which Nicole [and Arnauld] have said about those concerning infinite divisibility. "The value that can be gained from these speculations is not simply that of acquiring this sort of knowledge, which is pretty sterile in itself; but it is in learning to know the limits of our mind and in making it admit, in spite of itself, that there are things that exist though it is not capable of understanding them. For this reason it is good that we wear it out with these subtleties in order to check its presumption and to keep it from ever being fool-hardy enough to oppose its feeble light to the truths that the Church proposes to it on the pretext that it cannot understand them. For since all the strength of the mind of man is forced to succumb to the smallest atom of matter and admit that it sees clearly that the atom is infinitely divisible without being able to understand how this can be the case; is it not manifestly sinning against reason to refuse to believe in the marvelous effects of the almighty power of God, which is incomprehensible in itself, because our mind cannot understand them?"[20]

Notes

1. A. A. Luce, *The Dialectic of Immaterialism* (London: Hodder and Stoughton, 1963), p. 59.
2. A. A. Luce, *The Dialectic of Immaterialism*, chap. 4, cf. his *Berkeley and Malebranche* (Oxford: Oxford University Press, 1934), pp. 53–55; and R. H. Popkin, "Berkeley and Pyrrhonism" (first published in 1951), reprinted in Popkin's *The High Road to Pyrrhonism*, ed. R. A. Watson and J. E. Force (San Diego: Austin Hill Press, 1980).
3. Berkeley, *Theory of Vision Vindicated*, in *Works* I, p. 254.
4. Other articles that Luce thought had left their mark on the *Principles* are "Anaxagoras", "Epicurus", "Leucippus", "Rodon", "Rorarius", and "Zabarella" (Luce, *Berkeley and Malebranche*, p. 53).
5. Simon Foucher, *Critique of the Search for Truth* (first published in 1675), in *Malebranche's First and Last Critics: Simon Foucher and Dortous de Mairan*, trans. R. A. Watson and M. Grene (Carbondale: Southern Illinois University Press, 1995), p. 38.
6. "Pyrrho", Remark B, in Bayle, *Historical and Critical Dictionary: Selections*, trans. R. H. Popkin (Indianapolis: Hackett, 1991), pp. 197–99. Reprinted by permission of Hackett Publishing Company, Inc. All rights reserved. References hereafter to "Bayle" are to this volume. (We have omitted a number of Bayle's footnotes.)
7. The Abbé Foucher proposed this objection in his *Critique de la recherche de la vérité*. Father Malebranche made no reply to it. He realized how strong it was. [Bayle's note.]
8. Father Malebranche, in *Éclaircissement sur la recherche de la vérité*, shows that "it is extremely difficult to prove that there are bodies and that faith alone can convince us that bodies actually exist." [Bayle's note.]
9. Cf. chap. 28 of Arnauld's *Traité des vrayes & des fausses idées*, where he refutes the above-mentioned *Éclaircissement* of Father Malebranche, by reasons all based on this principle. [Bayle's note.]
10. Bayle, pp. 364–65.
11. Bayle, p. 354.
12. M. A. Fardella, *Universae philosophiae systema* (Venice, 1691), p. 511, quoted by Lewis Robinson in "Un solipsiste au XVIIIe siècle," *Année philosophique* 24 (1913), p. 16, note 1. Bayle's account of Fardella is taken from a review, so it

seems quite likely that he had not read Fardella himself. It may be because of this that he takes Fardella's view to be closer to Malebranche's than perhaps it really was. As a later comment confirms, he sees Fardella as agreeing with Malebranche that "faith alone can truly convince us of the existence of bodies." Fardella's book is very rare and we have not been able to consult it, but Robinson, who had read it, has it that Fardella argued, against Malebranche, that even faith does not oblige us to believe that material things exist.

13. It was in fact published in 1691.
14. *Journal des Sçavans*, July 30, 1696. [Bayle's note.]
15. Bayle, pp. 373–75.
16. Bayle, p. 377.
17. Bayle, p. 354.
18. Bayle, pp. 359–62.
19. Bayle, pp. 363–64.
20. Bayle, p. 372. The passage Bayle quotes is from *The Art of Thinking*, Pt. IV, chap. 1.

EIGHT

John Locke

It seems so obvious to modern readers that *Locke* was the most important influence on Berkeley that it can strike them as odd that Berkeley's earliest readers tended to see him not as Locke's philosophical heir but as Malebranche's. The attention we have given to Malebranche, and to the Cartesian tradition generally, does indeed indicate that, in our view, Berkeley's contemporaries were right in thinking that his debt to Malebranche was very significant. Yet it must now be stressed that any later commentators who may have overlooked this debt sinned only by omission. They were not wrong in believing that Locke's influence was fundamental. Locke's *Essay concerning Human Understanding* had been introduced into the undergraduate curriculum at Trinity College, Dublin, as early as 1692; and Berkeley, in the *Philosophical Commentaries*, refers to its author frequently and often in admiring terms, likening him at one point to "a Gyant" (*PC* 678). Berkeley had studied the *Essay* very carefully, paying close attention to its large themes and often to its minute details, too. We give, therefore, more extensive extracts from Locke than from any other of Berkeley's predecessors.

It is not possible, however, for us to give an adequate selection of texts from Locke here – to do so might require including virtually the whole of the *Essay*. Those wanting to make a comprehensive study of Berkeley's sources must turn to the *Essay* itself. We have pruned the possible selections so that they cover, not everything that is important in the *Essay*, and not everything that Berkeley reflected on, but, rather, some central tenets, starting with what Locke had to say about "ideas".

1. Ideas and Experience

The term "idea" appears in almost every section of Locke's *Essay*. Berkeley, too, uses it very frequently, but entries in the *Philosophical Commentaries* show that he had pondered *how* the term should be understood, and that he was aware that there were dangers in using it. At the end of the day his usage differs from Locke's, and he presumably had it in mind to make this clear when he wrote:

> Excuse to be made in the Introduction for the using the Word Idea viz. because it has obtain'd. But a Caution must be added. (*PC* 685)

In the event, no such excuse and no such caution appeared in the Introduction to the *Principles* – we have to look to the main body of the work for the sort of thing he had in mind; but in planning to include some sort of "excuse" early on, Berkeley was in effect following Locke, who, in *Essay* 1.1.8, had apologized for *his* use of the term. Moreover, one can detect in what Berkeley says about ideas in *Principles* §1 deliberate echoes of the opening sections of the first chapter of Book 2 of the *Essay*. Our selections from Locke begin, therefore, with his brief apology for his use of the term "idea", followed by the first five sections from Book 2, Chapter 1, which is entitled "Of Ideas in General, and their Original."[1]

1.1.8. Thus much I thought necessary to say concerning the occasion of this inquiry into human understanding. But, before I proceed on to what I have thought on this subject, I must here in the entrance beg pardon of my reader for the frequent use of the word *idea*, which he will find in the following treatise. It being that term which, I think, serves best to stand for whatsoever is the object of the understanding when a man thinks, I have used it to express whatever is meant by *phantasm, notion, species,* or whatever it is which the mind can be employed about in thinking; and I could not avoid frequently using it.

2.1.1. Every man being conscious to himself that he thinks, and that which his mind is applied about whilst thinking being the *ideas* that are there, it is past doubt that men have in their minds several *ideas* such as are those expressed by the words *whiteness, hardness, sweetness, thinking, motion, man, elephant, army, drunkenness* and others: it is in the first place then to be inquired, how he comes by them? I know it is a received doctrine that men have native *ideas* and original characters stamped upon their minds in their very first being. This opinion I have at large examined already;[2] and, I suppose, what I have said in the foregoing book will be much more easily admitted when I have shown whence the understanding may get all the *ideas* it has, and by what ways and degrees they may come into the mind; for which I shall appeal to everyone's own observation and experience.

§2. Let us then suppose the mind to be, as we say, white paper void of all characters, without any *ideas*. How comes it to be furnished? Whence comes it by that vast store which the busy and boundless fancy of man has painted on it with an almost endless variety? Whence has it all the materials of reason and knowledge? To this I answer, in one word, from *experience*; in that all our knowledge is founded, and from that it ultimately derives itself. Our observation, employed either about *external sensible objects, or about the internal operations of our minds perceived and reflected on by ourselves, is that which supplies our understandings with all the materials of thinking.* These two are the fountains of knowledge, from whence all the *ideas* we have, or can naturally have, do spring.

§3. First, *our senses,* conversant about particular sensible objects, do *convey into the mind* several distinct *perceptions* of things, according to those various ways wherein those objects do affect them. And thus we come by those *ideas* we have of *yellow, white, heat, cold, soft, hard, bitter, sweet,* and all those which we call sensible qualities; which when I say the senses convey into the mind, I mean, they from external objects convey into the mind what produces there those *perceptions.* This great source of most of the *ideas* we have, depending wholly upon our senses, and derived by them to the understanding, I call SENSATION.

§4. Secondly, the other fountain from which experience furnisheth the understanding with *ideas* is the *perception of the operations of our own minds* within us, as it is employed about the *ideas* it has got; which operations, when the soul comes to reflect on and consider, do furnish the understanding with another set of *ideas,* which could not be had from things without. And such are *perception, thinking, doubting, believing, reasoning, knowing, willing,* and all the different actings of our own minds; which we, being conscious of and observing in ourselves, do from these receive into our understandings as distinct *ideas* as we do from bodies affecting our senses. This source of *ideas* every man has wholly in himself; and though it be not sense, as having nothing to do with external objects, yet it is very like it, and might properly enough be called internal sense. But as I call the other *sensation,* so I call this REFLECTION, the *ideas* it affords being such only as the mind gets by reflecting on its own operations within itself. By REFLECTION then, in the following part of this discourse, I would be understood to mean that notice which the mind takes of its own operations, and the manner of them, by reason whereof there come to be *ideas* of these operations in the understanding. These two, I say, viz. external material things as the objects of SENSA-TION, and the operations of our own minds within as the objects of REFLECTION, are to me the only originals from whence all our *ideas* take their beginnings. The term *operations* here I use in a large sense, as comprehending not barely the actions of the mind about its *ideas*, but some sort of passions arising sometimes from them, such as is the satisfaction or uneasiness arising from any thought.

§5. The understanding seems to me not to have the least glimmering of any *ideas* which it doth not receive from one of these two. *External objects furnish the mind with the* ideas *of sensible qualities*, which are all those different perceptions they produce in us; and the *mind furnishes the understanding with* ideas *of its own operations*.

These, when we have taken a full survey of them and their several modes, combinations, and relations, we shall find to contain all our whole stock of *ideas*, and that we have nothing in our minds which did not come in one of these two ways. Let anyone examine his own thoughts and thoroughly search into his understanding and then let him tell me whether all the original *ideas* he has there are any other than of the objects of his *senses*, or of the operations of his mind, considered as objects of his *reflection*. And how great a mass of knowledge soever he imagines to be lodged there, he will, upon taking a strict view, see that he has *not any* idea *in his mind but what one of these two have imprinted*, though perhaps, with infinite variety compounded and enlarged by the understanding, as we shall see hereafter.

It seems clear that Berkeley intended the opening words of the *Principles* (§1) to be reminiscent of the opening sections of the first chapter of Book 2 of Locke's *Essay*. "It is evident to any one who takes a survey of the objects of human knowledge," Berkeley declares, "that they are either ideas actually imprinted on the senses, or else such as are perceived by attending to the passions and operations of the mind, or lastly ideas formed by help of memory and imagination, either compounding, dividing, or barely representing those originally perceived in the aforesaid ways." Berkeley knew full well, of course, and his readers would soon discover, that his position differed far more from Locke's than this opening statement suggests. For one thing, though his words here *suggest* that *all* the objects of human knowledge are "ideas", it soon emerges that, for him, we have no *ideas* of the mind and its operations. For another, where Locke holds that ideas are produced in us by "external material things," Berkeley will soon deny that there are any such things.

Still early on in the *Essay*'s second book, Locke divides ideas into the *simple* and the *complex*. Simple ideas – for example, those of *green, heat, willing*, and *existence* – are "the materials of all our knowledge" (2.2.2); complex ideas include such ideas as those of *a man, murder*, or *God*, which result from "combining several simple *ideas* into one compound one" (2.12.1). Berkeley seems initially to have accepted this distinction. However, numerous entries in the *Philosophical Commentaries* express doubt about whether many of Locke's supposedly simple ideas *are* in fact simple, and he does not make use of the distinction in the *Principles*. He does, however, have much to say about one important topic discussed by Locke in connection with simple ideas: the distinction between "primary" and "secondary" qualities.

2. Primary and Secondary Qualities

Locke defended the distinction between primary and secondary qualities and Berkeley attacked it. This distinction, in some form or other, was already widely accepted when Locke wrote the *Essay*, and it was generally regarded as central to the "new science", so we should not assume that Berkeley's attack was aimed solely at Locke; but Locke's version of the distinction was clearly one important target. Locke's main treatment of the doctrine is contained in *Essay* 2.8.7–26. We include most of that discussion here, starting with a section that suggests a certain complication in the way Locke will use the term "idea".

2.8.8. Whatsoever the mind perceives in itself, or is the immediate object of perception, thought, or understanding, that I call *idea*; and the power to produce any *idea* in our mind, I call *quality* of the subject wherein that power is. Thus a snowball having the power to produce in us the *ideas* of *white, cold*, and *round*, the powers to produce those *ideas* in us as they are in the snowball I call *qualities*; and as they are sensations or perceptions in our understandings, I call them *ideas*; which *ideas*, if I speak of sometimes as in the things themselves, I would be understood to mean those qualities in the objects which produce them in us.

§9. Qualities thus considered in bodies are:

First, such as are utterly inseparable from the body, in what state soever it be; such as in all the alterations and changes it suffers, all the force can be used upon it, it constantly keeps; and such as sense constantly finds in every particle of matter which has bulk enough to be perceived; and the mind finds inseparable from every particle of matter, though less than to make itself singly be perceived by our senses. V.g., take a grain of wheat, divide it into two parts, each part has still *solidity*, *extension, figure,* and *mobility*; divide it again, and it retains still the same qualities; and so divide it on, till the parts become insensible: they must retain still each of them all those qualities. For division (which is all that a mill or pestle or any other body does upon another in reducing it to insensible parts) can never take away either solidity, extension, figure, or mobility from any body, but only makes two or more distinct separate masses of matter, of that which was but one before; all which distinct masses, reckoned as so many distinct bodies, after division make a certain number. These I call *original* or *primary qualities* of body; which I think we may observe to produce simple *ideas* in us, viz. solidity, extension, figure, motion or rest, and number.

§10. Secondly, such *qualities* which in truth are nothing in the objects themselves but powers to produce various sensations in us by their *primary qualities*, i.e. by the bulk, figure, texture, and motion of their insensible parts, as colours, sounds, tastes, etc. These I call *secondary qualities*. To these might be added a third sort, which are allowed to be barely powers, though they are as much real qualities in the subject as those which I, to comply with the common way of speaking, call *qualities*, but for distinction, *secondary qualities*. For the power in fire to produce a new colour, or consistency in wax or clay, by its primary qualities, is as much a quality in fire as the power it has to produce in me a new *idea* or sensation of warmth or burning, which I felt not before, by the same primary qualities, viz. the bulk, texture, and motion of its insensible parts.

§11. The next thing to be considered is how *bodies* produce *ideas* in us; and that is manifestly *by impulse*, the only way which we can conceive bodies operate in.

§12. If then external objects be not united to our minds when they produce *ideas* in it and yet we perceive *these original qualities* in such of them as singly fall under our senses, it is evident that some motion must be thence continued by our nerves or animal spirits, by some parts of our bodies, to the brains or the seat of sensation, there to *produce in our minds the particular* ideas *we have of them*. And since the extension, figure, number, and motion of bodies of an observable bigness may be perceived at a distance *by* the sight, it is evident some singly imperceptible bodies must come from them to the eyes, and thereby convey to the brain some *motion*, which produces these *ideas* which we have of them in us.

§13. After the same manner that the *ideas* of these original qualities are produced in us, we may conceive that the *ideas of secondary qualities* are also *produced*, viz. *by the operation of insensible particles on our senses*. For it being manifest that there are bodies and good store of bodies, each whereof are so small that we cannot by any of our senses discover either their bulk, figure, or motion, as is evident in the particles of the air and water and others extremely smaller than those, perhaps as much smaller than the particles of air or water as the particles of air or water are smaller than peas or hail-stones: let us suppose at present that the different motions and figures, bulk and number, of such particles, affecting the several organs of our senses, produce in us those different sensations which we have from the colours and smells of bodies: v.g. that a violet, by the impulse of such insensible particles of matter, of peculiar figures and bulks, and in different degrees and modifications of their motions, causes the *ideas* of the blue colour and sweet scent of that flower to be produced in our minds. It being no more impossible to conceive that God should annex such *ideas* to such motions, with which they have no similitude, than that he should annex the *idea* of pain to the motion of a piece of steel dividing our flesh, with which that *idea* hath no resemblance.

§14. What I have said concerning *colours* and *smells* may be understood also of *tastes* and *sounds, and other the like sensible qualities*; which, whatever reality we by mistake attribute to them, are in truth nothing in the objects themselves but powers to produce various sensations in us, and depend *on those primary qualities*, viz. bulk, figure, texture, and motion of parts, as I have said.

§15. From whence I think it easy to draw this observation: that the *ideas of primary qualities* of bodies *are resemblances* of them, and their patterns do really exist in the bodies themselves; but the *ideas produced* in us *by* these *secondary qualities have no resemblance* of them at all. There is nothing like our *ideas* existing in the bodies themselves. They are, in the bodies we denominate from them, only a power to produce those sensations in us; and what is sweet, blue, or warm in *idea* is but the certain bulk, figure, and motion of the insensible parts in the bodies themselves, which we call so.

§16. *Flame* is denominated *hot* and *light*; *snow*, *white* and *cold*; and *manna*, *white* and *sweet*, from the *ideas* they produce in us. Which qualities are commonly thought to be the same in those bodies that those *ideas* are in us, the one the perfect resemblance of the other, as they are in a mirror, and it would by most men be judged very extravagant if one should say otherwise. And yet he that will consider that *the same fire* that at one distance *produces* in us the sensation of *warmth* does, at a nearer approach, produce in us the far different sensation of *pain*, ought to bethink himself what reason he has to say that his *idea* of *warmth*, which was produced in him by the fire, is actually *in the fire*; and his *idea* of *pain*, which the same fire produced in him the same way, is *not* in the *fire*. Why are whiteness and coldness in snow, and pain not, when it produces the one and the other *idea* in us; and can do neither, but by the bulk, figure, number, and motion of its solid parts?

§17. The particular *bulk, number, figure, and motion of the parts of fire or snow are really in them*, whether anyone's senses perceive them or no; and therefore they may be called *real qualities*, because they really exist in those bodies. But *light, heat, whiteness,* or *coldness are no more really in them than sickness or pain is in* manna. Take away the sensation of them; let not the eyes see light or colours, nor the ears hear sounds; let the palate not taste, nor the nose smell; and all colours, tastes, odours, and sounds, as they are such particular *ideas*, vanish and cease, and are reduced to their causes, i.e. bulk, figure, and motion of parts.

§18. A piece of *manna* of a sensible bulk is able to produce in us the *idea* of a round or square figure; and by being removed from one place to another, the *idea* of motion. This *idea* of motion represents it as it really is in the *manna* moving; a circle or square are the same, whether in *idea* or existence, in the mind or in the *manna*; and this, both *motion and figure, are really in the manna*, whether we take notice of them or no: this everybody is ready to agree to. Besides, *manna*, by the bulk, figure, texture, and motion of its parts, has a power to produce the sensations of sickness, and sometimes of acute pains or gripings in us. That these *ideas of sickness and pain are not in the* manna, but effects of its operations on us, and are nowhere when we feel them not: this also everyone readily agrees to. And yet men are hardly to be brought to think that *sweetness and whiteness are not really in manna*, which are but the effects of the operations of *manna*, by the motion, size, and figure of its particles, on the eyes and palate, as the pain and sickness caused by *manna* are confessedly nothing but the effects of its operations on the stomach and guts, by the size, motion, and figure of its insensible parts (for by nothing else can a body operate, as has been proved): as if it could not operate on the eyes and palate and thereby produce in the mind particular distinct *ideas* which in itself it has not, as well as we allow it can operate on the guts and stomach and thereby produce distinct *ideas* which in itself it has not. These *ideas* being all effects of the operations of *manna* on several parts of our bodies by the size, figure, number, and motion of its parts, why those produced by the eyes and palate should rather be thought to be really in the *manna* than those produced by the stomach and guts; or why the pain and sickness, *ideas* that are the effects of *manna*, should be thought to be nowhere, when they are not felt: and yet the sweetness and whiteness, effects of the same *manna* on other parts of the body by ways equally as unknown, should be thought to exist in the *manna*, when they are not seen nor tasted, would need some reason to explain.

§19. Let us consider the red and white colours in *porphyry*. Hinder light but from striking on it, and its colours vanish: it no longer produces any such *ideas* in us; upon the return of light it produces these appearances on us again. Can anyone think any real alterations are made in the *porphyry* by the presence or absence of light; and that those *ideas* of whiteness and redness are really in *porphyry* in the light, when it is plain *it has no colour in the dark*? It has, indeed, such a configuration of particles, both night and day, as are apt, by the rays of light rebounding from some parts of that hard stone, to produce in us the *idea* of redness, and from others the *idea* of whiteness; but whiteness or redness are not in it at any time, but such a texture that hath the power to produce such a sensation in us.

§20. Pound an almond, and the clear white *colour* will be altered into a dirty one, and the sweet *taste* into an oily one. What real alteration can the beating of the pestle make in any body, but an alteration of the *texture* of it?

§21. *Ideas* being thus distinguished and understood, we may be able to give an account how the same water, at the same time, may produce the *idea* of cold by one hand and of heat by the other, whereas it is impossible that the same water, if those *ideas* were really in it, should at the same time be both hot and cold. For if we imagine *warmth* as it is *in our hands* to be *nothing but a certain sort and degree of motion in the minute particles of our nerves, or animal spirits*, we may understand how it is possible that the same water may at the same time produce the sensation of heat in one hand and cold in the other; which yet figure never does, that never producing the *idea* of a square by one hand which has produced the *idea* of a globe by another. But if the sensation of heat and cold be nothing but the increase or diminution of the motion of the minute parts of our bodies, caused by the corpuscles of any other body, it is easy to be understood that, if that motion be greater in one hand than in the other, if a body be applied to the two hands, which has in its minute particles a greater motion than in those of one of the hands, and a less than in those of the other, it will increase the motion of the one hand and lessen it in the other, and so cause the different sensations of heat and cold that depend thereon.

> Locke's defense of the distinction between primary and secondary qualities and Berkeley's criticisms of it (in *PHK* §§9–15 and in the *First Dialogue*) have both prompted much discussion. Commentators have differed about whether Berkeley describes Locke's distinction accurately,[3] and whether Locke's actual case for the distinction is the one that Berkeley attributes to him.[4] It has also been argued that the question of whether Berkeley misrepresents *Locke* here, and on certain other matters, misses the point, given that Berkeley never explicitly mentions Locke in the main body of the *Principles* and that Locke was arguably *not* Berkeley's primary target when he attacked the distinction.[5] These are important issues, but we do not explore them here. What we think cannot be denied is that Berkeley had paid close attention to Locke's treatment of this doctrine. For example, Berkeley certainly did not overlook the tricky §8, for he cites it twice in the *Philosophical Commentaries* (entries 112 and 326), resolving to take special notice of it; the terms he uses, "primary qualities" and "secondary qualities", come from Locke (and ultimately from Boyle), not from the Cartesians; and the list of primary qualities Berkeley gives in *PHK* §9 corresponds more closely to Locke's than to what we find among the Cartesians. Though he was not addressing just Locke, Berkeley clearly had him in mind when discussing this distinction.

3. Substance

If we should not suppose that Locke is the only one under attack when Berkeley combats the doctrine of primary and secondary qualities, we should be even more wary of doing so when we consider his attack on the notion of material or corporeal substance, for this was a notion Berkeley took to be generally accepted by philosophers. It seems, moreover, equally clear that Locke himself, in his account of "the general name substance," is examining a received notion that he has some misgivings about. Exactly what those misgivings *are* is debatable, as is the question of what the idea of substance amounts to for Locke himself. As one prominent Locke scholar has observed in surveying the various interpretations, "There is even room for disagreement over whether Locke is advancing a theory of *substratum* or attacking it."[6] Finally, Berkeley once again never names Locke (or indeed any other philosopher) when examining the notion of substance in the *Principles* and *Dialogues*. For all that, it is clear that Berkeley had read the relevant passages in the *Essay* – not just Locke's better-known treatment of substance in 2.23, but an earlier discussion in 2.13, which forms our next selection. The context is a discussion of *space* as an idea quite distinct from that of *body*.

2.13.17. If it be demanded (as usually it is) whether this *space*, void of *body*, be *substance* or *accident*, I shall readily answer I know not, nor shall be ashamed to own my ignorance, till they that ask show me a clear distinct *idea* of *substance*.

§18. I endeavour as much as I can to deliver myself from those fallacies which we are apt to put upon ourselves, by taking words for things. It helps not our ignorance to feign a knowledge where we have none by making a noise with sounds, without clear and distinct significations. Names made at pleasure neither alter the nature of things, nor make us understand them, but as they are signs of and stand for determined *ideas*. And I desire those who lay so much stress on the sound of these two syllables, *substance*, to consider whether applying it as they do to the infinite incomprehensible GOD, to finite spirit, and to body, it be in the same sense; and whether it stands for the same *idea*, when each of those three so different beings are called *substances*? If so, whether it will not thence follow that God, spirits, and body, agreeing in the same common nature of *substance*, differ not any otherwise than in a bare different modification of that *substance*: as a tree and a pebble, being in the same sense body and agreeing in the common nature of body, differ only in a bare modification of that common matter; which will be a very harsh doctrine. If they say that they apply it to God, finite spirits, and matter in three different significations, and that it stands for one *idea* when GOD is said to be a *substance*, for another when the soul is called *substance*, and for a third when a body is called so: if the name *substance* stands for three several distinct *ideas*, they would do well to make known those distinct *ideas*, or at least to give three distinct names to them, to prevent in so important a notion the confusion and errors that will naturally follow from the promiscuous use of so doubtful a term; which is so far from being suspected to have three distinct, that in ordinary use it has scarce one clear distinct signification. And if they can thus make three distinct *ideas* of *substance*, what hinders why another may not make a fourth?

§19. They who first ran into the notion of *accidents*, as a sort of real beings that needed something to inhere in, were forced to find out the word *substance* to support them. Had the poor *Indian* philosopher (who imagined that the earth also wanted something to bear it up) but thought of this word *substance*, he needed not to have been at the trouble to find an elephant to support it, and a tortoise to support his elephant: the word *substance* would have done it effectually. And he that inquired might have taken it for as good an answer from an *Indian* philosopher that *substance*, without knowing what it is, is that which supports the earth, as we take it for a sufficient answer and good doctrine from our *European* philosophers that *substance*, without knowing what it is, is that which supports *accidents*. So that of *substance*, we have no *idea* of what it is, but only a confused, obscure one of what it does.

§20. Whatever a learned man may do here, an intelligent *American*, who inquired into the nature of things, would scarce take it for a satisfactory account if, desiring to learn our architecture, he should be told that a pillar was a thing supported by a *basis* and a *basis* something that supported a pillar. Would he not think himself mocked instead of taught with such an account as this? And a stranger to them would be very liberally instructed in the nature of books and the things they contained if he should be told that all learned books consisted of paper and letters, and that letters were things inhering in paper and paper a thing that held forth letters: a notable way of having clear *ideas* of letters and paper! But were the *Latin* words *inhaerentia* and *substantia* put into the plain *English* ones that answer them, and were called *sticking on* and *under-propping*, they would better discover to us the very great clearness there is in the doctrine of *substance* and *accidents*, and show of what use they are in deciding of questions in philosophy.

How to construe Locke's tale of the Indian philosopher (he tells it twice in the *Essay*) is debatable. One could take Locke's point to be that the Indian erred at the outset, by assuming that the earth "wanted something to bear it up," and that the Aristotelian and Scholastic philosophers made a similar error by thinking of "*accidents*, as a sort of real beings that needed something" – substance – "to inhere in." Or one could take Locke to have it in mind that, just as pillars are indeed supported by a "basis" (although the "intelligent American" does not know what the "basis" is), so substance is indeed some "thing", but that it is a mistake to suppose *we* have any clear conception of it. Either way, we could hardly conclude that Locke was an enthusiastic supporter of the notion of "substance", as that notion had traditionally been understood. Berkeley had certainly noted these sections, for in *PC* 89 he cites 2.13.19 when he writes, "Material substance banter'd by Locke." He would seem to mean by this that Locke is here ridiculing the notion of material substance.

Our next selection comes from Locke's better-known discussion of *substance* in 2.23, one of the *Essay*'s most important chapters but, again, one it is notoriously difficult to interpret. The title is "Of our Complex Ideas of Substances," and officially its concern is with complex ideas of "material sensible substances" (e.g., gold, bread, or a horse) and of "an immaterial spirit" (e.g., the soul, an angel, or God), but it ranges widely, and merits careful study as a whole. We can include here only the first five sections.

2.23.1. The mind being, as I have declared, furnished with a great number of the simple *ideas* conveyed in by the *senses*, as they are found in exterior things, or by *reflection* on its own operations, takes notice also that a certain number of these simple *ideas* go constantly together; which, being presumed to belong to one thing, and words being suited to common apprehensions and made use of for quick dispatch, are called, so united in one subject, by one name; which, by inadvertency, we are apt afterward to talk of and consider as one simple *idea*, which indeed is a complication of many *ideas* together: because, as I have said, not imagining how these simple *ideas* can subsist by themselves, we accustom ourselves to suppose some *substratum* wherein they do subsist, and from which they do result; which therefore we call *substance*.

§2. So that if anyone will examine himself concerning his *notion of pure substance in general*, he will find he has no other *idea* of it at all, but only a supposition of he knows not what support of such qualities which are capable of producing simple *ideas* in us; which qualities are commonly called accidents. If anyone should be asked what is the subject wherein colour or weight inheres, he would have nothing to say but, the solid extended parts; and if he were demanded what is it that that solidity and extension adhere in, he would not be in a much better case than the *Indian* before-mentioned who, saying that the world was supported by a great elephant, was asked what the elephant rested on, to which his answer was, a great tortoise; but being again pressed to know what gave support to the broad-backed tortoise, replied, something, he knew not what. And thus here, as in all other cases where we use words without having clear and distinct *ideas*, we talk like children who, being questioned what such a thing is which they know not, readily give this satisfactory answer, that it is *something*; which in truth signifies no more, when so used, either by children or men, but that they know not what, and that the thing they pretend to know and talk of is what they have no distinct *idea* of at all, and so are perfectly ignorant of it and in the dark. The *idea* then we have, to which we give the general name substance, being nothing but the supposed, but unknown, support of those qualities we find existing, which we imagine cannot subsist *sine re substante*, without something to support them, we call that support *substantia*; which, according to the true import of the word, is, in plain *English*, *standing under* or *upholding*.

§3. An obscure and relative *idea* of substance in general being thus made, we come to have the *ideas of particular sorts of substances* by collecting such combinations of simple *ideas* as are, by experience and observation of men's senses, taken notice of to exist together, and are therefore supposed to flow from the particular internal constitution or unknown essence of that substance. Thus we come to have the *ideas* of a man, horse, gold, water, etc.; of which substances, whether anyone has any other clear *idea*, further than of certain simple *ideas* co-existing together, I appeal to everyone's own experience. It is the ordinary qualities observable in iron, or a diamond, put together that make the true complex *idea* of those substances, which a smith or a jeweller commonly knows better than a philosopher; who, whatever substantial forms he may talk of, has no other *idea* of those substances than what is framed by a collection of those simple *ideas* which are to be found in them: only we must take notice that our complex *ideas* of substances, besides all these simple *ideas* they are made up of, have always the confused *idea* of *something* to which they belong, and in which they subsist; and therefore when we speak of any sort of substance, we say it is a *thing* having such or such qualities: as body is a *thing* that is extended, figured, and capable of motion; a spirit, a *thing* capable of thinking; and so hardness, friability, and power to draw iron, we say, are qualities to be found in a loadstone. These and the like fashions of speaking intimate that the substance is supposed always *something* besides the extension, figure, solidity, motion, thinking or other observable *ideas*, though we know not what it is.

§4. Hence, when we talk or think of any particular sort of corporeal substances, as *horse*, *stone*, etc., though the *idea* we have of either of them be but the complication or collection of those several simple *ideas* of sensible qualities, which we use to find united in the thing called *horse* or *stone*: yet, because we cannot conceive how they should subsist alone, nor one in another, we suppose them existing in and supported by some common subject; *which support we denote by the name substance*, though it be certain we have no clear or distinct *idea* of that *thing* we suppose a support.

§5. The same thing happens concerning the operations of the mind, viz, thinking, reasoning, fearing, etc., which we concluding not to subsist of themselves, nor apprehending how they can belong to body or be produced by it, we are apt to think these the actions of some other *substance*, which we call *spirit*; whereby yet it is evident that, having no other *idea* or notion of matter but *something* wherein those many sensible qualities which affect our senses do subsist, by supposing a substance wherein *thinking, knowing, doubting*, and a power of moving, etc., do subsist, *we have as clear a notion of the substance of spirit as we have of body*: the one being supposed to be (without knowing what it is) the *substratum* to those simple *ideas* we have from without; and the other supposed (with a like ignorance of what it is) to be the *substratum* to those operations which we experiment in ourselves within. It is plain then that the *idea* of corporeal *substance* in matter is as remote from our conceptions and apprehensions as that of spiritual *substance*, or *spirit*; and therefore, from our not having any notion of the *substance* of spirit, we can no more conclude its non-existence than we can, for the same reason, deny the existence of body: it being as rational to affirm there is no body, because we have no clear and distinct *idea* of the *substance* of matter, as to say there is no spirit, because we have no clear and distinct *idea* of the *substance* of a spirit.

Even in these opening sections Locke has covered a lot of ground, considering our "idea of substance in general," as well as our ideas of particular sorts of substances (e.g., wood or iron), and indeed not just our idea of material substance, but also our idea of "the substance of spirit." Berkeley, for his part, does not wish to dispense altogether with the notion of substance, for he holds that spirits are substances, and he is, moreover, quite happy to talk of wood, for example, as a substance, at one point in the *Commentaries* (*PC* 179) actually citing a section in the *Essay* (2.26.1) for the notion that "the substance wood [is] a collection of simple ideas." What Berkeley adamantly opposes is any notion of substances as things existing outside the mind, and any notion of an external "support" of mind-independent qualities. He attacks this notion on various grounds, including that sensible qualities (which for him are "ideas") can only exist in a *perceiving* thing, and that the materialists cannot attach any clear meaning to "support" in *their* talk of substance. Locke had pretty much conceded the last point, and to that extent Berkeley may have seen him as an ally. Nonetheless, Locke's position on substance differs in important ways from Berkeley's, for Locke remains committed to "corporeal substance in matter," and also to holding that our ideas of particular sorts of substances include "the confused idea" of *something* to which the observable qualities belong. Berkeley will dismiss any such notion of a mere "something" as an unacceptable abstract idea.

4. Abstract Ideas

In Book 3 of the *Essay*, Locke examines language, a subject of great interest to Berkeley. In the third chapter, Locke gives his account of abstract general ideas, another topic of great importance to Berkeley (and the *only* topic about which, in the *Principles*, Berkeley explicitly singles Locke out as an opponent). To this topic we now turn. Warnings are again necessary. For one thing, we know that Berkeley saw philosophy and the sciences as having been infected well before Locke by the supposition that there are abstract ideas,[7] so the attack on *Locke's* account of them in the Introduction to the *Principles* is intended merely to illustrate, by concrete example, the absurdity of belief in abstract ideas. For another, we know from the *Philosophical Commentaries* that Berkeley had pondered Locke's account of language and had been influenced by it in areas that went beyond what he focuses on in the Introduction to the *Principles*. He had, for example, criticized Locke's suggestion that words have a function in "recording" our own thoughts (*PC* 495 and 565), though he seems soon to have changed his mind about this (*PC* 607); he had himself taken it as an axiom that "All significant words stand for Ideas" (*PC* 378), but had come to reject that; he had noted Locke's own observation that "particles" (words like "but" and "and") do not stand for ideas (*PC* 661 and 667) and connected this with his own view that words signifying acts of the mind do not stand for "ideas". We will be concentrating on abstraction, beginning with the first three sections of Book 3.

3.1.1. GOD, having designed man for a sociable creature, made him not only with an inclination and under a necessity to have fellowship with those of his own kind, but furnished him also with language, which was to be the great instrument and common tie of society. *Man*, therefore, had by nature his organs so fashioned as to be *fit to frame articulate sounds*, which we call words. But this was not enough to produce language; for parrots and several other birds will be taught to make articulate sounds distinct enough, which yet by no means are capable of language.

§2. Besides articulate sounds, therefore, it was further necessary that he should be *able to use these sounds as signs of internal conceptions*, and to make them stand as marks for the *ideas* within his own mind, whereby they might be made known to others, and the thoughts of men's minds be conveyed from one to another.

§3. But neither was this sufficient to make words so useful as they ought to be. It is not enough for the perfection of language that sounds can be made signs of *ideas*, unless those *signs* can be so made use of as *to comprehend several particular things*: for the multiplication of words would have perplexed their use, had every particular thing need of a distinct name to be signified by. To remedy this inconvenience, language had yet a further improvement in the use of general terms, whereby one word was made to mark a multitude of particular existences, which advantageous use of sounds was obtained only by the difference of the *ideas* they were made signs of: those names becoming general which are made to stand for general *ideas*, and those remaining particular where the *ideas* they are used for are particular.

Berkeley would certainly not dissent completely from what Locke has said so far, for he accepts, naturally, that there are general terms, and he in fact agrees that there are general *ideas*, although for him a general idea is emphatically not an abstract idea, but one that "considered in it self is particular [and] becomes general, by being made to represent or stand for all other particular ideas of the same sort" (*PHK*, Introduction §12). His objection to Locke, then, centers on Locke's view that general ideas are *abstract*. Locke had already said something about abstraction earlier in the *Essay* (2.11.9ff.), and Berkeley quotes several sentences from this in *PHK*, Introduction §11, prior to commenting on Locke's suggestion that brutes cannot abstract while men can. What, in relation to Berkeley, is perhaps more important in the passage is its account of our supposed ability to form an abstract idea of some particular quality such as whiteness. We therefore give here only the first of the sections from this earlier discussion.

2.11.9. The use of words then being to stand as outward marks of our internal *ideas*, and those *ideas* being taken from particular things, if every particular *idea* that we take in should have a distinct name, names must be endless. To prevent this, the mind makes the particular *ideas* received from particular objects to become general; which is done by considering them as they are in the mind such appearances, separate from all other existences and the circumstances of real existence, as time, place, or any other concomitant *ideas*. This is called ABSTRACTION, whereby *ideas* taken from particular beings become general representatives of all of the same kind; and their names, general names, applicable to whatever exists conformable to such abstract *ideas*. Such precise, naked appearances in the mind, without considering how, whence, or with what others they came there, the understanding lays up (with names commonly annexed to them) as the standards to rank real existences into sorts, as they agree with these patterns, and to *denominate* them accordingly. Thus the same colour being observed to-day in chalk or snow, which the mind yesterday received from milk, it considers that appearance alone, makes it a representative of all of that kind; and having given it the name *whiteness*, it by that sound signifies the same quality wheresoever to be imagined or met with; and thus universals, whether *ideas* or terms, are made.

Berkeley elaborates on our supposed ability to frame abstract ideas of "qualities or modes" in *PHK*, Introduction §§7–8, and he is as opposed to any suggestion that we can form the idea of just one quality in abstraction from all other qualities, or that we can, for example, come by an abstract idea of extension in general, as he is to abstraction at any other level. However, Locke himself says no more about abstract ideas of individual qualities either here or in the third chapter of Book 3, where his first example of an abstract idea, and the general term that stands for it, is *man*.

3.3.6. The next thing to be considered is *how general words come to be made*. For since all things that exist are only particulars, how come we by general terms, or where find we those general natures they are supposed to stand for? Words become general by being made the signs of general *ideas*; and *ideas* become general by separating from them the circumstances of time and place and any other *ideas* that may determine them to this or that particular existence. By this way of abstraction they are made capable of representing more individuals than one: each of which, having in it a conformity to that abstract *idea*, is (as we call it) of that sort.

§7. But to deduce this a little more distinctly, it will not perhaps be amiss to trace our notions and names from their beginning and observe by what degrees we proceed and by what steps we enlarge our *ideas* from our first infancy. There is nothing more evident than that the *ideas* of the persons children converse with (to instance in them alone) are, like the persons themselves, only particular. The *ideas* of the nurse and the mother are well framed in their minds and, like pictures of them there, represent only those individuals. The names they first gave to them are confined to these individuals, and the names of *nurse* and *mamma* the child uses determine themselves to those persons. Afterwards, when time and a larger acquaintance have made them observe that there are a great many other things in the world that, in some common agreements of shape and several other qualities, resemble their father and mother and those persons they have been used to, they frame an *idea* which they find those many particulars do partake in, and to that they give, with others, the name *man*, for example. And *thus they come to have a general name*, and a general *idea*. Wherein they make nothing new, but only leave out of the complex *idea* they had of *Peter* and *James*, *Mary* and *Jane* that which is peculiar to each, and retain only what is common to them all.

§8. By the same way that they come by the general name and *idea* of *man*, they easily *advance to more general names* and notions. For, observing that several things that differ from their *idea of man* and cannot therefore be comprehended under that name have yet certain qualities wherein they agree with *man*, by retaining only those qualities and uniting them into one *idea*, they have again another and a more general *idea*, to which, having given a name, they make a term of a more comprehensive extension: which new *idea* is made, not by any new addition, but only as before, by leaving out the shape and some other properties signified by the name *man*, and retaining only a body, with life, sense, and spontaneous motion, comprehended under the name *animal*.

§9. That this is the *way whereby men first formed general* ideas, *and general names to them*, I think is so evident that there needs no other proof of it but the considering of a man's self, or others, and the ordinary proceedings of their minds in knowledge; and he that thinks general natures or notions are anything else but such abstract and partial *ideas* of more complex ones, taken at first from particular existences, will I fear be at a loss where to find them. For let anyone reflect and then tell me wherein does his *idea* of *man* differ from that of *Peter* and *Paul*, or his *idea* of *horse* from that of *Bucephalus*, but in the leaving out something that is peculiar to each individual, and retaining so much of those particular complex *ideas* of several particular existences as they are found to agree in. Of the complex *ideas* signified by the names *man* and *horse*, leaving out but those particulars wherein they differ, and retaining only those wherein they agree, and of those making a new distinct complex *idea*, and giving the name *animal* to it, one has a more general term that comprehends with man several other creatures. Leave out of the *idea* of *animal* sense and spontaneous motion, and the remaining complex *idea*, made up of the remaining simple ones of body, life, and nourishment, becomes a more general one, under the more comprehensive term, *vivens*. And not to dwell longer upon this particular, so evident in itself, by the same way the mind proceeds to *body, substance*, and at last to *being, thing*, and such universal terms which stand for any of our *ideas* whatsoever. To conclude: this whole *mystery* of *genera* and *species*, which make such a noise in the schools and are with justice so little regarded out of them, is nothing else but abstract *ideas*, more or less comprehensive, with names annexed to them. In all which, this is constant and unvariable: that every more general term stands for such an *idea* as is but a part of any of those contained under it.

What here seemed to Locke "so evident in itself" that it hardly needed prolonged treatment was to seem to Berkeley not just far from evident but, in fact, evidently false and so philosophically dangerous that he devoted much of the Introduction to the *Principles* to it. We cannot consider here whether Berkeley interpreted Locke aright, or whether his attack was fair, but it is worth noting that –

as the penultimate sentence of the last extract suggests – Locke had polemical aims of his own. His ultimate target was the Scholastic doctrine of "substantial forms", in the guise of objective "real essences", and he was here preparing the ground for his own doctrine that "the sorting of things is the workmanship of the understanding" (3.3.12), and, longer term, for his account, in Book 4, of what our knowledge of general truths consists in. Berkeley's polemical aims are different and, in fairness to Locke, that needs to be borne in mind when considering the famous passage in Book 4 about framing the abstract idea of a triangle – the passage Berkeley would make the target of what in *PC* 687 he called his "killing blow" against the doctrine of abstraction. That passage, which follows, occurs in the chapter entitled "Of Maxims," where Locke criticizes the Scholastic notion that certain highly abstract "axioms" are *praecognita* and *praeconcessa* (or truths "first known to mind," upon which "the other parts of our knowledge depend"). Against this, Locke is eager to stress that framing the more abstract concepts involved in these maxims is a pretty sophisticated task. In his account of this he included two sentences that, as Berkeley read them, seemed to imply that framing *any* abstract general idea is not just a sophisticated task but an impossible one.

4.7.9. *First*, That they are not the *truths first known* to the mind is evident to experience, as we have shown in another place, Book I, Ch. ii. Who perceives not that a child certainly knows that a stranger is not its mother; that its sucking bottle is not the rod, long before he knows that *It is impossible for the same thing to be and not to be*? And how many truths are there about numbers, which it is obvious to observe that the mind is perfectly acquainted with and fully convinced of, before it ever thought on these general maxims, to which mathematicians in their arguings do sometimes refer them? Whereof the reason is very plain: for that which makes the mind assent to such propositions being nothing else but the perception it has of the agreement or disagreement of its *ideas*, according as it finds them affirmed or denied one of another, in words it understands; and every *idea* being known to be what it is; and every two distinct *ideas* being known not to be the same, it must necessarily follow that such self-evident truths must be *first* known which consist of *ideas* that are *first* in the mind; and the *ideas first* in the mind, it is evident, are those of particular things; from whence, by slow degrees, the understanding proceeds to some few general ones; which, being taken from the ordinary and familiar objects of sense, are settled in the minds with general names to them. Thus particular *ideas* are *first* received and distinguished, and so knowledge got about them; and next to them, the less general or specific, which are next to particular. For abstract *ideas* are not so obvious or easy, to children or the yet unexercised mind, as particular ones. If they seem so to grown men, it is only because by constant and familiar use they are made so. For when we nicely reflect upon them, we shall find that general *ideas* are fictions and contrivances of the mind that carry difficulty with them, and do not so easily offer themselves as we are apt to imagine. For example, does it not require some pains and skill to form the *general idea* of a *triangle* (which is yet none of the most abstract, comprehensive, and difficult), for it must be neither oblique nor rectangle, neither equilateral, equicrural, nor scalenon; but all and none of these at once. In effect, it is something imperfect that cannot exist, an *idea* wherein some parts of several different and inconsistent *ideas* are put together. It is true, the mind in this imperfect state has need of such *ideas*, and makes all the haste to them it can, for the conveniency of communication and enlargement of knowledge, to both which it is naturally very much inclined. But yet one has reason to suspect such *ideas* are marks of our imperfection: at least, this is enough to show that the most abstract and general *ideas* are not those that the mind is *first* and most easily acquainted with, nor such as its earliest knowledge is conversant about.

5. The Existence of Things without Us

The reader who turns from Descartes' *Meditations* to Locke's *Essay* may be struck by how little inclined Locke seems to be to see skepticism about the existence of an external world as posing a serious philosophical challenge. The Cartesians had put this issue high on the philosophical agenda, but early in the *Essay* Locke simply introduces ideas of sensation as those received from "external sensible objects" and from then on the existence of such objects is, for the most part, taken for granted. This apparent casualness may seem the more surprising given that, at the beginning of Book 4, Locke tells us that "*the mind*, in all its thoughts and reasonings, hath no other immediate object but its own *ideas*, which it alone does or can contemplate," and then defines *knowledge* as "nothing but *the perception of the connexion and agreement, or disagreement and repug-*

nancy, of any of our ideas" – a characterization that, on the face of it, seems to rule out knowledge of anything other than ideas.[8] Locke's own understanding of the implications of his definition, and his seeming lack of concern that the mind can "contemplate" only ideas, are not issues we here examine.[9] We limit ourselves to noting that, apart from 4.2.14, which simply anticipates 4.11, the latter is the only place in the *Essay* where the very existence of external objects becomes an *issue* for Locke,[10] and that, even there, it is not treated as a matter of central importance. We include most of that discussion here.

4.11.1. The knowledge of our own being we have by intuition. The existence of a GOD, reason clearly makes known to us, as has been shown.

The *knowledge of the existence* of any other thing we can have only by *sensation*: for, there being no necessary connexion of *real existence* with any *idea* a man hath in his memory, nor of any other existence but that of GOD with the existence of any particular man, no particular man can know the *existence* of any other being but only when, by actual operating upon him, it makes itself perceived by him. For the having the *idea* of anything in our mind no more proves the existence of that thing, than the picture of a man evidences his being in the world, or the visions of a dream make thereby a true history.

§2. It is therefore the actual receiving of *ideas* from without that gives us notice of the *existence* of other things and makes us know that something doth exist at that time without us which causes that *idea* in us, though perhaps we neither know nor consider how it does it; for it takes not, from the certainty of our senses and the *ideas* we receive by them, that we know not the manner wherein they are produced: v.g. whilst I write this, I have, by the paper affecting my eyes, that *idea* produced in my mind which, whatever object causes, I call *white*, by which I know that that quality or accident (i.e. whose appearance before my eyes always causes that *idea*) doth really exist and hath a being without me. And of this, the greatest assurance I can possibly have and to which my faculties can attain is the testimony of my eyes, which are the proper and sole judges of this thing whose testimony I have reason to rely on, as so certain that I can no more doubt whilst I write this that I see white and black, and that something really exists that causes that sensation in me, than that I write or move my hand: which is a certainty as great as human nature is capable of concerning the existence of anything but a man's self alone and of GOD.

§3. *The notice we have by our senses of the existing of things without us,* though it be not altogether so certain as our intuitive knowledge or the deductions of our reason employed about the clear abstract *ideas* of our own minds, yet it is an assurance that *deserves the name of knowledge.* If we persuade ourselves that our faculties act and inform us right concerning the existence of those objects that affect them, it cannot pass for an ill-grounded confidence: for I think nobody can, in earnest, be so sceptical as to be uncertain of the existence of those things which he sees and feels. At least, he that can doubt so far (whatever he may have with his own thoughts) will never have any controversy with me, since he can never be sure I say anything contrary to his opinion. As to myself, I think GOD has given me assurance enough of the existence of things without me, since, by their different application, I can produce in myself both pleasure and pain, which is one great concernment of my present state. This is certain: the confidence that our faculties do not herein deceive us is the greatest assurance we are capable of concerning the existence of material beings. For we cannot act anything but by our faculties, nor talk of knowledge itself but by the help of those faculties which are fitted to apprehend even what knowledge is. But besides the assurance we have from our senses themselves, that they do not err in the information they give us of the existence of things without us when they are affected by them, we are further confirmed in this assurance by other concurrent reasons.

> Locke now offers four "concurrent reasons," which are, apparently, intended merely to confirm us in an assurance we already have – the assurance deriving from the senses themselves. The first is that we require sense organs in order to see or otherwise sense things, which indicates "exterior causes"; the third is that many of our ideas are accompanied by painful or pleasant sensations, whereas the same ideas, when called up in the memory, are not; and the fourth is that what is suggested by one sense (e.g., sight) can often be confirmed by another (e.g., touch). We include here only the second of Locke's "concurrent reasons".

4.11.5. *Secondly,* Because *sometimes I find that I cannot avoid the having those* ideas *produced in my mind.* For though, when my eyes are shut, or windows fast, I can at pleasure recall to my mind the *ideas* of *light*, or the *sun*, which former sensations had lodged in my memory: so I can at pleasure lay by that *idea*, and take into my view that of the *smell* of a rose, or *taste* of sugar. But, if I turn my eyes at noon towards the sun, I cannot avoid the *ideas* which the light or sun then produces in me. So that there is a manifest difference between the *ideas* laid up in my memory (over which, if they were there only, I should have constantly the same power to dispose of them and lay them by at pleasure) and those which force themselves upon me and I cannot avoid having. And therefore it must needs be some exterior cause and the brisk acting of some objects without me, whose efficacy I cannot resist, that produces those *ideas* in my mind, whether I will or no. Besides, there is nobody who doth not perceive the difference in himself between contemplating the sun as he hath the *idea* of it in his memory, and actually looking upon it: of which two, his perception is so distinct that few of his *ideas* are more distinguishable one from another, and therefore he hath certain knowledge that they are not both memory or the actions of his mind and fancies only within him, but that actual seeing hath a cause without.

None of Locke's "concurrent reasons" would convince a determined skeptic, but it is this second one that may particularly strike readers of Berkeley.[11] For here Locke moves quickly from the claim that there must be "some exterior cause" of our ideas of sense to the claim that this cause must be "the brisk acting of some objects without me, whose efficacy I cannot resist." Now Berkeley, too, will rest heavily on the premise that certain ideas are not, as he puts it, "creatures of my will." What is sometimes called Berkeley's "Passivity Argument", which is found in *PHK* §§28–29, thus starts from much the same point as Locke's argument, but Berkeley's conclusion is not that there must be external objects, but that "some other will or spirit" produces our ideas of sense.[12] Locke does not address the possibility that the external cause of our ideas of sense might be something *other* than external objects. He limits himself to acknowledging that a determined skeptic may simply dig his heels in and refuse to accept what has been said so far. He thus concludes with the following observations:

4.11.8. But yet, if after all this anyone will be so sceptical as to distrust his senses and to affirm that all we see and hear, feel and taste, think and do during our whole being is but the series and deluding appearances of a long dream, whereof there is no reality, and therefore will question the existence of all things or our knowledge of anything: I must desire him to consider that, if all be a dream, then he doth but dream that he makes the question, and so it is not much matter that a waking man should answer him. But yet if he pleases he may dream that I make him this answer, that *the certainty of* things existing *in rerum natura*, when we have *the testimony of our senses* for it, is not only *as great* as our frame can attain to, but *as our condition needs*. For our faculties being suited not to the full extent of being, nor to a perfect, clear, comprehensive knowledge of things free from all doubt and scruple, but to the preservation of us in whom they are, and accommodated to the use of life: they serve to our purpose well enough if they will but give us certain notice of those things which are convenient or inconvenient to us. For he that sees a candle burning and hath experimented the force of its flame by putting his finger in it will little doubt that this is something existing without him which does him harm and puts him to great pain: which is assurance enough, when no man requires greater certainty to govern his actions by than what is as certain as his actions themselves. And if our dreamer pleases to try whether the glowing heat of a glass furnace be barely a wandering imagination in a drowsy man's fancy, by putting his hand into it, he may perhaps be wakened into a certainty greater than he could wish that it is something more than bare imagination. So that this evidence is as great as we can desire, being as certain to us as our pleasure or pain, i.e. happiness or misery, beyond which we have no concernment, either of knowing or being. Such an assurance of the existence of things without us is sufficient to direct us in the attaining the good and avoiding the evil which is caused by them, which is the important concernment we have of being made acquainted with them.

Locke calls our knowledge of the existence of external objects "sensitive knowledge" – a "degree of knowledge" that goes "beyond bare probability" (4.2.14) but is "not altogether so certain" as the two highest degrees: intuitive and demonstrative knowledge. By contrast, Berkeley – for whom bodies are congeries of sensible ideas and so things we are directly acquainted with – boasted: "I am the farthest from Scepticism of any man. I know with an intuitive knowledge the existence of other things as well as my own Soul. this is wᵗ Locke nor scarce any other Thinking Philosopher will pretend to" (*PC* 563). Locke had said that in intuitive knowledge "the mind is at no pains of proving or examining but perceives the truth, as the eye doth light, only by being directed toward it" (4.2.1), and there is little doubt that when Berkeley claimed to have *intuitive* knowledge of the existence of other things, he was using the term in its Lockean sense. From early on, Berkeley claimed to be more certain of the existence of bodies than other philosophers, including Locke, had been. Already at *PC* 80, when Berkeley was still entertaining the view that a body is a combination of *powers* (a view he soon abandoned), he wrote, "I am more certain of ye existence & reality of Bodies than Mr Locke since he pretends onely to w^t he calls sensitive knowledge, whereas I think I have demonstrative knowledge of their Existence, by them meaning combinations of powers in an unknown substratum." Thus, in avowing, first, that he had *demonstrative* knowledge (Locke's second highest degree) that bodies exist, and then that he had *intuitive* knowledge (Locke's highest degree) that they do, Berkeley laid claim to greater certainty that there are bodies than even Locke had done.

* * *

Given the length of Locke's *Essay*, and the space available to us, it has not been possible here to do full justice to Locke's treatment of even the topics our selections deal with. To portray adequately his doctrines of substance and of primary and secondary qualities, for example, it would be necessary to exhibit more fully his doctrine that secondary qualities are powers in corporeal substances, and to show its relation to the scientific theory known as "corpuscularianism" that lies behind much that he writes in the *Essay*. It has not even been possible here to deal with every topic in the *Essay* that Berkeley himself explicitly commented on, such as Locke's "dangerous opinions" about the infinity and eternity of space and the possibility of matter thinking, to which Berkeley alludes in *PC* 695. Nor have we covered Locke's account of what he calls "real" knowledge. Still, it is not hard to imagine Berkeley's reaction to a passage like this one from Book 4, Chapter 4 (a chapter Berkeley reminded himself, at *PC* 549, "nicely to discuss"): "It is evident the mind knows not things immediately, but only by the intervention of the *ideas* it has of them. *Our knowledge*, therefore, is *real* only so far as there is a conformity between our *ideas* and the reality of things." Berkeley, very likely, had passages like this in mind when he wrote, at *PC* 606, "The supposition that things are distinct from Ideas takes away all real Truth, & consequently brings in a Universal Scepticism, since all our knowledge & contemplation is confin'd barely to our own Ideas." While Berkeley presumably recognized that Locke himself scorned skepticism, at least concerning the *existence* of bodies, he seems to have seen Locke's views as opening the door to it.

Notes

1. Our selections are taken from J. W. Yolton's edition of the *Essay* (London: Dent, 1974), in which Locke's spelling and punctuation have been somewhat modernized. References in what follows are by book, chapter, and section number and can thus be easily located in any edition.
2. In Book 1 of the *Essay*, Locke had attacked the doctrine that there is *innate* knowledge and given arguments against innate ideas.
3. See, for example, Reginald Jackson, "Locke's Distinction between Primary and Secondary Qualities" and W. H. F. Barnes, "Did Berkeley Misunderstand Locke?", reprinted from *Mind* (1929 and 1940), in C. B. Martin and D. M. Armstrong, *Locke and Berkeley: A Collection of Critical Essays* (Garden City, NY: Anchor Books, 1968).
4. See, for example, Peter Alexander, "Boyle and Locke on Primary and Secondary Qualities," reprinted from *Ratio* (1974), in I. C. Tipton, *Locke on Human Understanding: Selected Essays* (Oxford: Oxford University Press, 1977).
5. See David Berman, "On Missing the Wrong Target," *Hermathena*, no. 113 (1972), pp. 54–67. Berman notes that Luce, in *Berkeley and Malebranche*, calculated that, of the entries in *PC* marked with the letter "P" (for "Primary and secondary qualities"), "8 mention Malebranche or the Cartesians, and another 10 or 12 contain references to the *Search*," while only 3 "mention Locke and possibly 4 others refer to him."
6. M. R. Ayers, "The Ideas of Power and Substance in Locke's Philosophy," reprinted from *Philosophical Quarterly* (1975), in Tipton, *Locke on Human Understanding*, p. 78. Ayers goes on to give his own valuable account of what he takes Locke to be up to.
7. See *PHK*, Introduction §§6 and 17. He later told Samuel Johnson, "Abstract general ideas was a notion that Mr. Locke held in common with the Schoolmen, and I think all other philosophers" (*Works* II, p. 293).
8. Berkeley took note of the relevant point at *PC* 522.
9. Nor can we here do more than note a related puzzle. In his posthumously published *An Examination of P. Malebranche's Opinion of Seeing all Things in God*, Locke asks, "how can [Malebranche] know that there is any such real being in the world as the sun? Did he ever see the sun? No, but on occasion of the presence of the sun to his eyes, he has seen the idea of the sun in God, which God has exhibited to him; but the sun, because it cannot be united to his soul,

he cannot see. How then does he know that there is a sun which he never saw?" (§20). The point is pressed further when he later asks, "for how can I know that the picture of any thing is like that thing, when I never see that which it represents?" (§51). Many, including Berkeley, have thought that this very objection can be made to Locke's own theory of sense perception, just as much as Locke thought it could to Malebranche's. Against that, however, it has been argued that the reason Locke was not embarrassed by the objection was that he did not in fact hold the kind of representative theory of perception often attributed to him. For various opinions on this matter, see R. I. Aaron, *John Locke*, 3rd ed. (Oxford: Clarendon Press, 1971), pp. 101ff.; A. D. Woozley, in his Introduction to his abridged edition of Locke's *Essay* (London: Fontana, 1964), pp. 25ff.; H. E. Matthews, "Locke, Malebranche and the Representative Theory," reprinted from the *Locke Newsletter* (1971), in Tipton, *Locke on Human Understanding*; and C. J. McCracken, *Malebranche and British Philosophy*, pp. 132–34.

10. It has often been supposed that the same issue is raised in *Essay* 4.4.3 (a section from which we quote at the end of the present chapter) which poses the question, "How shall the mind, when it perceives nothing but its own *ideas*, know that they agree with things themselves?" Taken in context, however, it seems that Locke may not be questioning the *existence* of bodies, but rather raising, and answering, a question about the adequacy of our conceptions of them. See Kathy Squadrito, "The *Essay* 4.4.3," *The Locke Newsletter*, no. 9 (1978), pp. 55–61.

11. Berkeley himself alluded to it in *PC* 790: "Locke in his 4th book & Descartes in Med. 6. use the same argument for the Existence of objects viz. that sometimes we see feel etc against our will."

12. Berkeley was just as keen as Locke to point to the manifest differences between ideas of imagination and ideas of sense, both because doing so provided him with a premise for the Passivity Argument for God's existence and because it enabled him to sustain a distinction between the ideas of the imagination and the ideas constituting the real.

NINE

Henry Lee

Berkeley, we have noted, seems to have viewed Locke's philosophy as opening a door to skepticism. It was a view shared by some other early critics of Locke, among them Henry Lee, who in 1702 published *Anti-Scepticism: or, Notes upon each Chapter of Mr. Locke's Essay concerning Human Understanding*. Lee's overriding worry – like Bishop Stillingfleet's before him – was that *religious* certainties were threatened by Locke's restriction of knowledge to the perception of the agreement or disagreement of "ideas", but Lee also argued that this restriction rules out *any* knowledge of real things. We suspect, but cannot be sure, that Berkeley read Lee's *Anti-Scepticism*.[1] Certainly, if a copy was available to him in Dublin, it seems very likely that he would have read it, for it was, after all, a chapter-by-chapter examination of a work of central importance for him.

In many ways, Lee's views are remote from Berkeley's: he never doubts that there are objects external to the mind; he champions the doctrine of innate knowledge; he defends the Scholastics' "maxims" and the doctrine that these are *praecognita* and *praeconcessa*; and he accepts without qualms the distinction between primary and secondary qualities. Yet in his treatment of abstract ideas Lee clearly anticipates Berkeley, and in our view this adds to the likelihood that Berkeley knew his book. But even if he did not know Berkeley's book, Lee's work would not be without interest for us. Berkeley is sometimes accused of misinterpreting the *Essay*, so it is instructive to see how others of the time construed Locke's views. In Lee we have a thinker whose overall stance was very different from Berkeley's and yet who read the *Essay* in much the way Berkeley did, making some of the same criticisms Berkeley made. Both Berkeley and Lee hold that the doctrine of abstract general ideas is an error tainting Locke's whole account of knowledge; Lee, like Berkeley, focuses attention on the supposed abstract ideas of existence and unity; and Lee objects to Locke's account of abstraction on much the same grounds as Berkeley (right down to criticizing the passage in *Essay* 4.7 that Berkeley was to base his "killing blow" on). A. A. Luce once speculated on what the "source" of Berkeley's anti-abstractionism was; if there were need of a source, Lee would seem a good candidate.

One difference between Berkeley and Lee is that Berkeley is content to make the term "idea" central in his philosophy, whereas Lee, like Bishop Stillingfleet and John Sergeant (whose *Solid Philosophy Asserted, Against the Fancies of the Ideists* Berkeley alludes to at *PC* 840), was not. Lee here thought like Stillingfleet, who did not object to using "idea" in "a common sense," but who rejected Locke's use of the term, declaring: "I am for no new affected terms which are apt to carry men's minds out of the way; they are like *ignes fatui* which seem to give light, but lead those that follow them into bogs."[2] That Lee agrees with Stillingfleet about this can be seen in the following extract, which we include to set the scene.[3]

By the word *idea* [Locke] means, he says, *Whatsoever is the object of the understanding when a man thinks.* And this term, he says, he could not avoid frequently using. And there is no wonder at that, for if everything that is within the reach of thought be an *idea*, then all the world of which we have the least knowledge must consist only of several kinds of *ideas*, and so it must come to pass that the word must be used in no *certain* sense. And accordingly this author makes it stand sometimes for the *thoughts*, or *conceptions* themselves, in the mind, and sometimes for the *things* themselves without the mind that are the objects of its thoughts, and this often in the same sentence and without any distinction, which creates great difficulty in the understanding his meaning.

But that I may lead the reader the nearest way to the understanding this author's language, and save myself the necessity of repetitions, I shall here endeavour to show the *proper* sense of the word *idea*; and that it is a very inadequate object of thoughts in that sense, and, when used in any other, is apt to breed misunderstandings and confusions; and that all which can be meant by it may be expressed in other words that are less ambiguous and more intelligible. The word *idea*, we all agree, is derived from the Greek word εἴδω, which originally signifies *to see*, and therefore, in its strict or proper sense, that only can be called an *idea* which is a visible representation or resemblance of the object and, in some measure at least, *like* that thing of which it is the idea. Thus a man's face in the glass is properly the *idea* of that face; or, when we see any single object, the little picture or image formed at the bottom of the eye may properly be called the *idea* of the thing seen; and by a latitude in expression the picture of a man or of anything else may be called the *idea* of that man or thing represented. In all which cases there is a resemblance or some kind of likeness between the *thing* itself and its *idea*. So that in the proper original sense of that word there is no *idea* in the mind but when it is some resemblance, picture, image or likeness of that which is without it, and never occurs but in that act of the mind which is commonly and properly called *imagination*: and there is then indeed a kind of picture or image of that thing in the mind whilst it thinks of it. And therefore whenever it is used in any other case, it is metaphorical and improper. And though this is no more than what this author owns and proves in several places, and long before him Descartes, Hobbes, Gassendi, and most others that have written of late concerning those matters, yet it was necessary to be noted here to show the necessity of using *other* words to express things with any tolerable clearness: for this impropriety of the word would wear off by degrees, because common use will make any word proper. And besides most other words are metaphorical as well as this. But now this author has stocked our language with such a spawn of new words that one will need a new dictionary to understand English. *Simple, complex, abstract ideas; simple, compound, mixed modes*; which does not only corrupt our language, but, which is worse, raises such a mist that we are often deluded with the hopes of some great discoveries when there is hardly common sense to be gained.[4]

> Lee goes on to illustrate how Locke's talk of "ideas" leads to errors about certain matters, including the acceptance of a distinction between "simple" and "complex" ideas. This distinction, which was so prominent in Book 2 of Locke's *Essay*, is not one Berkeley himself uses in the *Principles* or the *Dialogues*. Although Berkeley never explicitly rejects "simple" ideas, it has been strongly argued that a rejection of them is implicit in his attack on abstraction.[5] Certainly, for Lee – and it would seem for Berkeley, too – "simple" ideas would have to be *abstract* ideas. The following extract typifies Lee's opposition to abstract ideas as such.

Figure, motion, rest, bulk, position may properly be called the *modes* of the bodies, because from the varieties of them, so far as we can learn, all the other qualities of bodies derive their distinctions and denominations. And when they are conceived or thought on by the mind, they may be called its *modes* of *perception*, but not its *simple ideas*, because we never have any ideas of them at all, *abstracted* from the particular bodies to which they belong: not of figure, without the body figured; nor of motion or rest, without the bodies moving or resting; of bulk or position, without the bodies which are said to be great or small, in this or that place. *Colours, smells, tastes, sounds, roughness, smoothness*, and other qualities which affect the organs of feeling, may be properly called, when *out* of the mind, the *modes, powers*, or *sensible qualities* of bodies; when *in* the mind its various *modes* of *sensation*, but not again *simple ideas*. For no one can form any idea at any time of any colour, of roughness or smoothness, or any other tangible quality, without conceiving at the same instant the idea of a particular body that is so coloured, rough or smooth. And if he does so, then it is a *complex* idea. And if anyone offer to conceive an idea of a smell, taste, or sound, his thoughts will run upon the bodies that produce them, and then they will be *complex* ideas. And therefore they are only modes of sensation, and of them the mind has no abstract or simple ideas. All the operations of the mind itself, such as *affirming, denying, understanding, judging, remembering*, are only its various modes of thinking or acting: but we have no ideas of them except we include the things affirmed, denied, understood, judged of, remembered or thought on; but then they are not *simple* ideas. And as for *substances*, we have no ideas of them abstracted from all their modes and properties, any more than we have of any one mode abstracted from its substance. And therefore *all* ideas are *complex*; and as for the whole tribe of *abstract general* ideas, they are mere fictions, they are only the common names of substances or their modes given them for their agreement with others: but there are no ideas, answering those general names, in the mind. All the ideas we have are of *particular visible substances*, in conjunction with their several modes. I am very sensible that the word *idea* has been much used of late to express other immediate objects of the understanding, besides such as are visible; but if anyone reflect upon his own thoughts he will easily find reason to judge it is altogether improper, and only metaphorical. To say we have an *idea* of God, properly speaking, is only to have such thoughts, notions or knowledge of his perfections, properties, excellencies or attributes by which he may be distinguished from all other beings; and the like of all other substances and modes, which I shall have occasion farther to explain in more proper places. And I noted it here only to show the impropriety and needlessness of the word *idea*, and that there are really in the mind of man no such things as simple or general abstract ideas: on which hypothesis this author's whole scheme about knowledge, so far as different from the common, is built.[6]

> Where for Berkeley an "idea" becomes "any sensible or imaginable thing" (*PC* 775), Lee restricts the term to images and does not hold that the things we perceive by sense are "ideas". For all that, the two thinkers agree that, properly speaking, there can be no "ideas" of operations of the mind, or of God, and, most strikingly, that there can be no abstract ideas as Locke understands them. Moreover, they both take the acceptance of abstract general ideas to be a quite fundamental error in Locke's philosophy, and one that infects the *Essay* as a whole. It is, says Lee, the hypothesis "on which . . . this author's whole scheme about knowledge . . . is built"; while for Berkeley "Abstract general ideas was a notion that . . . runs through [Locke's] whole book of Human Understanding."[7] We include next an intriguing snippet from Lee on what Locke took to be "simple ideas of both sensation and reflection." Once again it concerns what Lee takes to be abstract ideas.

> By *simple ideas of both sensation and reflexion* [Locke] understands such perceptions or notions which are produced in us both by the impressions upon the organs of our body, and the reflexion also the mind makes upon its own actions. And of this sort he reckons pleasure and pain, power, existence, unity. . . .
>
> But now how pleasure or pain, power, unity or existence come into the class of *simple ideas* is not easy to imagine. For what notion can any man have either of *pleasure* or *pain* alone, without considering, I mean, the causes of them, or subjects wherein they are? Or of *power*, without the object operating or operated upon? Or of *existence* or *unity*, without the thing existing, or the thing that is one? So that *pleasure* and *pain* seem to me only the names of our perceptions; *power*, *unity* and *existence* the names only of the acts of the mind itself exercised about things operating, existing and being one, and not any abstract ideas or objects of the mind.[8]

> Lee's overall standpoint remains quite different from Berkeley's, and while, for Lee, we have no simple idea of existence abstracted from

the "thing existing," the things existing will include objects that Lee thinks of as external. For his part, Berkeley certainly agrees with Lee that existence "is no simple idea," but what he adds is that it is not "distinct from perceiving & being perceiv'd" (*PC* 408).[9] In his hands, therefore, the denial of any abstract idea of existence, which had been so clearly anticipated by Lee, became one important weapon in his attack on external existence. The supposedly simple idea of *unity*, which again Lee objects to, is another that Berkeley, too, dismisses (*PC* 545). "To say no more, it is an *abstract idea*" (*PHK* §13).

We turn next to Lee's criticism of Locke's account of substance. Here too Lee's view is remote from Berkeley's, in that there is no suggestion that *substances* do not exist outside the mind; but Lee *is* highly critical of what he takes to be Locke's account of "pure substance", which he again links with the notion of abstraction.

This name of *substance* we give to anything whose existence we conceive independent upon everything else, and in which several properties or qualities are united or combined. And this, as old as it is, is taken to be a perfect definition of *substance* in general, because hereby the mode of its existence is distinguishable from that of *qualities* or *properties*: namely, its existence does not depend upon any other created substance or any quality or property, whereas qualities or properties do depend upon one substance or other, and have no qualities united in them. Thus *spirit* is distinguished from *perception* and *willing*, *body* is distinguished from *figure* and *motion*, and so of the rest of the qualities of either of those two sorts of substances.

But to clear this old notion of *substances* from the new difficulties with which my author has obscured it when he treats of the *nature* and *essence* of substances in general or of pure substance, it will be proper first to enquire and settle what we mean by those two words *nature* and *essence*, in which, I doubt, several great authors have fumbled as in the dark, by not understanding one another's meaning of those two common words. In order to that I must presume, because it seems agreed on all sides: 1. that *nature* and *essence* do not signify any principles, or anything else, really distinct from that of which they are said to be the nature or essence; 2. that there is nothing general but *names*: every substance is a *particular* substance, and every quality is a *particular* quality. And if this be allowed then, in propriety of speech, the *nature* or *essence* of every particular thing can be that only by which it is distinguished from everything else; the nature or essence of every *substance*, as distinguishable from every *quality*, is that its manner of existence is *independent*, and that it has several qualities united in it; and the nature or essence of every *quality*, as distinguishable from every *substance*, is that its manner of existence is *dependent*, and that it has no qualities united in it. Again, the nature or essence of any *particular* substance, as distinguishable from all other particular substances, is the combination of those properties or qualities which it has and others want; and the nature or essence of any *particular* quality is that particular modification of a substance which another has not, and by which it affects us.

And now I am ready to answer all my author's queries. Have we any notion of *substance* in general? Yes, as before defined, and that as distinct as *qualities* in general, or *ideas* either, if he mean by the word *ideas* that which is in the object of which he is said to have an idea. Have we any notion of a *particular* substance? Yes, and that as clear (though not so full or adequate) as of any one quality whatsoever. Will not this content? What would he have more? He would have a clear notion of *pure substance* (that is) abstracted from all properties or qualities whatever. I answer, there is no such substance in the whole world. Every substance has some qualities or other: a *spirit* its thinking, *space* its expansion, *body* its solidity. And then how can any man have a distinct notion of that from which you suppose all its properties (by which it should be distinguished) separated or abstracted. However thus far I can go, if that will gratify him: every man has as clear a notion of *pure substance*, abstracted from all its *qualities*, as he can of *qualities* in general abstracted from every *substance*. Let any man tell me what a kind of thing, or what is the *nature* or *essence* of motion, rest, figure, colour, thinking, *abstracted* from every *substance* moving, resting, figured, coloured and thinking, and I'll be bound to tell him what kind of thing, or what is the *essence* or *nature* of spirit or body separated from all its qualities or properties. No, no, there is really no such substance in the world abstracted from all qualities, nor no quality abstracted from all substances. And so we are even. We have as clear a notion of substance in *general*, or of any *particular* substance, as we have of quality in *general* or any *particular* quality. And therefore it is not fair, first to require us to abstract every property and quality which constitutes the essence or nature of it, and then ask us what it is. That is as impertinent as to ask what a man's estate is after we have stripped him of every foot of land, house, and all his goods wherein estate consists. But still there will be enough left for our conception of the difference between *substance* and *quality*, there will remain more than bare something, for quality is something as well as substance; but qualities cannot exist independent upon substance, nor cannot have other qualities united in them; but the existence of substance is independent and can have several sorts of qualities united in it.[10]

> Since Lee takes Locke's doctrine of abstract general ideas to be a quite fundamental error, it is not surprising that he comments adversely on the treatment of abstraction in the *Essay*, Book 2, Chapter 11, and Book 3, Chapter 3. The following is from Lee's comments on the second of these. It will be noted that although Lee does not find the role that Berkeley soon does for what *Berkeley* recognizes as "general" ideas,[11] and although Lee does concede that there is a proper sense in which an idea can be said to be *abstract* (but cf. *PHK*, Introduction §10), his firm rejection of abstract general ideas is strongly reminiscent of Berkeley's. The opening paragraph is (and is intended as) a summary of Locke's starting point, with which Lee does not quarrel.

Though all things that exist are particulars, yet we find most of our words are general, and do not signify particular things. But this could not be avoided, because if every particular thing should have a distinct name, names would be infinite and no one man's memory could retain them. And besides, if it were possible, yet it would not answer the great design of language; for that being to communicate our thoughts to one another, those words or names would be useless sounds unless we could suppose others to understand the distinction as well as ourselves. Though every crow, sheep, leaf on a tree, hair of our head, sand on the shore, be really distinct from each other, yet if each had a distinct name, the using that distinct name would not communicate our thoughts to others unless they knew that individual thing as well as ourselves. And therefore we find that, though jockeys may have names for their horses, and shepherds for some of their sheep, yet they cannot treat with others about them merely by their names, but must either show them, if present, or describe them by distinct marks, if absent. And this being impracticable in all individuals, distinct names, if they could be made or remembered, would be of no use in conversation. And therefore proper names are seldom given but to such things as mankind are concerned to maintain a distinct knowledge of: such are persons, countries, cities, rivers, mountains, towns and villages. But as for other individual things, though really as distinct in nature, and sometimes more, have not proper names, but have a general name; and if that general name be not understood by them we converse with, we are forced to set it forth by its peculiar qualities, as marks of distinction.

Thus far my author's notions are common with other people's. But when he comes to assign the use of general words, then he differs from the sense (at least in manner of expression) of most others. His fancy is *that words become general by being made the signs of general or abstract ideas.* But, for the clearing this matter, I shall endeavour, 1. to explain what an *abstract idea* is; 2. to show there are no *general* or *abstract* ideas in his sense; 3. what a *general word* signifies.

1. I conceive that properly an *abstract* idea is nothing else but the representation, image, picture or resemblance in the mind of a single or particular visible object, when the object itself is not present, does not actually affect the eye. Thus in the night a man may be properly said to have the *abstract* idea of the sun in his mind. So again one man may have the abstract idea of another man's face, of a particular country, city, house, river, rainbow, or of any particular substance that is visible, though at a distance, though absent, because whilst he thinks of them there is a perfect picture or image of them in the mind. And these are properly called *abstract ideas*, because the objects are at that time abstracted or separated from the mind that conceives them.

2. I say there can be no *general* or *abstract ideas* in my author's sense because no man can possibly think of more than one thing at one instant and therefore cannot form a *general* or *abstract idea*, as will clearly appear to anyone that will but reflect upon the actions of his own mind. When he hears the word *man*, has he any idea but of the sensible properties of some single person? When he hears the word *white*, does not his mind fix upon milk, snow, paper, which he conceives as in one certain place? And the like of sweetness in taste or smell, of sounds and all tangible qualities, if he does not fix his mind upon some particular object that may produce them? And the case is the same as to *figure, motion, rest,* and *bulk*: when any man thinks of them he does either only rumble over the word in his mind or fixes it upon some visible body that has that motion, figure, rest or bulk. And the like for *murder, procession, triumph.* If he thinks on murder, his mind runs upon the actions of stabbing, shooting, slashing of some particular person, and in some particular place. And so for all other mixed modes, the mind has no idea at all but of what is visible, or only ruminates the words. Thus I find it with myself, and appeal to every other man's sense.

3. It remains then only to be considered what these general words are the signs of, for they cannot be *general* or *abstract ideas*. There are no such. They are all of particular and only visible objects, at a distance from the mind. Now I cannot apprehend that general words are anything more than the signs of the mind's having observed that several particular things agree; and those words when used intelligibly by any person imply no more than that he has observed such an agreement. When I say, *This paper is white*, I don't compare it with any idea that I have in my mind of whiteness abstracted from particular bodies (for I have no such idea, or can form any) but with snow, milk, or some wall that uses to affect my sight in the same manner, and so give it that name of *white*, because it agrees with one or other of them in producing the like effect. When I give the name *man* to this particular person, it is only because he has all the visible properties which I have observed in other individual persons. I give the general name of *words* to this or that sound because it affects my ears as other words do. I call stabbing *murder* because it is contrary to the laws of nature and my country. And so for all sort of actions and the modes of them, which my author calls mixed modes: they are only general words because the several actions and modes agree in those particulars which entitle them unto that common name. Though stabbing and shooting be different actions, as much as hog and dog are different substances, yet I give them the common name of murder, because they agree in being equally contrary to law, just as I do in those two sort of substances – though they differ in shape and other qualities, yet, because they agree in having life and all the signs of sense, I call them both animals.[12]

There is one other notable passage on abstract ideas in Locke's *Essay* – the passage in 4.7, "Of Maxims", on which, notoriously, Berkeley was to base his "killing blow."[13] Berkeley is not particularly interested in the topic that is Locke's real concern in this chapter, and simply seizes on the one offending passage, but Lee is, wishing as he does to defend maxims as in some sense innate, and "of singular use in the ready proof of such propositions, as are not discoverable merely by the senses, where sensible ideas are not to be had." However, what is striking about our final selection from Lee is that, like Berkeley, Lee does seize on the passage about the triangle.

It must be owned, these truths [maxims] are not the first known to children, in that sense especially wherein my author means, namely that the terms wherein they are expressed are first known. It is great odds, I confess, that they know pleasure and pain, hunger and thirst, warmth and cold, before they know their names or form propositions about them. However, I guess they don't in their minds play with the abstract *ideas*, like babies, before they know that pleasure is pleasure, pain is pain, and that pain is not pleasure, and yet that knowledge is but that everything is the same with itself and not another. And when they grow old enough to be philosophers, they don't need to be taught those truths any more than they do that their sucking-bottle is not the rod, or a stranger not their mother; and that is all we mean when we say that such truths are innate. What my author says is wonderfully true, that the ideas of particular things are first in the mind (if he mean the thoughts of single objects) and that children by slow degrees proceed to general ideas (if he mean to more objects). But if he mean any more by general ideas, then I confess on this side of the country children go on cruel slowly, for they never grow to the maturity of having general ideas as long as they live. But if by general ideas he means only general names, they are like other people, give general names as fast as they can, learn wherein individuals agree or disagree with others. Nay, my author himself, though a great mathematician, seems sensible how hard it is to form the general idea of a triangle: for it must neither be oblique, rectangle, equicrural, nor scalenum; it must be all and none of these at once. From whence this corollary will fairly be inferred: that there is no such general or abstract idea possible to be formed. For he that can form the idea of a line that shall not be a particular line; of an angle, but shall be of no particular sort; of a figure, without a determinate kind; of an animal, and yet of no particular species; or of a species without an individual, shall pass for a sight and get more money in the country than an unicorn with many horns. For we look upon these only as common names of several individuals.[14]

> Even if one supposed that Berkeley did not read Lee's *Anti-Scepticism*, it need not mean that Lee should be of no interest to students of Berkeley. For it would still be interesting that Lee anticipates a number of Berkeley's criticisms of Locke, and interprets him in much the way that Berkeley did. However, our own suspicion is that Berkeley did read Lee, and that Lee played some role in

influencing him during the period in which he was penning entries in the *Philosophical Commentaries* and, in particular, developing his opposition to abstraction.[15]

Notes

1. The library at Trinity College, Dublin, did not acquire a copy of *Anti-Scepticism* until 1727. That does not, however, entail that Berkeley did not have access to the work at the relevant time. Locke was eagerly studied in Dublin. Moreover, the copy acquired in 1727 is inscribed with the name of William Palliser, Archbishop of Cashel, and was one item in a collection of books bequeathed to Trinity by Palliser in that year. This suggests one way in which Lee's book might have been available to Berkeley at a much earlier date, for that Berkeley had some connection with Palliser is indicated by the fact that it was to the Archbishop's young son, also William, that Berkeley dedicated his *Arithmetica* in 1707. Interestingly, it was towards the end of 1707, or early in 1708, that Berkeley's firm opposition to abstraction began to develop (see note 15). This may have been under the influence of Lee.
2. *The Bishop of Worcester's Answer to Mr. Locke's Second Letter* (1698), p. 71.
3. All selections are from Lee's *Anti-Scepticism* (London, 1702). References from here on give the pages that the selection is from; in parentheses we give the book and chapter of Locke's *Essay* that Lee is examining at that point.
4. Lee, pp. 1–2 (*Essay*, 1.1).
5. See, for example, Kenneth P. Winkler, *Berkeley: An Interpretation* (Oxford: Clarendon Press, 1989), ch. 3.
6. Lee, pp. 3–4 (*Essay*, 1.1).
7. Berkeley, *Works* II, p. 293.
8. Lee, pp. 53–54 (*Essay*, 2.7).
9. Supposing Berkeley did read Lee, had he also been struck by Lee's observation that *existence* is the name of an *act* of the mind? If so, he certainly went further than Lee, for Lee remains committed to existence without the mind. It is undeniable, however, that *PC* 408 (the first of the entries in the *Commentaries* with the marginal sign for "Existence") encapsulates what Berkeley sees as a major insight, and one connected with the thought that everything hangs on "the meaning & definition of the word Existence" (cf. *PC* 604 and *PHK* §3) and the claim that existence is no simple idea. It is not impossible that Berkeley read more into Lee's suggestion that it is merely the name of an act of the mind than Lee himself did, concluding that "existence" marks out an essential relationship to the mind.
10. Lee, pp. 110–11 (*Essay*, 2.23).
11. *PHK*, Introduction §12. There is, however, no parallel passage in the draft Introduction of 1708 (*Works* II, pp. 121–45). There, and in the *Philosophical Commentaries*, "general" ideas are always taken to be abstract.
12. Lee, pp. 202–204 (*Essay*, 3.3).
13. See above, pp. 110–11.

14. Lee, p. 274 (*Essay*, 4.7).

15. This appears to have been while he was writing the first of the two notebooks [Notebook B] that comprise the *Philosophical Commentaries*, which would have been in the second half of 1707, or thereabouts. As Luce says, "In the earlier part of notebook B there are two or three casual references to abstraction; but there is no evidence of any sustained interest in the theme" (*The Dialectic of Immaterialism*, p. 108; cf. Luce's note on entry 318 in his diplomatic edition of the *Commentaries*). That changes soon after, and by the end of 1708 Berkeley had written the draft Introduction for the *Principles*, vigorously attacking abstraction.

TEN

John Norris

Soon after the *Principles* appeared, John Percival reported to Berkeley that two prominent thinkers of the time, Samuel Clarke and William Whiston, had dismissed his views, "ranking" him with Malebranche and John Norris. Berkeley wrote back to Percival, "I know few writers whom I take myself at bottom to differ from more than them."[1] As this letter contains Berkeley's only recorded mention of Norris, it is not possible to say whether he had ever actually read Norris, still less whether he was at all influenced by him. There are, however, good reasons for including here a selection from Norris. Norris was Malebranche's foremost English follower and was well known when Berkeley was young; his many books were widely read, some of them going through edition after edition ("he can turn Metaphysicks into Money," declared John Dunton, the London bookseller); and his chief work, *An Essay towards the Theory of the Ideal or Intelligible World* (1701–1704), was a comprehensive defense, over 1,000 pages long, of the doctrine of the vision of things in God. It is not surprising, therefore, that Berkeley knew at least enough about Norris's views to be able to insist that they were very different from his own.

Berkeley may already have had Norris, as well as Malebranche, in mind at *PHK* §148, when, after declaring that "we need only open our eyes to see the sovereign Lord of all things with a more full and clear view, than we do any one of our fellow-creatures," he sought to dissociate his own standpoint from the doctrine that "we see God (as some will have it) by a direct and immediate view, or see corporeal things, not by themselves, but by seeing that which represents them in the essence of God." Despite this disavowal, it is not perhaps surprising that some of Berkeley's early readers, familiar with Norris's doctrine that an "ideal or intelligible world" exists eternally in the mind of God as the "uncreated archetype" of the natural world, linked Berkeley's view with Norris's. For Berkeley, too, could assert, through Philonous, that "I . . . acknowledge a two-fold state of things, the one ectypal or natural, the other archetypal and eternal," adding that "the former was created in time; the latter existed from everlasting in the mind of God."[2] In reality, however, Norris and Berkeley meant quite different things by the "natural world"; for Norris, it is an unperceivable material world, for Berkeley, the perceivable world of sensible ideas.[3]

The selection below does not include Norris's account of the nature of the "ideal or intelligible world" or his arguments for its existence. It is concerned, rather, to argue, as the title of the chapter it is taken from puts it, "That the Existence of the Intelligible is more Certain than that of the Natural or Sensible World," and that the evidence for the latter is weaker than we suppose. Norris embraced Malebranche's view that neither sense nor reason can prove the natural world's existence with certainty, but he departed from Malebranche by denying the validity of any appeal to Scripture to prove it. In this he agreed with Arnauld, though Arnauld had, of course, held that the appeal to faith is unnecessary, since reason can prove that bodies exist. Norris, by contrast, is concerned to press the view that neither sense, reason, nor faith can establish with certainty that bodies exist. While Norris in fact firmly disavowed skepticism about the existence of the corporeal world, Arthur Collier was to point out that Norris provided no very clear case for doing so. With the publication of this material in 1701, a year after Berkeley entered Trinity College, Dublin, the stage was thus in effect set for a straightforward denial of the existence of a material world.[4]

All that I pretend is that the house of wisdom, the ideal fabric, stands upon a more stable foundation than the frame of external nature, and that, as sure as this sensible world is, the intelligible world is yet surer. And that because we have (1) more, (2) better reasons to assure us of its existence.

First, *more* reasons. For this sensible world being no necessary emanation from the nature of God, but the free and (in that respect) contingent effect of his will and power, there is no proving a priori, or from the cause, that there should be such a world, nor consequently (that way) that there is one. The only argument producible for its existence must be from the effect, namely from those impressions which are made upon our senses in our conversing with bodies. What the force or moment of this argument is I am not now to consider. My present business is sufficiently served in remarking that, be the moment of it what it will, it is the only one that the thing has, or is capable of, in a natural way. But does not faith tell me so as well as sense? For is not the natural world the object of divine revelation as well as of sensible perception? I grant it is so. But then I ask again whether the certainty I have of this divine revelation does not ultimately depend upon the information of sense. Not I mean as *divine* (that being a matter of a more rational discussion, though even that too will be found in some measure to have its foundation in sense, as in the attestation of miracles), but purely and simply as revelation. That is, without considering at present the authority of such a revelation either as to its being from God or as to the truth and certainty of it supposing it be, all that I now inquire is whether I must not be beholden to my sense to inform me whether *de facto* there be any such revelation extant or no. And I think it cannot be denied but that I must. For I have no other certainty of the existence of such a revelation than I have of the existence of my Bible wherein it is contained. And then again I have no other certainty of the existence of my Bible, or of such and such characters in it, than I have of other bodies or of any of those figures whereby they are modified. So that, you see, all at last resolves into the testimony of sense, which therefore upon an ultimate and final consideration may be said to be the only argument I have for the existence of a natural world. The short is, revelation tells me there is such a world, but then it is my sense that tells me there is such a revelation, and therefore, ultimately and fundamentally speaking, I have but one argument to assure me that there is a natural world, and that is because my *sense* tells me so. But now as to the intelligible world, the existence of that (as may appear by that little specimen already given of it) is demonstrable by a great variety of argument: both the nature of God and the works of God prove it, all the arts and sciences proceed upon it, every eternal truth supposes it, and there is no talking intelligibly, nor so much as thinking, without it.

But the quality of reasons is more considerable than their number. And here also the intelligible world has the advantage, because we have not only more but also *better* arguments to assure us of its existence than the natural world can pretend to. This I expect (if anything) will give a rude shock to the prejudice of vulgar minds, who have been accustomed to think nothing so sure and certain as a material world, and with whom sensible objects are the greatest if not the only realities, and who in comparison of this great certainty are apt to think all other things so uncertain that, for the sake of this short but sure present, they will hazard their immortal souls and that eternal heaven of glory and happiness for which they were designed and for which they even breath and live. But yet as great a paradox as this may seem, I shall hint at a few things the more particular consideration of which will sufficiently clear and evince the truth of it.

In the succeeding pages, here omitted, Norris gives several reasons for claiming that we can be more certain of the existence of the intelligible world than of that of the material world. The intelligible world's existence can be proved a priori, from a consideration of God's nature – for God must have the ideas of all possible things eternally present in his mind; but we have at best only the a posteriori evidence of the senses for the material world's existence. A priori proofs are better than a posteriori ones, so our evidence for the existence of the intelligible world is superior. Then, pursuing a line familiar from the Platonist tradition, Norris argues that the objects of the intelligible world are immutable universals, whereas those of the material world are mutable particulars, and that only what is immutable and universal can, in the strict sense, be known. Lastly, evidence for the existence of the intelligible world is drawn from reason, whereas our only evidence for the existence of the material world comes from the senses. Reason, rightly employed, produces conclusions that are certain, whereas the evidence of the senses is uncertain. We can conclude, therefore, that we have more and better grounds for believing in an intelligible world than in a material world. Norris continues:

But to bring this matter to a closer issue, let us consider what this evidence of sense is which we have for a natural world. I believe there is such a world upon the evidence of sense. So the language of the world expresses it, in which nothing is more common and familiar than to talk of the reports of sense, and the testimony of sense, and the information of sense, and our senses tell us this or that, etc. And I should hardly be intelligible should I, without preparing the way for it, deliver myself any otherwise. But am I truly intelligible *now*? Indeed we are so used to this way of speaking that everybody fancies that they understand me and I am ready to think that I understand myself. But let me think again. Does my sense in very deed inform me that there is a world? Yes, you'll say, most plainly. But hold, let me answer my question myself, and that by another: What? Does my sense then *judge*, does it affirm, deny, or infer, make propositions, or draw conclusions? But not to answer to I know not what, let me first consider what I mean by *sense*. Do I mean by it that perception, sentiment, or feeling which follows upon some corporeal motion or impression mediately or immediately made upon the brain? Or do I mean the faculty or power of having such a perception by such an impression? Or else do I mean a certain texture or configuration of some parts of my machine whereby I am disposed for such an impression, and by that to such a perception? One of these I must mean, if I mean anything distinct. But the last belongs wholly to the body, and therefore, to be sure, there can be no such thing as judging there. And though the other two do indeed appertain to the soul, yet the former of them implying only a modification of it (that which we more properly call *sensation* than sense), and the latter a capacity or potentiality of being so modified, it is plain that there is nothing of judgement included in these neither. For these are not intellectual operations but only different states or manners of the soul's being, such as pleasure or pain, etc. Sense then is so far from telling me that there is a world that in strictness it tells me nothing, it being most evident that there is nothing of judging, and so nothing of telling, informing, reporting, or testifying in all this.

But what then is this *sensible evidence* which we are said to have of a material world, or what do people mean when they say that their *senses* do report to them or inform them of such or such things? Why truly I believe most people, when they use this way of speaking, do not know what they do mean, though the familiarity of the phrase may impose so far upon them as to persuade them that they do. And truly it is not very easy to tell presently what they *should* mean. However thus much I think is clear: that the proper, obvious and literal meaning is not intelligible, it being most certain that that which cannot judge of the existence of bodies (as sense cannot, because there is no such thing as judgement belonging to it) cannot properly make any report or give in any evidence or information about them.

But though my sense does not in strictness *judge* of the existence of bodies, yet does it not *feel* it? That would be pleasant indeed. He must have a very metaphysical sense that shall feel *existence*, but not a very metaphysical understanding that shall think he does. For to feel that a thing exists is the same as to feel a proposition. Well but, however, I may feel *bodies*, though I cannot feel their *existence*, and may not this be the evidence that I have of them from my senses? And an excellent evidence, too, if it can be had. For there is nothing more clear than sensation, and what I *feel* I am as certain of as of what I *know*. No principle or conclusion in geometry is more unquestionably evident to me than pleasure or pain is when I feel it. But do I indeed thus feel bodies? What, as I feel pleasure or pain? No, that cannot possibly be, for bodies are without me, but that which I feel must be within me. And indeed, to speak with philosophic accuracy, how contrary soever to popular prejudice, as ordinary as it is to say we feel such or such bodies when we have any sensation through their occasion, it is not the *bodies* that we truly feel, but the *sensation*. As for instance when I drink wine, it is not the wine that I feel, but pleasure. And so when I touch a coal of fire, it is not the fire that I feel, but pain. For I feel only that which is within me, and whereof I am inwardly conscious to myself, viz. that different modification of its being which my soul then has. In a word, I do not feel anything that is out of my self, but I feel my very self otherwise modified and existing after another manner than I did before. So that here is no such thing as sensation of bodies, but only simple sensation.

My sense then neither *judges* of bodies, nor *feels* them. And how then can it give any evidence concerning them? It goes no farther than a sensation, and that sensation goes no farther than my soul. And what is either of these as such to the existence of bodies that are without me? But, however, upon such sensations I naturally judge that there are such bodies. That indeed I do, and now you have hit it. But then this amounts to a plain confession that what you call the evidence of sense is indeed not the evidence of *sense* but the evidence of *reason*. I feel a sensation, and thence find myself naturally carried to judge or conclude that there are bodies, but then it is not the sensation but my reasoning or judgement upon that sensation that tells me or reports to me that there are such beings. And though, to distinguish this from other ways of reasoning, we may if we please, in the language of the people, call it *sense*, yet if we will conform to the exactness of truth in thinking, as we do to custom in speaking, we must remember that it is not really sense but reasoning or making a judgement upon sense. So then that sensible evidence which is alleged for a natural world proves after all to be indeed a rational evidence (though of a particular kind) and such as upon no other consideration, and in no other respect, is to be called a sensible one than merely as it proceeds upon a *ground* of sense, because as I said before it is reasoning upon a sensation or, if you will, concluding something without from something felt within. . . .

The true state of the question then will be (after this most distinct evolution of [the] matter) not which gives the best and surest evidence, my sense or my reason, but precisely this: when it is that I reason best, that is, with most clearness, or with most certainty, when I reason upon a sensation, or when I reason upon an abstract and intellectual principle or truth.

But if the state of the question be reduced to this, methinks there should be no great question about it.

Norris next argues that, although we cannot doubt that we have sensations, as soon as we try to make inferences from them we are liable to go astray. Thus I cannot doubt that I am now having a sensation, but there is almost nothing I can infer with certainty from the mere fact that I have it. However, when we reason from "an abstract and intellectual principle," we will never, if we take care, go astray. He continues:

Not that the [intellectual] principle itself is then better (for as was before observed, and may not be amiss again to inculcate, nothing can well be more clear than sensation), but only we may reason better upon it, and that because there is a more close and evident connexion of the principle with the conclusion when we reason upon a pure intellectual principle than when we reason upon sensation, especially as to the existence of bodies. For in reasoning upon an intellectual principle, I find the conclusion often times so nearly and visibly connected with the principle that I can be as certain of the conclusion as I am of the principle itself. But now it is not so when I reason upon a sensation, unless in one instance, and that is when I conclude my own existence from it, and then, indeed, *I am in pain, therefore I am*, or *I am in pleasure, therefore I am*, is as good an argument as *I think, therefore I am*. But it is otherwise when from sensation I conclude the existence of things without me. There is no such immediate connexion then, nor can I with reason pretend to be as certain (however otherwise persuaded or assured I may be) of the existence of those bodies which I prove from sensation, as I am of the sensation itself. For, as I do not properly feel bodies, so neither are bodies (or at least it may justly be doubted whether they are or not) the causes of what I feel, as the best philosophers will now acknowledge.[5]

Besides, when I reason intellectually I have oftentimes that intuitive evidence which is the ground of demonstration, and which (as the author [Locke] of the *Essay of Human Understanding* well observes) is found in every step of that reasoning which produces knowledge. I say I have here an intuitive view of the premises upon which my conclusion depends, by which means I can demonstrate a multitude of propositions in the most perfect and scientific manner. But when I reason upon sensation, I find this intuitive evidence fails me, except only in the case of my own existence, which accordingly is the only thing I can strictly demonstrate in that way of reasoning. . . .

[A]s to the existence of bodies, though it be a thing of no reasonable doubt, nor to be seriously questioned by any sober understanding, yet if a strict and rigorous demonstration should be required of it, I must confess that I know not how to give it upon a principle of sensation. And I think it is very plain that it is not so demonstrable. . . .

But though sense does not properly *feel* bodies, yet can anything be more plain than that we *see* them? There is, I confess, this peculiar in vision that is not in our other senses: that it includes an outward objective perception, as well as an inward sentiment or sensation. That is, I mean (as clearly as I can express it in so short a compass of words) that in vision the soul is not only otherwise modified in itself and otherwise conscious to itself, but that there is something seen or perceived by it that is really distinct from itself. But what is that *something*? Not the very bodies that are without us, and that because they *are* without us and sometimes far distant from us. Besides that (M. Malebranche well remarks) if one did see them in themselves, one could never see them when they were not, which yet very often happens. And accordingly even the common philosophy finds it necessary to allow that we see not bodies immediately but mediately, that is, not the bodies themselves but only the representative species or ideas of them. But, however, those species which we see come from those bodies which we do not see. That indeed would be a material instance. But are you sure of that? The contrary perhaps is demonstrable, and that from this very consideration just now borrowed; but this belonging to the 2nd part of this theory, it will be sufficient to the present purpose to suppose it only doubtful (and so without doubt it is) whether the species that represent bodies to us come from the bodies or no.[6] And if they do not derive from them, they are as such no positive proof of them. So that even our vision itself, and that even the most clear and awakened (not to make any advantage of the illusions of dreams), has no immediate, much less absolute or necessary, connexion with the existence of bodies. It is true, indeed, [that] upon the appearances of bodies, and those regular and uniform sensations which accompany those appearances, I find myself naturally determined to think that they exist. But before I can rationally conclude that they do so, or by a reflex act of my mind approve of that natural judgement, some other considerations must intervene, since neither my sensation, nor my judgement upon that sensation, is of itself any direct argument for it. And therefore I cannot but think M. Descartes was much in the right (how paradoxical soever he may seem to some less capable or less considerate judges) when he suspended the certainty, at least of sensible things, upon the existence of God. For thither we must have recourse at last for all the certainty that is to be had in this matter. And indeed those considerations which are taken from the truth and goodness of the excellent and most perfect Author of our natures, who there is no reason to suspect would give us senses to abuse and deceive us in the due and natural use of them, are sufficient to satisfy all sober and reasonable understandings of the real existence of bodies. But yet I think that even these do not *demonstrate* it, and that after all the thing is not capable of a strict metaphysical evidence. . . .

In short, then, as my sense does not tell me there are bodies, so neither does my reasoning upon sense absolutely conclude them. There is evidence enough from sensation to exclude all *reasonable* but not all *possible* doubt concerning the existence of bodies. For I can doubt, if I please to use my liberty of suspense to the utmost, of anything that is not absolutely evident, so evident as invincibly to determine my assent. . . .

[A]ccordingly, I conclude, upon an equal balancing of the evidence on both sides, that the existence of the intelligible world (as much an utopia as it may be fancied by some) is more certain than that of the natural. And I believe I might defy any man to prove the reality of the latter as well as even I myself have done that of the former.

Notes

1. See below, pp. 164–65.
2. *Third Dialogue*, in *Works* II, p. 254.
3. Norris used "natural world", "sensible world", and "material world" as synonyms. Berkeley, for whom the "sensible world" is simply all that is immediately perceivable by sense, would have rejected this usage.
4. The following excerpts are from *An Essay towards the Theory of the Ideal or*

Intelligible World, Part I (London, 1701), chap. 4, pp. 188–91, 196–201, 203–208, 210, 213–14. A second volume appeared three years later.

5. Norris alludes here to the doctrine of Occasionalism.

6. In Part II of the work, Norris argued against the Scholastic doctrine that perception involves "representative species" that come to us from bodies, defending instead Malebranche's doctrine that "we see all things in God."

ELEVEN

Arthur Collier

In 1713, the year in which Berkeley's *Three Dialogues* appeared, Arthur Collier, a Wiltshire clergyman, published *Clavis Universalis: or, a New Inquiry after Truth. Being a Demonstration of the Non-Existence, or Impossibility, of an External World*. In it, Collier does not deny, as does Berkeley, that a "material" world exists. But this difference between the two thinkers is largely verbal. What Collier does claim is that "all matter, body, extension, &c. exists *in*, or in dependence on, mind, thought, or perception, and that it is not capable of an existence which is not thus dependent." His doctrine, therefore, if not his terminology, is strikingly close to Berkeley's.

This raises the question of what connection, if any, there was between the two thinkers. Clearly Berkeley, whose *Principles* appeared three years before Collier's *Clavis*, was not influenced by Collier. And Collier seems to have developed his views independently of Berkeley: at any rate, he claims in his Introduction to be publishing his views after "a ten years' pause and deliberation," and there is indeed evidence that by 1708 he had already drafted a work denying that the visible world is external. Nor would it be surprising if Collier's views were formed quite independently of Berkeley's, for Collier was deeply under the influence of Malebranche and John Norris (who was rector of Bemerton, the parish neighboring Langford Magna, where Collier was rector). We have seen that Malebranche held that neither sense nor reason can demonstrate that an external world exists, to which Norris added that even an appeal to Scriptural revelation fails. It is not hard to imagine that a thinker, deeply under their joint influence, might push on, even without knowing of Berkeley's views, to deny an external world.

A few passages in *Clavis*, however, are markedly reminiscent of

Berkeley's *Principles*. A noted Berkeley scholar, G. A. Johnston, therefore suggested that Collier may have come across the *Principles* before he was ready to publish his own views and that at a very few points (all but one in the Introduction to *Clavis*) Berkeley's influence may show through.[1] In fact, some of the pronouncements that Johnston refers to could have been made by someone who had read Malebranche and Norris, whether he had read Berkeley or not, but others (including one we will draw attention to later) do sound peculiarly Berkeleian; so Johnston's speculation that the published *Clavis* reveals *occasional* traces of Berkeley's influence may just possibly be correct. Nevertheless, it remains the case that for the most part the arguments of *Clavis Universalis* differ from those of the *Principles*, and that any influence Berkeley may have exerted would have come late, and well after Collier had reached his own position. It is interesting to note, too, that nowhere in his work does Collier mention Locke or show any familiarity with Locke's *Essay*. This lends support to what other chapters in the present volume may have suggested – that there was a route to a denial of an external world that did not pass through Locke.

Clavis is divided into two parts. In Part I, Collier does not question the supposition that there is an "external world", but undertakes to prove that the "visible world", or the world we perceive by our senses, is not external to the perceiver, and so cannot be identified with the external world. Then, in Part II, he tries to prove that no world exists other than the "visible world". There is also an Introduction, from which our first extract is taken.

The question I am concerned about is in general this, whether there be any such thing as an external world. And my title will suffice to inform my reader that the negative of this question is the point I am to demonstrate.

In order to which, let us first explain the terms. Accordingly, by *world* I mean whatsoever is usually understood by the terms *body*, *extension*, *space*, *matter*, *quantity*, &c., if there be any other word in our English tongue which is synonymous with all or any of these terms. And now nothing remains but the explication of the word *external*.

By this, in general, I understand the same as is usually understood by the words *absolute*, *self-existent*, *independent*, &c., and this is what I deny of all matter, body, extension, &c.

If this, you'll say, be *all* that I mean by the word *external*, I am like to meet with no adversary at all, for who has ever affirmed that matter is self-existent, absolute, or independent?

To this I answer: What others hold, or have held in times past, I shall not here inquire. On the contrary, I should be glad to find by the event that all mankind were agreed in that which I contend for as the truth, viz. that matter is not, cannot be, independent, absolute, or self-existent. In the meantime, whether they are so or no will be tried by this:

Secondly, and more particularly, that by *not independent, not absolutely existent, not external*, I mean and contend for nothing less than that all matter, body, extension, &c. exists *in*, or in dependence on, mind, thought, or perception, and that it is not capable of an existence which is not thus dependent.

This perhaps may awaken another to demand of me, how? To which I as readily answer: just how my reader pleases, provided it be *somehow*. As, for instance, we usually say an *accident* exists in, or in dependence on, its proper subject, and that its very essence, or reality of its existence, is so to exist. Will this pass for an explication of my assertion? If so, I am content to stand by it in this sense of the words. Again, we usually say (and fancy too we know what we mean in saying) that a body exists in, and also in dependence on, its proper *place*, so as to exist necessarily in some place or other. Will this description of dependence please my inquisitive reader? If so, I am content to join issue with him and contend that all matter exists *in*, or as much dependently *on*, mind, thought, or perception, to the full, as any body exists in place. Nay, I hold the description to be so just and apposite as if a man should say a thing is like itself. For I suppose I need not tell my reader that when I affirm that all matter exists in mind after the same manner as body exists in place, I mean the very same as if I had said that mind itself is the place of body, and *so* its place as that it is not capable of existing in any other place, or in place after any other manner. Again, lastly, it is a common saying that an object of perception exists in, or in dependence on, its respective faculty. And of these objects, there are many who will reckon with me light, sounds, colours, and even some material things, such as trees, houses, &c. which are seen, as we say, *in* a looking-glass, but which are, or ought to be, owned to have no existence but *in*, or respectively *on*, the minds or faculties of those who perceive them. But to please all parties at once, I affirm that I know of no manner in which an object of perception exists *in*, or *on*, its respective faculty which I will not admit in this place to be a just description of that manner of *in-existence* after which all matter that exists is affirmed by me to exist in mind. Nevertheless, were I to speak my mind freely, I should choose to compare it to the in-existence of some, rather than some other, objects of perception, particularly such as are objects of the sense of vision, and of these, those more especially which are allowed by others to exist wholly in the mind or visive faculty, such as objects seen in a looking-glass, by men distempered, light-headed, ecstatic, &c., where not only colours, but entire bodies, are perceived or seen. For these cases are exactly parallel with that existence which I affirm of all matter, body, or extension whatsoever.

Having endeavoured, in as distinct terms as I can, to give my reader notice of what I mean by the proposition I have undertaken the defence of, it will be requisite in the next place to declare, in as plain terms, what I do not mean by it.

Accordingly, I declare in the first place that in affirming that there is no external world, I make no doubt or question of the existence of bodies, or whether the bodies which are seen exist or not. It is with me a first principle that whatsoever is seen, is. To deny or doubt of this is errant scepticism, and at once unqualifies a man for any part or office of a disputant or philosopher; so that it will be remembered from this time that my enquiry is not concerning the *existence*, but altogether of the *extra-existence*, of certain things or objects. Or, in other words, what I affirm and contend for is not that bodies do not exist, or that *the* external world does not exist, but that such and such bodies, which are supposed to exist, do not exist externally; or, in universal terms, that there is no such thing as an *external* world.

Secondly, I profess and declare that, notwithstanding this my assertion, I am persuaded that I see all bodies just as other folks do; that is, the visible world is seen by me, or, which is the same, *seems* to me to be as much external or independent, as to its existence, on my mind, self, or visive faculty, as any visible object does, or can be pretended to do or be, to any other person. I have neither, as I know of, another nature, nor another knack of seeing objects, different from other persons', suitable to the hypothesis of their existence which I here contend for. So far from this, that I believe, and am very sure, that this *seeming* or (as I shall desire leave to call it) *quasi* externeity of visible objects, is not only the effect of the will of God (as it is his will that light and colours should *seem* to be without the soul, that heat should *seem* to be in the fire, pain in the hand, &c.), but also that it is a natural and necessary condition of their visibility. I would say that though God should be supposed to make a world, or any one visible object, which is *granted* to be not external, yet by the condition of its being seen it would and must be *quasi external* to the perceptive faculty, as much so to the full as is any material object usually seen in this visible world.

Moreover, thirdly, when I affirm that all matter exists dependently on mind, I am sure my reader will allow me to say I do not mean by this that matter or bodies exist in *bodies*. As for instance, when I affirm or say that the world which I see exists in my mind, I cannot be supposed to mean that one body exists in another, or that all the bodies which I see exist in that which common use has taught me to call *my body*. I must needs desire to have this remembered, because experience has taught me how apt persons are, or will be, to mistake me in this particular.

Fourthly, when I affirm that this or that visible object exists in, or dependently on, my mind, or perceptive faculty, I must desire to be understood to mean no more than I say by the words *mind* and *perceptive faculty*. In like manner I would be understood when I affirm in general that all matter or body exists in, or dependently on, mind. I say this to acquit myself from the imputation of holding that the mind *causes* its own ideas, or objects of perception, or lest anyone by a mistake should fancy that I affirm that matter depends for its existence on the *will* of man, or any creature whatsoever. But now, if any such mistake should arise in another's mind, he has wherewith to rectify it, in as much as I assure him that by *mind* I mean that part, or act, or faculty of the soul which is distinguished by the name *intellective*, or *perceptive*, as in exclusion of that other part which is distinguished by the term *will*.

Fifthly, when I affirm that all matter exists in mind, or that no matter is external, I do not mean that the world, or any visible object of it, which I (for instance) see, is dependent on the mind of any *other* person besides myself, or that the world, or matter, which any other person sees is dependent on mine or any other person's mind or faculty of perception. On the contrary, I contend as well as grant that the world which John sees is external to Peter, and the world which Peter sees is external to John. That is, I hold the thing to be the same in this as in any other case of sensation: for instance, that of sound. Here two or more persons who are present at a concert of music may indeed in some sense be said to hear the *same* notes or melody, but yet the truth is that the sound which one hears is not the very same with the sound which another hears, because the souls or persons are supposed to be different; and therefore, the sound which Peter hears is external to or independent on the soul of John, and that which John hears is external to the soul or person of Peter.

Lastly, when I affirm that no matter is altogether external, but necessarily exists in some mind or other, exemplified and distinguished by the proper names of *John*, *Peter*, &c., I have no design to affirm that every part or particle of matter which does or can exist must needs exist in some *created* mind or other. On the contrary, I believe that infinite worlds might exist, though not one single created (or rather merely created) mind were ever in being. And as in fact there are thousands and ten thousands, I believe, and even contend, that there is a universe or material world in being which is at least numerically different from every material world perceived by mere creatures. By this I mean the great *mundane idea* of created (or rather twice-created) matter, *by* which all things are produced, or rather (as my present subject leads me to speak) *by* which the great God gives sensations to all his thinking creatures, and by which things that are not are preserved and ordered in the same manner as if they were.

And now I presume, and hope, that my meaning is sufficiently understood when I affirm that all matter which exists, exists in, or dependently on, mind; or, that there is no such thing as an external world.[2]

Turning now to Part I of *Clavis*, we find Collier allowing, for the sake of argument, that there may *be* an external world, but insisting that the world we see is not external. In the extract that follows, he supports this claim with three arguments: that a visible object such as the moon has properties quite different from those we suppose the external object (the moon in the heavens) to have; that a visible object can vary radically in its appearance from one time to another; and that an object can be seen only if it is immediately present to the mind, which nothing external to the mind can be. Arguments similar to these had been used by Malebranche and Norris. The first three paragraphs, however, are likely to remind *us* of Berkeley's *New Theory of Vision*, where Berkeley does not explicitly deny the existence of an external (tangible) world, but holds that it should not be confused with the visible world, using (in §44) the example of the moon, just as Collier does. But we do not suggest that Collier was *following* Berkeley here. Malebranche had taken a similar line, illustrating it with the example of the moon, sun, and stars.[3]

First, then, I am content for a while to grant that there is an external world, and in this world an external moon in a place far distant from us, which we call the heavens. Still, the question returns whether the moon which I *see* be that external moon here supposed to be in the heavens. Well now, the moon which I see is a luminous or bright object. But is the moon supposed to be in the heavens a luminous thing or body? No, but a dark or opacous body, if there is any truth in the unanimous assent of all philosophers. Again, the moon which I see is a plain surface; but is the moon in the heavens a plain surface? No, all the world agree that the moon in the heavens is rotund or spherical. Again, the moon which I see is semicircular or cornuted; but is this the figure of the moon supposed to be in the heavens? No, we all affirm that the moon in the heavens is round or circular. Again, lastly, the moon which I see is a little figure of light, no bigger than a trencher, nay so little as to be entirely coverable by a shilling. But is this a just description of the moon supposed to be in the heavens? No, the moon in the heavens is by all allowed to be a body of a prodigious size, of some thousands of miles in its diameter. Well then, what follows from all this but that the moon in the heavens is not the moon which I see; or that the moon which I see is not in the heavens, or external to my perceptive or visive faculty?

Secondly, as we have seen that the moon which I see is not the same with any moon supposed to be in the heavens, and consequently that the moon which I see is not external, by a comparison of the visible or seen moon with that which is supposed to be external, so the same thing will appear by a comparison of visible things with visible, or of the same thing (as I must here speak, for want of more proper words) with itself. But to explain:

At this instant I see a little strip of light which common use has taught me to call *the moon*. Now again I see a larger, which is still called by the same name. At this instant I see a semicircle; a while after I see a circle of light; and both these are called the moon. Again, now I see a circle of light of such or such a magnitude; a while after I see a circle of light of a much greater magnitude; and both these, as before, I am taught to call *the* moon. But really and truly, instead of *one*, I see *many* moons, unless things different are the same. How then can I believe that the moons which I see are either *one* or *all* of them external? That they are *all* so cannot be pretended, for no one ever dreamt of more than one external moon; and I am as confident, on the other hand, that no one will pretend that either one of them is external, as in exclusion of the rest. I conclude then that they are all alike external, that is, that neither of them is so; and consequently (there being nothing in this but what is equally true of every other object of the visible world) that no visible object is, or can be, external.

But why such long fetches to prove a simple truth? It is no wonder that my reader (who perhaps has never thought of this subject before) should overlook the exact point of the question, when I myself can scarce keep it in view. I would beg leave therefore to remind myself and him that the question in hand does not any way proceed [upon], or so much as need the mention of, any bodies supposed to be external, and *unknown* to us; but the question is whether the extensions, figures, bodies (or whatever else you'll call them) which I see *quasi* without me be indeed without me or not.

But can the resolution of any case be more plain and simple than of this? For is there any other possible way of *seeing* a thing than by having such or such a thing *present* to our minds? And can an object be *present* to the mind, or visive faculty, which is affirmed to be *external* to it? Then may we think without thinking on any thing, or perceive without having any thing in our mind. If then the *presentialness* of the object be necessary to the act of vision, the object perceived cannot possibly be external to, at a distance from, or independent on, us. And consequently, the only sense in which an object can be said to exist without us is its being *not seen* or perceived. But the objects we speak of are supposed to be seen, and therefore are not external to us, which is the point to be demonstrated.

[To this I might add another, which (if possible) is a yet more simple manner of proceeding to the same conclusion. And it is this: The objects we speak about are supposed to be visible, and that they are visible or seen is supposed to be *all* that we know of them or their existence. If so, they exist as visible, or, in other words, their visibility is their existence. This therefore destroys all or any distinction between their *being*, and their being *seen*, by making them both the same thing, and this evidently at the same time destroys the externeity of them. But this argument has the misfortune of being too simple and evident for the generality of readers, who are apt to fancy that light itself is not seen but by the help of darkness; and so, without insisting any farther on this head, I proceed to some other points which may *seem* to be more intelligible.][4]

The final paragraph here bears a remarkable resemblance to Berkeley's *esse* is *percipi* principle – a principle that, for Berkeley, represented a decisive step beyond the sort of consideration suggested by the varying appearances of things; so it is worth noting that it is the only passage in *Clavis* that is in square brackets, perhaps suggesting an afterthought, and that it contains the one sentence outside the Introduction to *Clavis* cited by G. A. Johnston in arguing that, at a late stage, Collier may have read Berkeley. If so, Collier may not have seen the argument's full force. Berkeley uses it to oppose the notion of external existence as such, but in *Clavis* it appears in Part I where Collier is not denying that there is, or may be, an external world, but insisting merely that the "visible world" is not external to the mind.

So far, Collier has argued only that the visible world is not the external world, but in Part II he gives nine arguments to show that there is no external world. A number of these have their source in arguments of Malebranche and Norris, while two others rest on paradoxes about infinite divisibility and motion that bear some resemblance to arguments in Bayle's "Zeno of Elea" (Remark G) and may indicate that Collier knew that article. Collier's arguments are often weak and his style turgid, his writing lacking in either the rigor or the grace that marks Berkeley's. We give here part of his first argument as a sample. (Collier's claim here that neither reason nor sense can prove that an external world exists may recall Berkeley's argument in *Principles* §18, but it is almost certainly modeled on similar arguments in Malebranche and Norris.)

I affirm, in the first place, that (abstracting from any argument directly proving this point) we are bound *already* so far to conclude that there is no external world, as that it is against all the laws of fair reason and argument to suppose or make mention of any such world. For if a visible world, as such, is not external, an external world, as such, must be utterly invisible, and if invisible, unknowable, unless by revelation.

For, first, an external world (if there be any such thing) is, I suppose, allowed by all to be a *creature*; but the being of a creature is not to be proved by *reason*, for reason converses only in things necessary or eternal, whereas a creature, as such, is contingent and temporary; so that in vain shall we seek to reason to assure us of the existence of an external world.

Then, secondly, it is here supposed that we should seek to as little purpose to the testimony of *sense*, since an external world, as such, is here supposed to be absolutely invisible. Whether we have any notice from *revelation* of the being of any such world shall be considered in its proper place. In the meantime I here suppose also, thirdly, that we have no such notice, so that, as the case stands at present, an external world is a being utterly *unknown*.

But now I have always received it as a law that we ought never to reason but upon *known* ideas; and if this be just and reasonable, an external world, as being *unknown*, ought to have as little place in our reasonings as if we knew for certain that there was no such world. . . .

I pretend not this to be demonstration of the point simply, as if I should say that a thing being unknown were a direct argument of its not being at all; but yet this is something so near of kin to a demonstration, and so every way serving all the ends and purposes of a demonstration, that whoever has the advantage of it on his side has as little to fear from an adversary as he that can produce ten thousand demonstrations. For this is an evident principle or rule of reasoning, that a thing unknown ought never to be supposed, and therefore till it be supposed, it is the very same thing as to us as if there were no such thing at all.[5]

> After giving eight more arguments by which he demonstrates, to his own satisfaction at least, that there certainly *is* no external world, Collier replies to the reasons offered, by three thinkers he admired, for their belief in such a world: Descartes' argument from our natural inclination to believe in it; Malebranche's from the authority of Scripture; and Norris's claim that, although the existence of such a world cannot be proven, it would be "errant scepticism" to doubt it. Collier's replies to all three are of interest, but we give here only his response to "the late judicious Mr. Norris." This way of referring to Norris makes it clear that Collier either wrote or modified this section after Norris died in 1711, and hence after the *Principles* had appeared, so it is *possible* that Berkeley's influence shows through here in Collier's insistence that he does not deny "the *existence* of *bodies*." Collier says that he has "repeated the same thing some hundreds of times," but, although he had made the point in the Introduction, in a passage that G. A. Johnston thought might show Berkeley's influence, this theme has not been a recurring one in *Clavis*.
>
> The chapter in Norris that Collier here discusses is the one from which the extracts in our previous chapter were taken.

OBJECTION III

That the late judicious Mr. Norris, who (in his *Ideal World*, vol. I, chap. IV) purposely considered this question of an external world, was yet so far from concluding as I have here done, that he declares it to be no other than errant scepticism to make a serious doubt or question of its existence.

ANSWER

I have chosen to place this in the form of an objection, that I may seem rather to defend myself than voluntarily oppose this author, for whose writings and memory I have a great esteem. But what shall I say in this case? Must I give up all the arguments by which I have shown that there is no external world, in complaisance to this censure, because it is the great and excellent Mr. Norris's? But has he supported this saying by any arguments in favour of that which he calls it *scepticism* to doubt of? Has he proved an external world to be of the number of those evident truths which are of no reasonable doubt, nor to be seriously questioned by any sober understanding? Or so much as pretended to answer any argument alleged for its non-existence? No, not a word of this is to be found in the whole chapter, unless the argument from *inclination*, which is the subject of the former objection, will be here named against me. Well then, and must this too pass for an argument, notwithstanding that I have shown the weakness of it? And so, must all that I have hitherto contended for submit to the power of this great authority, on peril of my being thought a sceptic?

But is not this the way to be betrayed into the very dregs of scepticism, to make a doubt of one's own most evident perceptions for fear of this imputation? . . .

But to speak particularly to the author's censure, with which we are at present concerned:

Is it so much as true in *fact* that he has said any such thing as is affirmed in the objection? This perhaps even a sceptic will contend fairly with me, for facts are the things they are observed to be most fond of. Well, let this be tried (as it ought to be) by his own words.

There are two, and as I remember but two, passages in this chapter which speak at all to this purpose. One is page 188, the other 205. In the first of these I immediately find these words: "Much less would I be suspected of indulging a sceptical humour, under colour of philosophical doubting, to such an extravagance as to make any serious question of that general and collective object of sense, a natural world." The other is this: "But as to the existence of bodies, though it be a thing of no reasonable doubt, nor to be seriously questioned by any sober understanding," &c.

Here the thing that is not to be doubted of (at the hazard of the sobriety of our understanding, and upon peril of scepticism) is the *existence* of bodies, the *existence* of a natural world, which is supposed to be the object of *sense*. Well, and what is this to me? Have I been doubting of the *existence* of *bodies*? Or of the natural or *sensible* world? Let the meanest of my readers be my witness, that I have been so far from doubting of anything of this, that I have even contended on all occasions that nothing is or can be more evident than the *existence* of *bodies*, or of a *sensible* world. Have I repeated the same thing some hundreds of times, and yet still is there need to have it observed that an *external* world is the moot point between us? That not the *existence* but the *extra-existence* of the sensible world is the point I have been arguing against? And that not a natural, supposed to be a *sensible*, world, but an *external* world, *as such*, is impossible? But there is not a word of an *external* world in the two sentences before-mentioned, and therefore nothing in the least against the conclusion which I am concerned for.

True, you'll say, but this was only a mistake in the manner of expressing it, for the whole drift and argument of this chapter supposes the subject to be an external world. I answer:

Right, that is the thing I have been all this while expecting, viz. a little of his argument in the place of his authority; and you see this we must come to before there can be any decision.

But alas! To what purpose? For I find these words in the very title of his chapter, viz. "That the existence of the intelligible is more certain than that of the natural and sensible world." This destroys, and doubly destroys, all again. For, first, here he speaks not of [an] *external*, but *sensible*, world; and of this, not of its external existence, which is the point I have been arguing against, but simply of its existence, which is the point I have been arguing for. And yet:

Secondly, his end proposed is not to aggravate, but lessen, its certainty. And this is the drift and argument of the whole chapter, at least of about thirty pages of it, the rest being employed in a digression concerning the comparative certainty of faith and reason.

But is this the main design and purpose of this chapter, to *lessen* the evidence of an external world? To show (as he plainly does, and for which I refer my reader; to show, I say) that neither *reason*, nor *sense*, nor *revelation*, are sufficient to assure us of the existence of any such thing; nay, that the argument used by Descartes, before mentioned, in which he places his last resort, falls short, and is deficient, for which we have his own express words in the 208th page. And can that same author say, in the midst of all this, that the existence of an external world *is a thing of no reasonable doubt, nor to be seriously questioned by any sober understanding,* &c.? Surely it could be no mistake that he omitted the word *external*, unless he designed to question his own understanding, and formally pronounce himself a sceptic.

Well, you'll say, but it is a matter of fact that he has argued against *something*. I answer, he has so, for it is evident to demonstration that he has argued against himself; and not only so, but also as sceptically as is possible.

For after all nothing is more evident than that his censure and arguments proceed upon the very same subject, and that is, not the *external* existence, but the existence *simple*, of the natural world. This natural world is sometimes by him called *bodies*, sometimes the *visible* or *sensible* world. Being about to aggrandize the evidence, or objective certainty, as to us, of his intelligible or ideal world, he endeavours to show that it is much more certain to us than the existence of the natural, or *sensible*, world, and that because we have,

1. *more*,
2. *better reasons to assure us of its existence.*

These are his very words, as may be seen in the 188th page, even in that very page in which the censure is found on all those who so much as offer to question the existence of the natural world. But now the fact is that he does question its existence, both here and throughout the whole course of this chapter. What can be more evidently inconsistent, more evidently sceptical, than this manner of proceeding? What! Doubt of the existence of bodies, *sensible* bodies? Well may this be called *indulging a sceptical humour under the colour of philosophical doubting.* And is this so called too by the very person who does it? This is not only to be guilty of scepticism himself, but also to be self-condemned.

The sum of the whole matter is this: If by the existence of the sensible world Mr. Norris in this censure is said to mean not the existence simple, but the extra-existence of it, his arguments directly contradict his censure, which is a full answer to his authority in this matter. If on the other hand he be said to mean as he himself speaks, this is, first of all, nothing at all to me, who doubt not of the *existence*, but only of the *extra-existence*, of the *sensible* world. Then, secondly, he is in this as much contrary to himself as on the other supposition, in that he formally doubts of, and even argues against, that which he calls it scepticism to doubt of. And, thirdly, which is as bad as any of the rest, he doubts formally of a point which is not capable of being doubted of, viz. *the simple existence of the visible world.* To all which, lastly, I may and also must add this, that this second supposition is something more than an *if*, it being evidently the case in fact that his whole discourse in this place is only of the existence simple of the sensible or visible world, and not a word of its extra-existence, on the concession of its existence simple, is so much as mentioned or implied.[6]

Collier argues effectively here against Norris, whose desire to establish the certain existence of the "intelligible" world had led him to stress how inconclusive by comparison the case for the "sensible" or "natural" world was, and who in fact held that we do not *see* "bodies" at all. For the most part, however, the quality of Collier's arguments in *Clavis* is much inferior to Berkeley's, which again suggests that *Clavis* was largely written prior to any influence the *Principles* may have had on Collier. What is of primary interest, therefore, is the evidence the work provides that by the early eighteenth century the time was ripe for *someone* to develop a thesis denying a world external to the mind. Apparently Berkeley and Collier did so at virtually the same moment, and at least largely independently. Later, in 1730, Collier published a second work, *A Specimen of True Philosophy*, in which he developed his views further, arguing that the visible world is in the mind, the mind in the Logos, and the Logos in God. If Collier did read the *Principles*, he sought to hide the fact, for, referring to what he had argued in *Clavis*, he declared that "except [for] a single passage or two in Dr. Berkeley's three dialogues, printed in the same year," *Clavis* was "the only book on that subject, which I ever heard of in the world."[7]

Notes

1. Johnston considers the relationship between Berkeley and Collier in *The Development of Berkeley's Philosophy* (London: Macmillan, 1923), Appendix I.
2. *Clavis Universalis* (London, 1713), pp. 2–10.

3. Malebranche, *Search*, Book 1, esp. Chapters 7 and 14.
4. *Clavis*, pp. 33–37.
5. *Clavis*, pp. 59–63.
6. *Clavis*, pp. 123–130.
7. *A Specimen of True Philosophy*, reprinted in *Metaphysical Tracts by English Philosophers of the Eighteenth Century*, ed. S. Parr (London, 1837), p. 114. (*Clavis* seems to have been published shortly before the *Three Dialogues*, so can hardly have been influenced by the latter work.) There is some evidence, based on an earlier letter, that Collier's claim here may have been disingenuous (see Johnston, p. 366n), but we leave that question open.

PART TWO

Reactions to Berkeley's Philosophy

TWELVE

First Reactions

David Hume was to complain that his *Treatise of Human Nature* fell "dead-born from the press." In the months following the publication of the *Principles* (in 1710) Berkeley, too, must have felt that his book had been dead-born. He knew that the position he took in it ran counter to entrenched views, but he believed that his arguments were powerful and would convince attentive readers. He can only have been distressed, therefore, when, in August 1710, Sir John Percival[1] reported from London that people were refusing to read the book when they heard from Percival – who had not yet read it himself – what its thesis was. Percival also reported a theological objection – one Berkeley was to take very seriously – that had been raised by Lady Percival (although she had not read the book either). By October, Percival could inform Berkeley that two noted figures of the day, Samuel Clarke and William Whiston, *had* read his book but pronounced its first principles false. When no review had appeared by early in 1711, Berkeley, growing desperate for some public recognition of the work, wrote to Jean Le Clerc, asking him to review it in his *Bibliothèque Choisie*. Berkeley told Le Clerc that the *Principles* "until now, like the *Essay of Vision* that I published in 1709, so far as I can judge, has scarcely attracted the attention of anyone outside this island, although many copies were delivered to Master Churchill, Bookseller in London."[2] Le Clerc did not reply, but Berkeley soon saw a review that Le Clerc had written of the *New Theory of Vision*, in the course of which he took issue with Berkeley's critique of abstract ideas. Berkeley now wrote a second letter to Le Clerc, responding to the review. Le Clerc did not answer the letter, nor did he review Berkeley's new book.

The first reactions to the *Principles*, in short, were inauspicious.

This clearly influenced Berkeley's decision not to press ahead immediately with finishing Part II of the *Principles*, but instead to present his views in a different form in the *Three Dialogues*. There he sought to take account of the objections that his views had thus far met. In this chapter we give extracts from the correspondence between Percival and Berkeley, from Le Clerc's review of the *New Theory of Vision*, and from Berkeley's second letter to Le Clerc, to illustrate early reactions to Berkeley and Berkeley's response to them.

1. Letter from Percival of 26th August 1710 and Berkeley's Reply

In July 1710, Berkeley wrote to Percival (to whom he had sent a copy of the *Principles*, although it had not yet arrived) asking him to "procure me the opinion of some of your ingenious acquaintances who are thinking men and addicted to the study of rational philosophy and mathematics." On the 26th of August, Percival, who had by now received the book, replied:

'Tis incredible what prejudices can work on the best geniuses, nay and even on the lovers of novelty, for I did but name the subject matter of your book to some ingenious friends of mine and they immediately treated it with ridicule, at the same time refusing to read it, which I have not yet got one to do, and indeed I have not yet been able to discourse myself on it because I had it so lately, neither when I set about it may I be able to understand it thoroughly for want of having studied philosophy more. A physician of my acquaintance undertook to describe your person, and argued you must needs be mad, and that you ought to take remedies. A Bishop pitied you that a desire and vanity of starting something new should put you on such an undertaking, and when I justified you in that part of your character, and added the other deserving qualities you have, he said he could not tell what to think of you. Another told me an ingenious man ought not to be discouraged from exercising his wit, and said Erasmus was not the worse thought of for writing in praise of folly, but that you are not gone so far as a gentleman in town who asserts not only that there is no such thing as matter but that we have no being at all. My wife, who has all the good esteem and opinion of you that is possible from your just notions of marriage-happiness, desires to know if there be nothing but spirit and ideas, what you make of that part of the six days' creation which preceded man.[3]

> Berkeley's reply is notable for several things: its implied recognition that his view does contradict "vulgar and settled opinion"; his plea that Percival should not inform potential readers that the *Principles* denies the existence of matter (even though Berkeley remains "entirely persuaded" of that thesis); and his response to Lady Percival's query about the creation.

I am extremely obliged to you for the favourable representation you made of me and my opinions to your friends and the account you have given me of their judgments thereupon; and am not at all surprised to find that the name of my book should be entertained with ridicule and contempt by those who never examined what was in it, and want that common justice of trying before they condemn. But my comfort is that they who have entered deepest into the merits of the cause, and employed most time and exactness in reading what I have written, speak more advantageously of it. If the raillery and scorn of those that critique what they will not be at the pains to understand had been sufficient to deter men from making any attempts towards curing the ignorance and errors of mankind, we should have been troubled with very few improvements in knowledge. The common crys being against any opinion seems to me so far from proving it false that it may with as good reason pass for an agreement of its truth. However I imagine whatever doctrine contradicts vulgar and settled opinion had need been introduced with great caution into the world. For this reason it was I omitted all mention of the non-existence of matter in the title-page, dedication, preface, and introduction, that so the notion might steal unawares on the reader, who possibly would never have meddled with a book that he had known contained such paradoxes. If, therefore, it shall at any time lie in your way to discourse with your friends on the subject of my book, I entreat you not to take notice to them I deny the being of matter in it, but only that it is a treatise of the *Principles of Human Knowledge* designed to promote true knowledge and religion, particularly in opposition to those philosophers who vent dangerous notions with regard to the existence of God and the natural immortality of the soul, both which I have endeavoured to demonstrate in a way not hitherto made use of.

Two imputations there are which (how unjust soever) I apprehended would be charged on me by censorious men, and I find it has happened accordingly. The first, that I was not myself convinced of the truth of what I writ, but from a vain affectation of novelty designed imposing on the world: – whereas there is nothing I esteem more mean and miserable, I may add more wicked, than an intention to cheat men into a belief of lies and sophisms merely for the sake of a little reputation with fools. God is my witness that I was, and do still remain, entirely persuaded of the non-existence of matter, and the other tenets published along with it. How desirous soever I may be to be thought well of, yet I hardly think that anyone in his wits can be touched with a vanity to distinguish himself among wise men for a mad man. This methinks should satisfy others of my sincerity at least, and that nothing less than a full conviction not only of the truth of my notions but also of their usefulness in the most important points, could have engaged me to make them public. I may add that the opinion of matter I have entertained some years; if therefore a motive of vanity could have induced me to obtrude falsehoods on the world, I had long since done it when the conceit was warm in my imagination, and not have staid to examine and revise it both with my own judgment and that of my ingenious friends. The second imputation I was afraid of is, that men rash in their censures, and that never considered my book would be apt to confound me with the sceptics, who doubt of the existence of sensible things and are not positive as to any one truth, no not so much as their own being (which I find by your letter is the case of some wild visionists now in London), but whoever reads my book with due attention will plainly see that there is a direct opposition betwixt the principles contained in it and those of the sceptics, and that I question not the existence of anything that we perceive by our senses.

As to your Lady's objection, I am extremely honoured by it, and as I shall reckon it a great misfortune, in case any prejudice against my notions should lessen the good thoughts, you say, she is pleased to entertain of me, so I am not a little careful to satisfy her in point of the creation's consistency with the doctrine in my book. In order to which I must beg you will inform her Ladyship that I do not deny the existence of any of those sensible things which Moses says were created by God. They existed from all eternity in the Divine intellect, and then became perceptible (*i.e.* were created) in the same manner and order as is described in Genesis. For I take creation to belong to things only as they respect finite spirits, there being nothing new to God. Hence it follows that the act of creation consists in God's willing that those things should be perceptible to other spirits, which before were known only to Himself. Now both reason and scripture assure us there are other spirits (as angels of different orders, &c.) besides man, who, 'tis possible might have perceived this visible world according as it was successively exhibited to their view before man's creation. Besides, for to agree with the Mosaic account of the creation it is sufficient if we suppose that a man, in case he was then created and existing at the time of the chaos, might have perceived all things formed out of it in the very order set down in Scripture, which is no ways repugnant to our principles. I know not whether I express myself so clearly as to be understood by a lady that has not read my book. Much more I might say to her objection, if I had the opportunity of discoursing with her, which I am sorry to hear we may not expect before next summer. I have a strong presumption that I either should make a proselyte of her Ladyship, or she convince me that I am in error. My reason is, because she is the only person of those you mentioned my book to, who opposed it with reason and argument.

As for the physician I assure him there are (besides several others) two ingenious men in his own profession in this town, who are not ashamed to own themselves every whit as mad as myself, if their subscribing to the notions contained in my book can make them so. I may add that the greatest Tory and greatest Whig of my acquaintance agree in an entire assent to them, though at this time our party men seem more enflamed and stand at a wider distance than ever.[4]

2. Letter from Percival of 30th October 1710 and Berkeley's Reply

When Percival wrote in October, he still had not read the *Principles*, but he could, at any rate, report that it had been "perused" by two well-known figures, William Whiston, Newton's successor at Cambridge, and Samuel Clarke, a philosopher famous in his day, although now remembered chiefly for his correspondence with Leibniz. Both seem to have been sent copies of the *Principles* by Berkeley himself, for later, in his *Memoirs of Dr. Clarke*, Whiston recorded that he and Clarke had each received "a book" – presumably the *Principles* – from Berkeley. Whiston there adds, "I, being not a metaphysician, was not able to answer Mr. Berkeley's subtile *premises*, though I did not at all believe his absurd *conclusion*." He had therefore asked Clarke to answer Berkeley's arguments, "which task he declined."[5] The reaction of Clarke and Whiston, as reported by Percival, is the first we have from any reader of the *Principles*, and here for the first – but by no means the last – time we find Berkeley's views associated with Malebranche's.

> There are here two clergymen who have perused your last book, Dr Clarke, and Mr Whiston, both deservedly esteemed men of excellent learning, though the last is a little different from the orthodox in some points, inclining as 'tis said to Arianism. Not having any acquaintance with these gentlemen I can only report to you by second hand that they think you a fair arguer, and a clear writer, but they say your first principles you lay down are false. They look on you as an extraordinary genius, and profess a value for you, but say they wished you had employed your thoughts less on metaphysics, ranking you with Father Malebranche, Norris and another whose name I have forgot,[6] all whom they think extraordinary men, but of a particular turn, and their labours of little use to mankind for their abstruseness.
>
> This is what I believe you are armed against as foreseeing the objection which possibly may proceed merely from a largeness of disposition, not caring to think after a new manner which would oblige them to begin their studies anew, or else it may be the strength of prejudice. For my part I don't design their opinion shall prevent my reading this book. . . . [7]

Berkeley was understandably distressed by the view that Clarke and Whiston took of his work, for both men were eminent and Clarke in particular was, in T. E. Jessop's words, "London's arbiter of philosophical soundness."[8] On the 27th of November, Berkeley replied to Percival.

> Your last . . . obliged me with the account that my 'Treatise of the Principles,' &c., had been perused by Dr. Clarke and Mr. Whiston. As truth is my aim, there is nothing I more desire than being helped forward in the search of it, by the concurring studies of thoughtful and impartial men: on both which accounts no less than for their uncommon learning and penetration those gentlemen are very deservedly much esteemed. This makes me very solicitous to know particularly what fault they find in the principles I proceed upon; which at this time cannot but be of great advantage to me [in] that it will either convince me of an error, and so prevent my wasting any more time and pains that way, or else it will prove no small confirmation of the truth of my opinions, in case nothing solid can be objected to them by those great men. This

makes me trouble you with the two enclosed letters to be sealed and sent by you to those gentleman respectively, if you shall think it convenient, or if not I must entreat you to get your friend to obtain from them the particulars which they object, and that you will transmit them to me; which will in truth be a deed of charity, much greater than that of guiding a mistaken traveller into the right way, and I think either good office may be with like reason claimed by one man from another.

As to what is said of ranking me with Father Malebranche and Mr. Norris, whose writings are thought too fine spun to be of any great use to mankind, I have this to answer: that I think the notions I embrace are not in the least coincident with, or agreeing with, theirs, but indeed plainly inconsistent with them in the main points, insomuch that I know few writers whom I take myself at bottom to differ more from than them. Fine spun metaphysics are what I on all occasions declare against, and if anyone shall shew me anything of that sort in my 'Treatise' I will willingly correct it.

I am sorry that I am not yet favoured with your own free thoughts on this subject. Would you but think away a few leisure hours in the morning on it, I dare say no one would understand it better. And, whether I am mistaken or no, I doubt not but your own thoughts will sufficiently recompence your labour.[9]

Berkeley was to be disappointed in his attempt to elicit Whiston's and Clarke's objections to his views. Percival did see to it that the letters Berkeley had entrusted to him were delivered, by two intermediaries, but by the end of December Percival was able to report that Clarke did not wish to respond, "because he was afraid it might draw him into a dispute upon a matter which was already clear to him." There the matter ended. Percival did not know Clarke himself and the intermediary, who did, "declined further speaking to Dr Clarke, who he said was a modest man, and uninclined to shock any men whose opinion in things of this nature differed from his own."[10] Berkeley found Clarke's conduct "unaccountable", and still hoped for some response,[11] but neither Clarke nor Whiston replied.

3. Le Clerc's Review of the *New Theory of Vision* and Berkeley's Reply

In March 1711, Berkeley wrote to Jean Le Clerc, urging him to publish a review of the *Principles* in his *Bibliothèque Choisie*. Le Clerc was an indefatigable scholar who for four decades kept readers informed, by his reviews and digests of new works, of the latest developments in the "republic of letters". He was a much read and respected reviewer, and Berkeley would have known that a review by him would bring his book to the attention of a very wide audience. Lack of critical comment on his work, Berkeley told Le Clerc, is "a great hindrance to my studies inasmuch as I should like to subject the first part of my treatise on its own to the examination of the learned, so that either I can gird myself to its conclusions and put together the second part, being confirmed in that line of argument by their approval, or else correct whatever errors they might have discovered before I proceed, or lastly, being warned that my ideas derive from false principles, so that I can withdraw from them, and not waste any more effort working them out." If Le Clerc were unable to publish a review of the *Principles*, Berkeley asked that he "communicate to me, at least by private letter, the errors that you might have found in it."[12] Berkeley got no reply to this letter, but he soon saw Le Clerc's review of the *New Theory of Vision* (the first review of that work to appear). Although much of the review was simply a summary of the book, Le Clerc objected to Berkeley's attack on abstract ideas (an attack limited in the *New Theory of Vision* to denying that we can form an abstract idea of extension). Berkeley now wrote a second letter, replying to Le Clerc's comments on his position on abstract ideas, a position that also played, of course, an important role in the *Principles*. We give next two passages from Le Clerc's review. The first focuses on what Berkeley says in *New Theory of Vision* §§122–25; the second concentrates on the closing sections in that work.

[Mr. Berkeley next] considers the abstract idea that we form of extension in general – an idea stripped of any sort of quality, as we are now considering nothing but extension. He maintains that this is an altogether incomprehensible thing, and that one can form no idea of a line, for example, or of a surface, that is without color, and is neither long nor short, rough nor smooth, square nor round, etc.

It seems to me, however, that such an idea can be formed, and length, for example, can be conceived without width or depth or any other quality whatsoever. It seems to me that I have a very clear idea of length, and similarly of width and depth considered in general, whether separately or together. But here we must be careful to distinguish *the pure intellect* from *the imagination*. We cannot imagine anything that is not clothed in some sensible qualities; but by pure intellection we can form abstract ideas whereby we consider just one thing, as when we think of a point or the beginning of a line, and of the figure described by a point in motion – the figure we call a *line* – without determining in any way its length or attributing to it any other quality. I grant that our habit of joining imagination to intellection, and even of confusing them with each other, can make for difficulties here. But Mr. *Berkeley*, who is used to thinking deeply, will be able to distinguish them if he makes an effort to.

He next undertakes to show that the abstract idea of extension is not the object of geometry, but rather that the figures used in geometry are its objects; and that the abstract idea of a triangle described by Mr. *Locke* is an altogether incomprehensible thing. We cannot, indeed, imagine a triangle without representing to ourselves a particular triangle. But it seems to me that we can think in general of a figure, bounded by three straight lines that form three angles at their intersection, without thinking, in any way, of the size of these angles or of the length of the lines. . . .

He ends his work with some reflections on the object of geometry, which he maintains is not visible extension [but tangible extension], for men measure a tangible extension by another tangible extension. He holds that visible figures serve the same purpose in geometry as the words that are used in it do – and who would take words to be the object of that science? Visible figures serve only to represent to the mind the tangible figures they are connected with, though they differ from words in this: words are subject to change and are not the same everywhere, whereas figures are the same in all times and places. A [visible] square, for example, represents the same tangible figure in America as it does in Europe. This voice of nature is not liable to misinterpretation as are the languages invented by men, and it is this that accounts in part for the clarity and evidence of geometry.

The author next shows that if there were spirits that possessed sight but not touch, they would not be able to learn geometry. Mr. *Berkeley* concludes from all this that neither abstract extension nor visible extension is the object of geometry. As far as visible extension is concerned, geometers would have no problem in agreeing with him, for we don't see points, lines, or surfaces, as these are described by geometers. But the points, lines, and surfaces considered in geometry are not tangible things either. Geometers hold that the figures seen on paper are only aids in focusing the mind, enabling it to find in itself those truths that cannot be represented exactly to sight. For example, one conceives that the center of a circle is a point that has no parts, and to which an infinity of lines can be drawn from the circumference. This can never be shown to the eyes, since there is no [visible] point that has not got some size; but the mind nonetheless conceives it by pure intellection. I grant that the imagination often helps intellection, but it very often hinders it, too.

Our author ends by saying that because the object of geometry has not been well understood, we are often, in mathematics, engaged in difficult labors that are of little use. He even believes that he has found something that seems to him true, though far removed from the usual roads of geometry. He does not know whether it would be well received, were he to publish it in an age when so many discoveries have been made by means of this science, because a great part of those discoveries might perhaps lose their reputation and people no longer apply themselves to the subject with the same ardor they now do, if what he believes to be the case should really prove to be so.[13]

It is no small thing, in effect, to risk the ire of the mathematicians, but one must put what one takes to be the truth above any other consideration. It is not the author alone who is unconvinced that everything in nature happens in the mathematical way it is nowadays imagined it does. Perhaps in bodies themselves there is some principle that we have no idea of and that is the cause of their chief effects. One would gladly see what the author has found that is contrary to the usual opinions of the mathematicians.[14]

In his second letter to Le Clerc, dated 14th July 1711, Berkeley replied to these criticisms.

As for your remarks concerning the abstract ideas of extension and figure, I consider that I must answer the following.

First, to what you say on page 81, *viz.* that I could form that sort of idea by means of the Pure Intellect, if only I carefully distinguished this faculty from the Imagination, I reply that I cannot in any way form an abstract idea of the triangle or of any other figure whatsoever. And I cannot understand in what manner I could achieve this by distinguishing (as Metaphysicians commonly do) the Intellect from the Imagination, which is something that I have often attempted to achieve but to no avail, employing to that end the power and capacity of all my mind, whatever this may be or by whatever name one calls it.

Second, even if one admitted this distinction, it seems that the pure intellect has to do only with spiritual things, which are known through a meditation within the soul itself, and does not, by any means, pertain to ideas arising from sensation, for example Extension. I regard it as most certain that I cannot conceive any thing or any sensible quality – and therefore Extension – otherwise than as a representation of a sensible thing. Nor can I, by any power of the mind, separate the ideas from these sensible things and display them to the soul as things distinct from them. And it is plainly impossible and repugnant to reason that they enter the senses as distinct and separate from each other.

Third, it must also be remarked that it is one thing to think of one quality only, another to form its idea in the soul to the exclusion of any other thing or quality. I can, for example, while inquiring into the nature and the laws of motion, turn and direct the attention of my soul principally or exclusively towards motion itself, but I cannot form an idea of it without, at the same time, apprehending in my mind a thing which is moving.

Furthermore, my arguments set forth in the Introduction, in section 126 etc, of my book *The Principles of Human Knowledge* make it superfluous to discuss this topic any further.

As for the rest, with respect to what you say on page 86 concerning the Object of Geometry, it must be noted that the word *tangible* admits of a double sense. In the strict sense, it designates only what can be stroked and touched by the hands. In a wider sense, it embraces not only things that can be perceived by touch in one way or another, but also ideas fashioned by the mind on the basis of things perceived by touch. So, when I assert that "the Object of Geometry is tangible Extension," this must be understood in the latter sense. Assuredly, figure, angle, line, point, (all objects) which Geometers contemplate in their mind, although they themselves are not objects of sensory perception, are nevertheless referred to touch, to which, in some way, they owe their origin, when by an operation of the mind they are formed on the pattern of Ideas that were originally imprinted by means of that sense.[15]

Pierre Bellemare has noted that the *New Theory of Vision* would not have led Le Clerc to expect anything so radical from Berkeley's next book as a denial of matter, and has suggested that, upon reading the *Principles*, Le Clerc may, like Clarke and Whiston, have linked Berkeley with Malebranche and Norris – thinkers to whom Le Clerc was very hostile. If so, this may have influenced his decision not to review it.[16]

* * *

Clearly, there was much to disappoint Berkeley in the reception his new book was getting. It was not, he thought (rightly it seems), being much read outside Ireland, perhaps owing in part to poor service from his London bookseller.[17] His own defender, Percival, appears still to have read no further than the Introduction by the beginning of December 1710. The Earl of Pembroke, to whom Berkeley had dedicated the *Principles*, was reported by Percival to have said that Berkeley was "an ingenious man [who] ought to be encouraged," but, also, that "he could not be convinced of the non-existence of matter."[18] If we add Percival's earlier discouraging reports on the book's reception in London, and Le Clerc's failure to respond to Berkeley's request that he review it, it is hardly surprising that Berkeley decided not to proceed at once with completing Part II of the *Principles*, but, instead, to present his case in a new guise.[19]

The result was the *Three Dialogues between Hylas and Philonous*. Here, Berkeley not only reformulated the arguments of the *Principles*, he also put into the mouth of Hylas the very few critical points that had already been put to him, and had Philonous answer them. Thus Hylas, like Lady Percival, objects that immaterialism seems to be inconsistent with the Biblical account of the creation of the world before there were human perceivers, and Philonous's reply corresponds to that which Berkeley gave to Lady Percival.[20] Also, Hylas asks Philonous whether his doctrine is not "very like a notion entertained by some eminent moderns, of *seeing all things in God*?" – an allusion to the doctrine of Malebranche and Norris, two thinkers with whom Clarke and Whiston had associated Berkeley – and Philonous takes pains to distance his view from theirs. Berkeley expands on this reply in the third edition, concluding that "upon the whole there are no principles more fundamentally opposite" than Malebranche's and his own.[21] Le Clerc's objection, too, finds its way into Hylas's mouth. "But what say you," Hylas asks, "to *pure intellect*? May not abstracted ideas be framed by that faculty?" Philonous replies, as Berkeley had replied to Le Clerc, that whatever "pure intellect" is, its concern is with such "spiritual objects, as *virtue, reason, God*, or the like," not with extension, and he invites Hylas to try to "frame the idea of any figure, abstracted from all particularities of size, or even from other sensible qualities."[22]

More speculatively perhaps, it may be that Berkeley's statement in the Preface to the *Dialogues* that the book represents an attempt to "treat more clearly and fully of certain principles laid down in the First [Part of the *Principles*], and to place them in a new light" was prompted by the charge of Clarke and Whiston that the "first principles you lay down are false." And Percival's report on the first reactions of his friends in London may have influenced how Berkeley introduces his topic in the *Dialogues*, with Hylas telling Philonous, "You were represented in last night's conversation, as one who maintained the most extravagant opinion that ever entered into the mind of man, to wit, that there is no such thing as *material substance* in the world." But be that as it may, it is clear that in the months following the publication of the *Principles*, Berkeley was gaining a reputation as one who, while an ingenious fellow, was essentially a purveyor of paradoxes. In 1711 the first review of the *Principles* appeared, but it too did not show the kind of understanding that Berkeley had hoped for.

Notes

1. Percival, later first Earl of Egmont, met Berkeley in Dublin in 1708, and it was to Percival that Berkeley dedicated the *New Theory of Vision*. An account of their long friendship and correspondence is given in Benjamin Rand, *Berkeley and Percival* (Cambridge: Cambridge University Press, 1914), hereafter cited as "Rand".
2. Pierre Bellemare and David Raynor, "Berkeley's Letters to Le Clerc (1711)," *Hermathena*, no. 146 (1989), p. 9.
3. Rand, pp. 80–81.
4. *Works* VIII, pp. 36–38.
5. Quoted, from Whiston's *Memoirs of Dr. Clarke* (1730), in Joseph Stock's *An Account of the Life of George Berkeley* (London, 1776), pp. 52–53.
6. A reasonable guess is that this third man was Leibniz. The spotlight is about to turn on Berkeley when, in his *Memoirs of Dr. Clarke*, Whiston complains of "the pernicious consequence [that] metaphysical subtilties have sometimes had, even against common sense and common experience," but Whiston also instances Leibniz's doctrine of pre-established harmony and Locke's "dispute with Limborch about human Liberty" (ibid., p. 52).
7. Rand, pp. 87–88.
8. *Works* II, p. 4.
9. *Works* VIII, pp. 40–41.
10. Rand, pp. 92–93.
11. *Works* VIII, pp. 43–44.

12. Bellemare and Raynor (see note 2), p. 9.
13. Le Clerc is here paraphrasing the rather opaque sentence with which Berkeley concluded the first edition of *A New Theory of Vision*. Berkeley omitted it from the revised 1732 edition.
14. *La Bibliothèque choisie* (Amsterdam), vol. 22, 1st part (1711), pp. 80–82, 85–88.
15. Bellemare and Raynor, pp. 12–13. When Luce included the two letters to Le Clerc in *Works* VIII, he was uncertain whether Berkeley had actually sent them, for he had seen only the draft versions of them in the British Library. The original letters, however, are among Le Clerc's papers in the library of the University of Amsterdam, and are published by Bellemare and Raynor together with an English translation (the letters are in Latin) and two useful commentaries, one historical (by Bellemare), one philosophical (by Raynor).
16. Bellemare and Raynor, pp. 17–18. Le Clerc had announced, in *La Bibliothèque choisie*, vol. 23, 1st part (1711), pp. 235–36, that a review of the *Principles* would appear in the next issue, but he postponed and then dropped the project.
17. *Works* VIII, p. 42.
18. Rand, p. 92.
19. The second part of the *Principles* was never completed. Berkeley lost the unfinished manuscript of it while in Italy, and never rewrote it.
20. *Works* II, pp. 250–56. Although Berkeley had not discussed this issue in the *Principles*, it is clear from *PC* entries (e.g., 60, 436, 723) that he had already thought about it.
21. *Works* II, pp. 213–14. There is a much more muted reference to Malebranche's doctrine in *PHK* §148.
22. *Works* II, pp. 193–94. "Pure intellect" is not mentioned in the *New Theory of Vision* or the *Principles*, but Berkeley had mentioned it twice in *PC*, first denying that it could deal with lines and triangles (*PC* 531), then dismissing it altogether: "Pure Intellect I understand not" (*PC* 810).

THIRTEEN

Early Reviews

In the summer of 1711, the *Journal des Sçavans* reviewed the *Principles*, thereby fulfilling Berkeley's hope that an important journal would take note of it. Four more reviews of the *Principles* or the *Three Dialogues* would appear during the next two years. In this chapter, we give all save one of these early reviews, the two longer ones here translated for the first time.[1]

1. *Journal des Sçavans* (September 1711)

The *Journal des Sçavans* was one of the best-known learned journals of the time and – after Percival's reports on the reactions to the *Principles* in London – we may suppose that Berkeley was gratified that the review neither ridiculed his book nor dismissed it out of hand. He cannot, however, have been pleased by its carelessness and its failure to grasp much that was central to his position. The review is really no more than a highly selective summary. It focuses on such things as Berkeley's denial that we can know either by sense or by reason that matter exists, and his claim that we might have all the sensations we now have even if matter did not exist, but it neglects his more important arguments for the claim that *matter* is either a word without meaning or a concept that is contradictory. Nor would one know, from the review, that Berkeley holds that, on his view, "the distinction between realities and chimeras retains its full force" (*PHK* §34), for the review repeatedly implies that Berkeley thinks the things we perceive are not real. Thus, it says that, for him, the "apparent mechanism" in nature "has the same effect on [us] as if the objects of our perceptions were real," and that, for him, "extension exists in the soul only as a perception, not as a reality." This tendency recurs in the review's last paragraph, where Berkeley is represented as holding that the wine at the wedding of Cana, although "only ideal", would have the same effect as "if it had been real and effective wine," leaving the reader with the impression that, for Berkeley, what was perceived at Cana was not real wine – quite the opposite of what he claimed at *PHK* §84.

Mr. Berkeley has lately published a book entitled *A Treatise concerning the Principles of Human Knowledge: Part I*, [etc.]. (Dublin, 1710, in 8°, 214 pages.)

In the Preface, the author asserts that after a long and serious investigation he has found that the principles he makes use of in his work are evidently true, and are capable of undeceiving those who have fallen into Pyrrhonism, or who want a demonstration stronger than that of the existence of God, and of the immortality of the soul.[2]

He then undertakes to prove his principle, which is that neither body nor matter exists, and that there is no being or substance other than spirits. These spirits possess understanding and will, which enables them to exercise power: for it is absurd, according to him, to imagine a power where there is no will that can direct and apply it. Everything else that we take to exist external to us is nothing, he says, but ideas of a wholly passive nature. These ideas come to us by way of our senses, he adds. They are no more dependent on us than those we form by imagination or by memory.[3] It is some other spirit who makes us perceive them. They have no existence apart from that of being perceived, and they cease to be or to exist when our mind or some other mind ceases to perceive them.

When several of these ideas or sensations are found constantly together, as a certain color, a certain odor, a certain taste, a certain figure, etc., they make a combination to which we give, for example, the name *apple*.

To prove so seemingly strange an hypothesis, here is how Mr. Berkeley argues. We cannot know, he says, either by our senses or by our reason that there exists outside us any such substance as matter or bodies. By our senses we do not perceive anything but sensations, which nothing external to us can resemble. One grants this with respect to those qualities that are called accidental, such as heat, color, etc. But it is usually supposed that figure, extension, motion, and the arrangement of parts are inherent qualities or modifications of matter and that the sensations we have of these qualities correspond to or resemble them. Now if this were the case, Mr. Berkeley continues, then, having once received in my mind the sensation or perception of the shape of a body by one of my senses, that same perception would necessarily be produced in my mind again if the same body were to make an impression on another of my senses, for that body would have caused, by this latter sense, a perception of shape that resembled the quality [in the body] and that, consequently, would be the same idea as the one I got from the first sense. But such is not the case, he says; a man born blind, who gains his sight, does not perceive by sight the same figures he was already familiar with from touch.

Nor can reason persuade us that there are external bodies. For were it to persuade us of that, it would have to do so by means of our sensations, since they are the sole means we have of taking account of such bodies. But our sensations do not prove the existence of a body, for sensations can be just as vivid when we are delirious as when we are calm. Now the perceptions formed in a state of delirium certainly do not resemble the bodies they represent, since they are not caused by something outside us. All that we can conclude from our sensations, Mr. Berkeley continues, is that they are caused by something external to us – some thing or principle that must be endowed with power and volition, which does not at all conform to the idea we have of body. Thus one cannot conclude that there are bodies outside us, for one conceives of matter as incapable of acting on spirit, and all the sensations we have could come to us even if no bodies exist outside us, for one can easily conceive that an intelligence that had no body could receive all the same sensations we do, from which it would draw the same conclusion we do – that bodies exist; and yet it would be deceived.

Were one to say that, though indeed matter cannot by itself act on mind and that it thus seems useless, it can nevertheless serve as an instrument and occasion for our having sensations, I [Berkeley] reply that the name *instrument* is here used very inappropriately, for there can be no application of one [matter] to the other [mind]. Equally, matter cannot be conceived as an occasional cause, as when it is said that God prescribes to himself a law to produce in us such and such a sensation, when such and such a body is present to us: for in what way is this body present to us if we do not perceive it, perception being the only way something can be made present to a mind? Since this body contributes nothing to the sensation I have, and I can have the same sensation without it, what reason have I to conclude that such a body exists? We would first have to prove that it exists, and then show that it is the occasion of our having this sensation.

Next Mr. Berkeley notes the advantages his hypothesis has. With it, an infinity of hitherto insoluble difficulties disappear – whether matter can think, whether it is extended and infinitely divisible, whether it can act on spirit, how it can be created out of nothing, etc. So long as men believed that the objects of their inquiries were external to them, it was impossible for them to be sure of anything. As the whole of their science consisted only in the conformity of their ideas with the nature of things, and they could know that conformity only by means of sensations, they could establish no fixed and certain principle, for they could never be certain of the perfect conformity of their sensations with external objects – sensations, after all, change constantly, depending on whether one looks at a thing from near or far away, or through a microscope. From this principle, the author concludes that time is just the succession of our ideas – to suppose it something else, he says, is to use a word without a meaning. This also proves, according to him, that our soul always thinks, and that its essence consists in this continuous thinking. Space, he adds, is just the ease with which I find I can move what I imagine to be my body. One cannot conceive space without conceiving a body in motion; taken in any other sense, it [*space*] is a word without meaning, by which we are, nonetheless, fooled, because we think that each word must stand for some particular idea. If my body were the only one in the world, he continues, I would say that all the rest is space, by which I would mean simply that I could move my body in any direction without meeting any resistance. Were that body annihilated, there would be no more motion, and so no more space. To say that extension is infinitely divisible, he adds, is a manifest contradiction, if one understands by extension a simple perception; for it is impossible for a finite being to perceive something infinitely large, infinitely small, or infinitely numerous; and when geometers say, e.g., that a line of one inch contains 10,000 parts, it is only because that line serves to represent another line in which that many parts are contained – parts that, because of their size, can be perceived. But they do not mean that these same parts are in the smaller line, they just make that supposition so that their calculations will work out.

Next Mr. Berkeley replies to objections that can be made to his hypothesis. We will just report some of these, with his replies.

Objection: When something is no longer perceived, it no longer exists.

Reply: (1) One can raise the same difficulty about the accidental qualities of a body, such as color, etc. (2) This hypothesis doesn't differ from that according to which the conservation of things is the same as a continuous creation. (3) God's creatures can continue to exist in another spirit, even when I do not perceive them.

Objection: If extension exists only in a soul, then the soul will itself be extended.

Reply: (1) Then the soul is colored, too, since colors exist only in us. (2) Extension exists in the soul only as a perception, not as a reality.

Objection: How can it be that all men are deceived [about the existence of matter]?

Reply: Upon finding that they have various perceptions that they are not the authors of – perceptions that come to them from without and that they cannot avoid – men have ascribed them to external objects, which they have supposed resemble these perceptions, attributing to things a power that they cannot have and so cannot exert on us.

Objection: Various mathematical truths will no longer hold [if this hypothesis is accepted], such as that the earth is in motion – something no one perceives.

Reply: The motion of the earth is just a consequence that follows from what we judge that we would see if we were located on a different planet. Furthermore, since the order, connection, and dependence that God has established in the ideas he imprints on our minds are the same as the laws of nature, the truths of physics and mathematics are left wholly intact.

Objection: What is the good of all that apparent mechanism that we see in the planets, in the changing of the seasons, etc.?[4]

Reply: It exercises man's faculties, gives him a plan of conduct, and has the same effect on him as if the objects of our perceptions were real. These objects are only signs and tokens of what we should expect, just as fire is not the cause of pain, but a warning in advance of it.

Objection: Won't miracles now be nothing but a change in our ideas?

Reply: The wine at Cana was not less wine, for it produced the same effect and revealed the same infinite power, surpassing that of creatures, as it would have if it had been real and effective wine. Miraculous productions, though they be, on this hypothesis, only ideal, have the same effect on our minds as if we took them to exist outside us.[5]

2. *Mémoires de Trévoux* (May 1713)

It was to be well over a year, it seems, before there was another review of the *Principles* – and it hardly merits the name "review". One has to wonder if its author had even read the work; the one paragraph that purports to state Berkeley's position is suspiciously like the third paragraph of the *Journal des Sçavans* review. (Even the reviewer's translation of the full title of the work follows that given in the earlier review, including certain differences from the title in English.) Moreover, the aim of the review was almost certainly not so much to inform readers of Berkeley's position as to strike a blow against Malebranche. A favorite target of the Jesuits, Malebranche was at this time engaged in bitter conflict with the *Mémoires de Trévoux*, the influential Jesuit journal in which this review appeared. By characterizing Berkeley as "a bona fide Malebranchist," and even more by identifying an unnamed solipsist as a "Malebranchist", the review could intimate the absurdities to which Malebranche's doctrine leads.

Mr. Berkley [*sic*], a bona fide Malebranchist [*Malbranchiste de bonne foi*], has pushed unreservedly the principles of his sect far beyond common sense, and has concluded that there are neither bodies nor matter, and that spirits alone exist. These spirits are nothing but individuals that have the faculty of receiving ideas, of willing and acting in conformity with their ideas and their will. All that we imagine to be corporeal are only ideas that another spirit imparts to us, and that have no existence outside us, and that cease to be when they cease to be perceived.

A Treatise concerning the Principles of Human Knowledge, First Part, [etc.]. The author promises a second part.

One of us knew in Paris a Malebranchist who has gone even further than Mr. Berkley, very seriously maintaining in a long dispute that it is very probable he is the sole created being that exists and that not only are there no bodies, but there is no created spirit other than him; it is for those who believe that *we see only an intelligible world* to prove that this is carrying their principles too far.[6]

Insubstantial though it was, this review appears to have been influential in coloring Berkeley's subsequent reputation. It was, it seems, the basis for a claim made by Christian Wolff, in 1720, that in Paris there was a "Sect of Egoists" who denied the existence of anything but the "I". Soon after, C. M. Pfaff attacked this sect in his *Oratio de egoismo* (1722), now taking Berkeley as a target. Pfaff also seems to have been the first to identify Berkeley with skeptics like Bayle. It is at least doubtful, however, that Pfaff ever actually read Berkeley. Harry Bracken notes that Pfaff cites no work of Berkeley's, but instead cites the above review and the other reviews presented in this chapter, observing too, with Lewis Robinson, that all the later eighteenth-century references to "Egoism" as a philosophical movement seem to be traceable, directly or indirectly, back to the *Mémoires de Trévoux* review.[7] More often than not, the only thinker actually named in this connection was Berkeley. This is the case, for example, in the articles on the egoists in the *Encyclopédie* and in the Jesuits' *Dictionnaire de Trévoux*.[8]

3. *Mémoires de Trévoux* (December 1713)

In December, the *Mémoires de Trévoux* struck again at Berkeley, now on the basis of the *Three Dialogues*. Again Malebranche seems to have been the real target. Malebranche's name is not mentioned on this occasion, but in suggesting that Berkeley reduces the material world to "an intelligible world" and thinks that "we see bodies only in God," as well as by its reference to "attention to universal reason," the review sent a clear signal to readers familiar with Malebranche's doctrine and vocabulary that Berkeley is a left-wing Malebranchean, pushing his master's doctrine to its natural and absurd end.[9]

Mr. Berkley [*sic*] continues obstinately to maintain *that there are no bodies, and that the material world is just an intelligible world.* He attacks the new philosophers with their own principles: I. Extension, he says, has no more existence than sensible qualities have, it is only an idea in our mind. II. We see bodies only in God, hence it is unnecessary for them to exist outside of God. You will ask, no doubt, what then is the creation that Moses has left us the history of? The creation, according to Mr. Berkley, is only the decision that God has made to imprint on minds the ideas of bodies. Hasn't Mr. Berkley made good use of his meditations and of his attention to universal reason? *Three Dialogues between Hylas and Philonous.* At London, by Clements, in 8°. 1713.[10]

A further bizarre twist in the Jesuits' attack on Berkeley came in 1718, when Père Tournemine, one of the editors of the *Mémoires de Trévoux*, published "The Atheism of the Immaterialists Refuted," in his preface to Fénelon's *Oeuvres philosophiques*. By denying the existence of the natural world, the immaterialists hope to strip "the true philosophers of all the means of proving the existence of God," thereby freeing themselves from moral obligations. Only one immaterialist work is cited: "the English book of one Berkey [*sic*]." [11]

4. *Journal Litéraire* (May & June 1713)

The following review – again of the *Three Dialogues* – stands in sharp contrast to those of the *Mémoires de Trévoux*. It was not, to be sure, a favorable review, and it failed to understand key features of Berkeley's doctrine. It dwells, for example, on the arguments in the *First Dialogue*, but has no grip on their dialectical role, with the result that it does scant justice to some more central arguments for immaterialism. Furthermore, like many others, the reviewer regularly speaks as if Berkeley denies the existence of "bodies", while failing to make clear that, for Berkeley, there is a profound difference between the *unperceivable* material substances he rejects and the *perceivable* bodies he firmly believes exist. Nonetheless, the review does take Berkeley sufficiently seriously to attempt to counter some of his actual arguments. Harry Bracken has gone so far as to say of it that, "early as it was, [it] turned out to be, so far as I know, the most philosophically mature discussion that was published during Berkeley's life." [12]

Three years ago the author of these dialogues published, at London, the first part of *A Treatise concerning the Principles of Human Knowledge*; the views he set forth in that work being entirely new, he believed it necessary, before publishing its second part, to clarify further certain principles he there lay down, and to set them in a new light. To this end, he has just published the dialogues we are here speaking of, which are, nevertheless, written in a way that allows them to be read even if one hasn't seen the first work. The same author has also published *An Essay towards a New Theory of Vision*, also in English, which went through a second printing in Dublin, in 1709. One sees in all these works the character of an author more attached to advancing paradoxes and wholly new opinions than to carefully examining the opinions that he refutes.

The speakers in the dialogues, of which we will give an abstract, are Hylas and Philonous. The latter, who is the victor, and who converts the former to his view, maintains that there are no bodies and that the only things that can exist are spirits; he holds that all that we call *bodies* are only ideas that cannot have an existence separate from the spirits that have these ideas. Our author believes that he has demonstrated his view, that it is without serious problems, and that it provides the simplest means to silence atheists as well as skeptics, and to recall men from paradoxes to common sense.

The reader will doubtless be surprised by the strangeness of this view, but a reading of the book will keep him from holding what the author holds. Still, whatever one thinks of Philonous's views, it has to be admitted that the ordinary view, which is defended by Hylas (who apparently puts forward all the reasons the author can think of in defense of it), appears even less defensible. The debate between our interlocutors is not sufficiently orderly to permit us to follow them in an abstract; we will content ourselves with setting out Mr. Berkeley's view as clearly as we can. Indeed, we will give here a fairly extended account of it, relative to the size of the book, not doubting that the reader will be curious to see in some detail what can be advanced on behalf of an opinion as peculiar as Mr. Berkeley's.

Let us begin with the reasons he urges for his claim that nothing similar to what is called *material substance* exists, or, put in other terms, that sensible things do not exist in the way we usually take them to. He begins by noting that only things immediately perceived by the senses should be called sensible things: "When I see one part of the sky red, and another blue, I am forced to conclude that there must be a cause of that diversity of colors; but one cannot say that that cause is a sensible thing, since it is only the colors themselves that I immediately perceive."[13] Our author adds that by the senses we only perceive light, colors, figures, sound, odor, taste, and what can be perceived by touch; he concludes from this that if it can be shown that nothing similar to these sensible qualities can exist outside us, it will follow that nothing that can be perceived by the senses exists outside us. Consequently, what we call *body*, and take to be the subject that these different sensible qualities are related to, is a chimera; *sensible things* are only different combinations of *sensible qualities* and have no subject, external to us, to which they can be related.

To prove that sensible qualities cannot exist outside us, Mr. Berkeley divides them into two classes: primary qualities and secondary qualities. The former are extension, figure, solidity, gravity, motion, and rest. All the others he calls *secondary*, such as heat, odor, taste, sound, and colors. Our author begins by examining the latter, and he shows that in bodies there is nothing similar to these secondary qualities – that is, to the sensations we have of heat, odors, etc.

Nobody doubts this truth and one would have willingly excused Mr. Berkeley from dwelling as fully on this subject as he has – answering objections that surely nobody would dare put to him. When one says that a body has any of these secondary qualities, one does not mean that that body feels anything similar to what it causes us to feel; one only means that that body, by the configuration of its parts, or by the motion that it communicates to the matter surrounding it, or by what it reflects off of itself, has the property of producing a certain motion in our nerves, which gets communicated, via the brain, to the soul, where it gives rise to some one of those ideas that we call *sensations*.

Also Mr. Berkeley takes up an objection that might be made to him in this regard about colors and sound, and contents himself with the reply that it is contradictory to say that sound is a motion, since motion can only be perceived by sight and touch.

But our author should have noted that one does not say that *sound* is a *motion*, but rather that sound is the effect of motion – namely, the motion that, by means of the organ of hearing, produces in our soul an idea that we call *sound*. Much the same can be said of what he says about colors.

It isn't on secondary qualities that the question of the non-existence of bodies turns, but rather on showing that extension, figure, solidity, gravity, motion, and rest are only sensations of the soul, and that they can exist only as ideas. Here are some of the main arguments of our author. To prove that size and shape are not in bodies, he notes that a thing cannot at the same time be of several different sizes, yet a very small body, barely visible to us, would appear enormous to an animal even smaller than that body itself. Again, an *inherent quality* of a thing cannot be changed unless the thing itself changes; yet we see that a body, as we approach it or recede from it, appears to us larger or smaller; hence, one cannot say that size is an inherent quality. A third argument of Mr. Berkeley's runs thus: When, on putting two hands in water, we have found that the water felt hot to one and cold to the other, we have rightly concluded that heat is not in water: should we not, in the same way, conclude that extension and figure are not in an object, when it appears small, smooth, and round to one eye, but large, rough, and angular to the other? Yet this is just what happens when one eye looks at something through a microscope and the other looks at it unaided.

To comment on all these arguments with a single remark, we will content ourselves with noting that the author fails to take account of the different relations objects can stand in to us. When those relations change, although the object remains in itself the same, it is no longer the same in its relation to us; the example of heat proves nothing, for one would err in saying that heat is not in the water, if, to prove it, one had only the reason given here by our author. Would it show good grace, for example, to conclude that when Mr. Berkeley remembers one thing but forgets another, memory is not a faculty of his soul? Would it not be unfair, by destroying in the same way his other [mental] faculties, to maintain that he has no soul at all? Since he himself has already annihilated his body, what would become of him?

The reasoning of our author about motion is of the same nature. If *motion* is in the body, it cannot be at the same time swift and slow, "but *motion* is swift in proportion to the time it takes one to traverse a given space, etc. Time is measured by the succession of ideas in our minds, and these ideas can succeed one another more quickly in one mind than in another. Therefore, etc." Solidity too is not in bodies, for it is relative to our senses: a body that appears hard and that resists one animal, will appear soft and non-resisting to another.

The author should have noted that what one usually calls *solidity* is that property in bodies whereby they prevent other bodies from occupying the space they are in; solidity, in that sense, is not relative to our senses: water, fluid though it be, will (if it cannot escape) resist a bit of iron just as much as would the hardest body.

Mr. Berkeley, to bring the dispute to a close and anticipate all the objections that might be made to his reasoning, adds that it suffices, to achieve this end, to show that there is no extension. If extension is only an idea, then bodies too can be nothing but ideas. The essence of Mr. Berkeley's proof consists in this: One cannot conceive extension separated from all those sensible qualities that are called secondary, from which our author concludes that extension cannot exist without some of these qualities, and, since these qualities exist only in our mind, extension cannot be something external to us; hence it is nothing but an idea. If this reasoning confuses anyone, he can put it in other terms, and he will find that Mr. Berkeley proves very well that the impression that extension, insofar as it is sensible, makes on our minds is an idea; or, what amounts to the same thing, that the idea of extension is an idea.

So much for what our author says of sensible qualities; we move on to a more metaphysical argument – one he returns to often and regards as by itself capable of settling the whole question. Nothing is sensible save what is immediately perceived; and what is immediately perceived is an idea – something that cannot exist in an unperceiving being such as the thing we call *body*. Ideas change with changes in the positions of objects, and hence they cannot be representations of those objects, which remain the same as they were. Furthermore, an idea can resemble only another idea; and hence what our ideas represent to us can exist only in another spirit. That which doesn't think cannot be the cause of thought. Furthermore, a being incapable of acting cannot be the cause of any effect, and one cannot say that motion is an action of matter – motion being just an idea, as our author claims to have proven by the argument recounted above.

By such proofs, Mr. Berkeley claims to overturn what we usually say, viz., that external objects, by the various impressions they make on our sense organs, set up a motion in our nerves that is communicated to the brain and thereby produces in our souls the ideas we call sensations. Our author asks, does one conceive that thing that is the brain? If one conceives it, he says, then it is an idea, and it would be absurd, in order to explain how an idea is produced in our soul, to have recourse to ideas imprinted on another idea [i.e., the brain]. If one *doesn't* conceive the thing that is the brain, then far from proposing a reasonable hypothesis, one doesn't know what one is talking about. There is no connection between a motion in the nerves and sensations of sound, colors, etc. Since the opinion that bodies exist is false, one is obliged to doubt everything.[14]

What is specious in Mr. Berkeley's reasoning is this: he supposes that only a spirit – something itself capable of having ideas – can give rise to ideas in another spirit. Say what he will on this subject, he can never show that God is not powerful enough to have made inanimate beings and rendered them capable, by means unknown to us, of acting on spirits in a way that produces ideas in them. It comes down, then, to a matter of knowing whether God has used this means to produce in us the ideas we receive when in the presence of the objects we call sensible, or whether God himself is the immediate cause of our ideas, as Mr. Berkeley believes. One cannot deny that God, as our author says, can do anything by himself without making use of any instrument. The question is whether God has not willed to employ some instrument, and whether he has not established certain laws in accordance with which some things come about in consequence of other things. It is up to the reader to judge whether it is conceivable that God, having willed that the world be such as it is, has at the same time willed to be the immediate author of our ideas. Can one imagine that God, having two means whereby to produce in men the ideas they have of sensible things, has willed to make men believe that he uses a means that he does not in fact use – both means being, for an all-powerful being, equally easy and equally suited to make known his power and his wisdom? It is true that our author, in his third dialogue, denies that God makes us believe that there are bodies, maintaining that this is just a prejudice that leads us quite astray. I leave to everybody's reflections what to make of this.

Now we come to a curious feature of Mr. Berkeley's views. After holding forth on the beauty of the universe, on the admirable order that reigns in it, on the divine mechanism whereby so many great bodies, at such great removes from each other, are made subject to and, as it were, dependent on each another, he adds that it would be madness to deny the existence of all these things. From which he concludes that, since they cannot exist outside us, nor have any existence separated from the spirits for whom they are sensible, it must be that their existence consists *in being perceived.*

When we consider, further, that it does not depend on us whether we perceive or do not perceive the objects we would will to, it is clear that the existence of objects does not depend on the perceptions we have of them. It must be, therefore, that they exist in some other spirit who perceives them, from which our author concludes, "Since one cannot doubt that the sensible world exists, it is also quite certain that an infinite omnipresent spirit exists, who contains that world and supports it."

One should not fear, says our author in another place, that one destroys sensible things by saying that they are only ideas. For these ideas are very different from those that our imagination provides us with; the latter are not so distinct and are wholly dependent on our wills. By contrast, the ideas that come to us by the senses are more vivid and clear, being produced in the soul by a spirit different from it. This view, Mr. Berkeley adds, does not lead to making God the author of our sins, for though it makes him the author of all physical actions, physical actions are always [morally] indifferent, the culpability of an act depending on what goes on in the soul of him who acts.

This then, briefly put, is the opinion of our author and his argument against the atheists, which he takes to be a direct and immediate demonstration, founded on incontestable principles.

Next Mr. Berkeley examines the thought of a famous philosopher of our time[15] about *the vision of bodies in God,* and he remarks that, given that view, it would be useless for bodies to exist, since our soul would perceive only the representative ideas of them in God, without perceiving bodies themselves. Our author also deals at length with how one should understand what Moses said about the Creation. When it is said that God created something, what is meant is that God willed to communicate certain ideas to particular spirits that he had already created.

Besides the argument against the atheists, Mr. Berkeley claims to find in his views many other advantages that are not to be had by those who believe in the existence of bodies. Philosophers have been forced to say that they do not know the nature of things, whereas he knows them: things are nothing but the ideas he has of them. Thus fire is hot and colors are in objects, in holding which, he says, he agrees with all men – but he should add, *in the words they use*. When a peasant says that the whiteness of his horse is in the horse itself, and when Mr. Berkeley says the same, do they mean the same thing? And how well would Mr. Berkeley – who claims to agree so strongly with what common sense teaches everybody – be received by the peasant if he declared to him that the horse only exists in the heads of those who are looking at it?

The author claims to show the advantages his system has in many other regards over the opinion of those who believe in the existence of bodies – an opinion which, according to Mr. Berkeley, leads to a great many paradoxes and absurd and untenable opinions. We will not look further at this: what we have already said makes clear enough what Mr. Berkeley means by these paradoxes and untenable opinions. We will content ourselves, before concluding this abstract, with noting some consequences of our author's opinion. Here are some he himself speaks of in these dialogues.

As I approach an object, with each step I take it is a different object that I see. When I look at an object through a microscope, I do not see the same object I see with the naked eye. The object I feel [by touch] is not the same object as the one I see. It is only to avoid confusion in language that in these cases we give the same name to different objects and speak of them as if they were the same thing.

Other consequences that one can draw from Mr. Berkeley's system: The hand that strikes the blow cannot be seen. The stick I use to strike with is not the one that I hold in my hand. The man who injured me is not the same as the one I bring before the court; and the one seen hanged from the gallows is not the one who committed the theft. I cannot speak to someone unless an infinite spirit intervenes to raise up, in the mind of him to whom I speak, the ideas I want him to have. By the same token, even for me to write this requires that God make visible these letters to all those who cast their eyes on this paper.[16]

* * *

Given Berkeley's eagerness to learn how his ideas were being received, we can only suppose that, if he learned of these early reviews, he made an effort to obtain them. One may equally suppose that he would have been disappointed by their neglect of some of his central arguments and the assumption that he denied the reality of "bodies". He had, it is clear, expected the strength of his arguments to win others to his view, if they would but read him carefully. He may even have thought that in time his views would gain the kind of widespread acceptance that Locke's enjoyed. Certainly, by 1713 he was on the lookout for signs that he was winning converts. Shortly before the publication of the *Three Dialogues*, he announced to Percival that "the first proselyte I have made by the Treatise I came over [to London] to print" was John Arbuthnot, the Queen's physician and someone noted for his learning, "being a great philosopher, and reckoned among the first mathematicians of the age."[17] Percival himself was now more encouraging than he had been earlier. "I hear your new book [the *Three Dialogues*] is printed though not yet published, and that your opinion has gained ground among the learned; that Mr Addison is come over to you; and now what seemed shocking at first is become so familiar that others envy you the discovery and make it their own."[18] Furthermore, Percival, when he had read the book "through and through," judged that the dialogue form made for a more effective presentation of Berkeley's position. "The new method you took by way of dialogue, I am satisfied has made your meaning much easier understood, and was the properest course you could use in such an argument, where prejudice against the novelty of it was sure to raise numberless objections that could not anyway so easy as by dialogue be either made or answered."[19]

Time was not to confirm these hopes. For one thing, in the same letter Percival questioned Arbuthnot's supposed conversion: "I hear Dr Swift has said you have not made a convert of Dr Arbuthnot."[20] Berkeley's reply is revealing. He and Arbuthnot have some disagreement about the necessity of nature's laws, "but this does not touch the main point of the non-existence of what philosophers call material substance, against which he has acknowledged he can object nothing."[21] Berkeley here optimistically ignored the chasm that can separate those who whole-heartedly embrace a view from those who find no way to object to it. In fact, Berkeley was to find very few supporters. Indeed, as Bracken notes in his seminal study of the early reception of Berkeley's immaterialism, in the two decades following the publication of the *Three Dialogues* many references to Berkeley "do little more than find in him a source of low-class intellectual comedy."[22]

We close this chapter with an example – a brief extract from an anonymous piece published in *The Tribune* in 1729 and rediscovered by David Berman. The author (probably, Berman thinks, James Arbuckle) describes

> . . . a Treatise written by a celebrated philosopher and *virtuoso* of our own nation. The book goes pretty much upon the principles of the famous Father Malebranche; but, in an uncommon strain of thinking, carries the matter much farther than I believe that author, or any of his followers, ever imagined. He supposes that there is no such thing as matter in the universe; but that *extension*, *solidity*, and those others commonly known by the name of its *primary* qualities, are equally fictitious with the *secondary* qualities, such as *heat*, *sounds*, *colours*, and the like, which by the universal suffrage of all modern philosophers are granted to have no real existence without us. . . .

As a result of reading Berkeley's book, the author has a dream in which he is transported into "the *ideal world*", which at first seems "not less lovely than that from whence I had imagined myself so lately expelled." He is, however, given a "*philosophical mirror*" in which he sees, for example, that an apparent battle is "no more than a fanciful battle between two numerous bands of *sensations* and *reflexions*." Rocks become "fugitive heaps of *primary* and *secondary qualities*" and lemons "clusters of *yellow imaginations*." The dream ends when a "*phantom* resembling a clergyman" steps on his toes "which put me to so much pain, that I could hardly stoop to lift up the book mentioned in the beginning of this paper, which had fallen out of my hand, and very much hurted one of my corns."[23]

No critic of Berkeley as serious as the *Journal Littéraire* reviewer seems to have appeared – at least in print – before Andrew Baxter in 1733.

Notes

1. The review we do not include was a negligible notice of the *Three Dialogues*, consisting almost entirely of quotations, which appeared in *Memoirs of Literature* (1713). It is reprinted in David Berman, ed., *George Berkeley: Eighteenth-Century Responses* (New York: Garland, 1989), vol. 1, pp. 105–6. Later on, reviews appeared of the *Three Dialogues*, 2nd ed., in *Acta Eruditorum* (1727); of the Italian translation of the Introduction to the *Principles* along with the *New Theory of Vision*, in *Bibliothèque Italique* (1732); and of the French translation of the *Three Dialogues*, in *Mémoires de Trévoux* (1750) and in *Mercure de France* (1750). Another review of the French translation of the *Dialogues* – one prepared privately in 1750 for the Court of Saxe-Gotha – is reprinted (with English translation) in Sébastien Charles, "L'abbé Raynal, author of an unnoticed review of Berkeley's *Dialogues*," *Berkeley Newsletter*, no. 15 (1997–98), pp. 14–18.
2. An example of the reviewer's tendency to garble Berkeley's words. What Berkeley says in the Preface is that his book will be useful "to those who are tainted with scepticism, or want a demonstration of the existence and immateriality of God, or the natural immortality of the soul."
3. Another example of carelessness. What Berkeley actually says (in *PHK* §§28–29) is that, in imagining, "I can excite ideas in my mind at pleasure, and vary and shift the scene as oft as I think fit"; but that the situation is quite different with respect to the ideas of sense. These "have not a like dependence on my will." Berkeley contrasts our passivity in sensing with our activity in imagining, whereas the reviewer implies that for Berkeley we are passive in both.
4. Where the reviewer speaks of "planets", Berkeley says "plants" (*PHK* §60).
5. *Journal des Sçavans* [Amsterdam edition] (September 1711), vol. 50, pp. 321–30. Our translation is based on the original French version, reprinted in Harry M. Bracken, *The Early Reception of Berkeley's Immaterialism: 1710–1733*, 2nd ed. (The Hague: Martinus Nijhoff, 1965), Appendix B; the original is also reprinted in Berman (see note 1 above), vol. 1, pp. 95–104.
6. *Mémoires de Trévoux* (May 1713), pp. 921–22. The original French version is reprinted in Bracken, Appendix D, and in Berman, vol. 1, pp. 107–9.
7. See Bracken, pp. 19–23.
8. *Dictionnaire de Trévoux*, new ed. (Paris, 1771), vol. 3, p. 599b, cited in Bracken, p. 21. On the *Encyclopédie*, see below p. 234.
9. The 1750 review of the French translation of the *Three Dialogues* in the *Mémoires de Trévoux* went further, claiming that Berkeley had admitted, privately, that he had written this work only "to expose the absurd and ridiculous consequences which follow from the doctrine of Malebranche." (Quoted in Bracken, p. 29.)
10. *Mémoires de Trévoux* (December 1713), pp. 2198–99. The original French version is reprinted in Bracken, Appendix E, and in Berman, vol. 1, pp. 110–11.
11. The relevant pages are reprinted in Bracken, Appendix F.
12. Bracken, pp. 49–50.

13. Here and elsewhere the passages put in quotation marks by the reviewer are paraphrases of Berkeley, not strict translations.

14. The reviewer fails to make it clear that it is *Hylas* who, at this point in the *Dialogues*, is driven to the conclusion that sensible things do not have a real existence and so to the position of "an arrant *sceptic*." Philonous steadfastly maintains that his view frees one from skepticism (*Works* II, pp. 210–12).

15. Malebranche.

16. *Journal Littéraire* (May and June 1713), vol. 1, pp. 147–60. Our translation is based on the original French version reprinted in Bracken, Appendix C; the original is also reprinted in Berman, vol. 1, pp. 113–26.

17. *Works* VIII, pp. 65–66.

18. Rand, *Berkeley and Percival*, p. 117. Joseph Addison was one of the great essayists of the age.

19. Rand, p. 120.

20. Rand, p. 121.

21. *Works* VIII, p. 70.

22. Bracken, p. 1.

23. From "A Dream Representing the World to be Better," reprinted in Berman, vol. 1, pp. 127–33.

FOURTEEN

G. W. Leibniz

Unbeknown to Berkeley, one very prominent philosopher did read the *Principles* at an early stage. This was G. W. Leibniz (1646–1716), the only major philosopher of the seventeenth century to read that work.[1] Leibniz found a good deal to object to in Berkeley and, in a letter to Bartholomew des Bosses, passed this severe judgment: "The Irishman who impugns the reality of bodies does not seem to give reasons that are sufficient, nor to explain his thought satisfactorily. I suspect he belongs to that genus of men that wants to be known for paradoxes."[2] On the last page of his copy of the *Principles*, Leibniz wrote a short comment on the work, noting some things he objected to in it: the rejection of abstract ideas, the reduction of ideas to images, the criticisms of pure mathematics, and the denial of the infinite divisibility of extension. However, his comment also shows that Leibniz recognized important affinities between his views and Berkeley's. For although Leibniz protests against saying that matter does not exist, he also holds that matter is not a *substance* (rather, it is a well-founded phenomenon) and, moreover, that the only true substances are "perceivers". Nor can he have failed to recognize similarities between Berkeley's reasons for rejecting Newton's doctrine of absolute space, time, and motion, in *PHK* §§110–117, and his own.[3] Here is Leibniz's comment.[4]

Much in this is right and agrees with my way of thinking. But it is paradoxically expressed. We need not say that matter is nothing, but it suffices that we say it is a phenomenon, like the rainbow – not a substance, but what results from substances, and that space is no more real than time, space being nothing other than the order of coexisting things [*ordinem coexistentiarum*], as time is the order of successively existing things [*ordinem subexistentiarum*]. True substances are monads or perceivers. But the author should have pressed on, to an infinity of monads from which all things are constituted, and to their pre-established harmony. He wrongly, or at least needlessly, rejects abstract ideas, restricts ideas to images, and scorns the subtleties of arithmetic and geometry. Worst of all, he rejects the division of extension to infinity, even if he might rightly reject infinitesimal quantities.[5]

Notes

1. Hobbes, Descartes, and Spinoza died before Berkeley was born; Locke and Bayle died before any of his works were published; Malebranche was still alive when the *Principles* and *Three Dialogues* appeared, but he could not read English.
2. *Die philosophischen Schriften von G. W. Leibniz*, ed. C. I. Gerhardt (Berlin, 1875–90), vol. 2, p. 492.
3. André Robinet has suggested that Leibniz may have gotten from *PHK* §§110–17 some ammunition for his battle with Samuel Clarke over Newton's doctrines, a battle that began late in 1715. See Robinet, "Leibniz: Lecture du *Treatise* de Berkeley," *Études philosophiques*, no. 2 (1983), p. 221.
4. For the Latin text of this comment, as well as a list of Leibniz's marginal markings in his copy of *PHK*, see Robinet, pp. 217–23. It is not known just when Leibniz read *PHK*, but presumably before 15th March 1715, the date of the letter to Des Bosses.
5. In discussing geometry in *PHK* §§123–32, Berkeley rejects the possibility of the infinite divisibility of extension and the notion of infinitesimal quantities. For his part, Leibniz holds that any part of extension can be divided into extended parts, and so accepts infinite divisibility, but he also holds that every actual quantity is determinate and bounded, and hence further divisible. As a consequence, he seems to have viewed infinitesimal quantities as "ideal concepts" that are required in mathematics, even if they cannot, in a rigorous metaphysical sense, be said to be real things. See Leibniz's letter to Varignon of 2nd February 1702, in *Leibniz, Philosophical Papers and Letters*, ed. L. E. Loemker (Dordrecht: Reidel, 1969), pp. 542–44; and *New Essays concerning Human Understanding*, II.17.1–3.

FIFTEEN

Andrew Baxter

Bishop Warburton called Andrew Baxter "a great genius", and predicted that the "time will come, if learning ever revive among us, when the present inattention to his admirable Metaphysics, established on the Physics of Newton, will be deemed as great a dishonour to the wisdom of this age, as the neglect of Milton's poetry was to the wit of the past." By contrast, Berkeley's demonstration of the non-existence of matter, according to Warburton, "is the poorest, lowest, and most miserable of all sophisms."[1] Both in his belief in Baxter's genius and in his disdain for Berkeley as a philosopher, Warburton was wildly out; ironically, if Baxter is now remembered at all, it is chiefly as a critic of Berkeley. It must be granted, however, that Warburton's warm reaction to Baxter, and his low esteem for Berkeley, were, if not justifiable, at any rate understandable. Baxter's was certainly not a great mind, but it was a far from contemptible one, and Berkeley's metaphysics struck most people, not just Baxter, as outrageous. In a long section entitled "Dean Berkeley's scheme against the existence of matter, and a material world examined, and shewn inconclusive" in his *Enquiry into the Nature of the Human Soul* (1733), Baxter offered what was in fact the first sustained critique of Berkeley's *Principles*. Its opening sets the tone.

Some men deny all *immaterial*, and others all *material* substance; so that between them they leave *nothing at all* existing in nature. These two opposite parties help to expose each other; and it is hard to say, everything considered, whose share is greatest in the absurdity of expunging all being out of existence. Yet thus much we may observe, that the existence of *both* substances must be very plain, since each side maintains that the existence of the substance which they themselves assert must be self-evident: for it would be absurd in either of the parties to suppose arguments necessary to prove that anything at all exists. Our dreams having no real external objects, and some of the ancient writers having suggested that this might be made a ground for doubting whether there were really any such objects, a late ingenious and learned author hath taken the hint, not only to doubt of the reality of matter and a material world, but to pretend to demonstrate the existence of any such thing impossible and contradictory. The attempt certainly is surprising. If his books had been written with a design to excite men to try what they could say, in case such a kind of scepticism should begin to prevail, or as an exercise in a university, to show how far wit and invention might go to maintain a paradox, there had been little in it; but when a person of great capacity and learning seems serious, and writes pieces, one after another, to support this kind of scepticism, and continues in these sentiments for such a number of years, if it be not carrying an ungenteel sort of a *banter* a great deal too far, one cannot tell what to think of it. For it seems impossible that a man should be seriously persuaded that he has neither country nor parents, nor any material body, nor eats, nor drinks, nor lies in a house, but that all these things are mere illusions, and have no existence but in the fancy.

That which makes it necessary here to examine this scheme, which denies the possibility of matter, is because all the arguments I have offered for the being of a God in Sects. I and II, Vol. I, are drawn from the consideration of this *impossible thing*; viz. from the *inertia* of matter, the *motion* of matter, the *cohesion* of matter, &c., and everyone sees what impropriety, or rather what repugnance, there must be to speak of the *vis inertiae* of ideas, the *motion* or *gravity* of ideas, the *elasticity* or *cohesion* of ideas. Whence these arguments must amount to nothing, if there be nothing but ideas instead of the objects of our ideas, as being drawn from properties which can belong to no subject, and which therefore must be impossible. Thus there must either be no truth in what I have said, or in what this author advances, for two such opposite accounts of nature cannot both be true; and if the conclusions in these two Sections be solid, this itself will be a weighty argument against his scheme. However, I shall here endeavour to show the inconclusiveness of it from reasons particularly applied, and try at least to remove so weighty an objection, if I cannot add more light to what hath already been said.[2]

Baxter thus has his own philosophical axe to grind, and this colors much that he says, as does his assumption that, in excluding "matter", Berkeley must be denying the reality of his country, parents, and house. Baxter intends to show that Berkeley's case for his outrageous scheme is "inconclusive", and he begins by putting considerable weight on the claim that neither the existence nor the non-existence of matter can be *demonstrated*. For Baxter, to demonstrate the existence of *anything* requires that it be shown to exist necessarily, which is possible only if existence belongs to its *nature* or *essence*. Of God alone is this the case. The existence of anything else is contingent on God's having willed that it exist. On the other hand, so long as the idea of matter contains no internal inconsistency (and Baxter supposes that, for Berkeley, it is the *existence* of matter, not the *idea* of it, that is contradictory), the non-existence of matter cannot be demonstrated either. We omit this material, as well as Baxter's claim that there is something self-defeating in Berkeley's attempt to convince others of his opinion, when, for Berkeley, even books, writing and printing are "ideas, or dreams", and when, indeed, Berkeley has no way of knowing whether there *are* any others to be convinced. We rejoin Baxter as he is about to pay rather closer, if highly selective, attention to the actual text of the *Principles*.

The great reason why this author pretends to doubt of the existence of material substance, or to demonstrate it impossible, is because we are percipient of nothing but our own perceptions and ideas; and because figure, colour, resistance, &c. is not this substance. Now (to observe here the extent of this kind of doubting) this argument will equally show spiritual substance to be a contradiction in terms, as well as matter: for we are percipient of nothing but our own perceptions and ideas with respect to the *soul* of another man, as well as with respect to his *body*; or if this be true in either, it is true in both. *Activity* and *perceptivity*, the only properties whereby we infer the existence of spiritual substance, are not that substance, but qualities belonging to it, any more than figure, motion, &c. are corporeal substance. If then this argument is good for anything in the first case, it is as good in the second; and if it demonstrate matter out of existence, it equally demonstrates all substance out of existence, save the mind thus percipient, without excepting the Deity himself. So that, brought to its genuine and undissembled issue, it ends in that kind of knowledge, mentioned once or twice above, called *Egomism*. Dean Berkeley, I think, is not far from owning this. In Sect. 138 of what he calls his *Principles* he hath these words: "If therefore 'tis impossible that any degree of these powers [willing, thinking, and perception of ideas, to wit] should be represented in an idea or notion, 'tis evident *there can be no idea or notion of a spirit.*" Here we may observe that, if we neither have any idea or notion of spiritual substance itself, nor of these properties whereby we could only come to the knowledge of such a substance (*activity* and *perceptivity*, the examples of which he assigns), it seems impossible that such a thing could ever have entered into the thoughts of men. These particulars ought to be well considered by those who run so greedily into this scheme. It is true, *thinking, willing,* &c. cannot be painted in the imagination, as objects having figure and magnitude may; but might not this author thus prove that we can have no idea or notion of *virtue, justice, truth*? And if this consequence be fair, as it seems to be, this scheme is a complication of all the species of scepticism that have ever yet been broached. *Notion* extends not only to the images of corporeal objects in the fancy, but to whatever is the object of the understanding.[3]

Baxter's attack on Berkeley has not received as much attention in the literature as perhaps it deserves, and, not surprisingly, it is Baxter's assumption that Berkeley is making everything "illusory" that has been noted most. The preceding extract has, however, been noticed, with Hone and Rossi in particular seeing in it an anticipation of "Hume's famous amplification of Berkeley's argument [against matter] to 'show spiritual substance to be a contradiction as well as matter.' "[4] Things may not be quite as simple as that, for, in the first place, Baxter's argument here is intended as a *reductio*, and Baxter (unlike Hume) is firmly committed to there *being* spiritual substances; and, in the second place, Baxter seems to be chiefly concerned with difficulties Berkeley faces over the issue of the existence of *other* minds, or *other* spiritual substances. The words "save the mind thus percipient" suggest that he is less than acutely aware that Berkeley *may* be in trouble even when it comes to the judgment that he at least is a substance. There seems, however, to be some recognition of the more general problem when Baxter adds that, by denying that we have any "idea or notion" of spirit, Berkeley apparently makes it "impossible that such a thing could ever have entered into the thoughts of men." It is hardly surprising that Baxter was struck by the words he quotes, for in the first edition of the *Principles* Berkeley did indeed deny that we have any "idea or notion" of spirit, and he there said more about how we do *not* know spirits than he did about how we do know them. It is possible that Baxter's remarks played a role in certain changes Berkeley made in the second edition of the *Principles* and third edition of the *Dialogues*, published a year after Baxter's book, which included removing the words "or notion" from the passage Baxter quotes. The question of how Berkeley can justify belief in other minds is one that Baxter returns to in the next brief extract.

If Dean Berkeley, to evade the inconsistency mentioned . . . of disputing with and endeavouring to convince nobody at all for aught he knows, should say that God excites the ideas of men's souls in him (provided he will allow that there can be any idea, or notion, of souls), then all his certainty for the existence of men's souls is because God would not excite the ideas of these beings in us, to make us believe they were, unless they really were. And this would be founding his belief of immaterial substance precisely upon the reason which Dr. Clarke hath brought to show that we cannot possibly be deceived in concluding that material substance really exists without the mind. That is, he cannot avoid proceeding in contradiction to himself, and his own tenets, without having recourse to the force of the Doctor's demonstration, and that demonstration overthrows his tenets. This I take to be a hard dilemma upon the scheme.[5]

It may seem odd that Baxter here appeals not to Descartes, but to Samuel Clarke, for an argument for the existence of matter based on God's veracity. The explanation can be found in part in Baxter's use of Ephraim Chambers's *Cyclopaedia, or an Universal Dictionary of the Arts and Sciences* (London, 1728). At least four articles of that work ("Abstraction", "Body", "External", and "Matter") give quotations – some extensive – from the *Principles*, though the quotations are often mangled, and they hardly give an adequate picture of Berkeley's views (they fail to bring out, for example, either the role God plays in Berkeley's immaterialism or the effort Berkeley makes to show that, on his view, things remain "real"). Baxter sometimes cites Chambers for quotations from Berkeley (although it is clear he also consulted the first edition of the *Principles*). The article "Body" gives, in addition to extensive quotations from Berkeley, Clarke's argument for the existence of matter from God's veracity, and, in a footnote, Baxter refers to that for Clarke's argument. (Bracken has suggested that Baxter's "task of labelling Berkeley a sceptic was made a good deal easier by his acquaintance with the negative

Berkeley of Chambers' distorted version.")[6] Moreover, Baxter regarded Clarke as an ally in a number of areas; in particular, they were at one in seeing matter as having very limited natural powers – limitations that play an important role in Baxter's proofs of the existence of God.

Baxter's attack on Berkeley continues with a passage in which scorn is poured on Berkeley – seen as the arch skeptic – for supposing that, by denying the existence of matter, he can refute skepticism and atheism. "This is, I think," says Baxter, "as if one should advance that the best way for a woman to silence those who may attack her reputation is to turn a common prostitute." We rejoin Baxter with a long extract, which we include without further comment, in which he presents a detailed analysis of what he takes to be Berkeley's central argument for his immaterialism.

It may not perhaps be foreign to the purpose to take notice here of the contradiction in terms which is pretended to be in asserting the existence of matter. It is (if anywhere) in Sect. 4 of Dean Berkeley's *Principles*; for in Sect. 7 he speaks of having *demonstrated* his conclusion, and in Sect. 21 he says, *Arguments a posteriori are unnecessary for confirming what, if he mistakes not, has been sufficiently demonstrated a priori*; therefore in Sect. 22 he apologizes for dilating on that which may with the utmost evidence be *demonstrated in a line or two*, to anyone that is capable of the least reflection. In short, all that I could find for it is in that fourth section, and contained in the following questions. "For what are the forementioned objects [*houses, mountains, rivers*], but the things we perceive by sense? And what, I pray you, do we perceive, besides our own ideas or sensations? And is it not plainly repugnant, that any of these, or any combination of them, should exist unperceived?" This is but a sorry affair to be the subject of three new pieces. We shall consider it query by query, as it is proposed. And first, *What are the forementioned objects, but the things we perceive by sense?* This query seems not to agree well with the next. Here it is allowed that *we perceive things* by sense, or by the mediation of sense (for these things seem at a distance from the sense), which are supposed and called *objects* (of sense it would seem); and in the next it is taken for granted that we *perceive nothing* but our own sensations, that is, nothing by means of the senses. This is what one may call sleight-of-hand reasoning. Let us join both questions in one. *What are the objects of our sensations, but those very sensations themselves?* This question, proposed thus somewhat less jugglingly, implies or supposes the truth of this proposition, *Our sensations have no objects existing without the mind*, which is really the whole point in controversy. And to take this for granted is to beg the thing to be proved, or to suppose the debate at an end. Those *mountains, rivers, houses*, we all suppose to exist without the mind; and although we should be wrong, it remains to prove that we are wrong, that being the whole of the dispute. To *affirm* this, or *ask* if it be not so, will never do anything. We may farther add, since he allows objects perceived by sense in this query, that *sensations* cannot be objects to themselves: a sensation may become the object of a reflex act of the mind upon it, and it can become an object to the mind in no other manner. But when a sensation thus becomes the object of a posterior perception, it is not the object to itself. When a man beholds the circulation of the blood by the help of a microscope, he doth not admire his own simple *perception*, more than when he beholds a pebble, but something which he thinks, at least, the *cause* and *object* of it. We might as well say, when a man laughs at some ridiculous thing, he laughs at his own laughter only. However, we may answer the question categorically: That these *forementioned objects* (rivers, houses, mountains) are *the very things* we perceive by sense. This is a proper answer enough to such a question; and we may add that these *objects* excite sensations in the mind by motion, or acting on the organs, whether by reflecting the rays of light, by raising an undulation in the air, by immediate contact, &c., and this motion is propagated by the nerves to the brain, where the soul (there present) is apprized of them thus acting. Now, it is no matter whether what we say be true or not; though it be only a *conjecture formed at random*, if it assigns to sensations their distinct objects, without a contradiction in terms, this puts D. B. [Dean Berkeley] to the trouble of another demonstration as much as if it were the real case that obtains.

His second question is, *And what I pray you do we perceive, besides our own ideas and sensations?* A consistent answer to this follows from what was said just now. We perceive, besides our sensations themselves, the *objects* of them; or we perceive objects existing from without, by the mediation of sensation, or motion produced, since we are conscious not only of sensation excited, but that it is excited by some cause besides ourselves, for we suffer it, often against our will. This cause we call matter; and D. B. says it is *God Almighty*. Hitherto there is no contradiction. He says it is one thing, and we say it is another; and so far he hath no reason to say we contradict ourselves, more than we have to say the same of him, nay nor so much. It is pleasant to observe D. B.'s address: he would have us to allow that *matter is a sensation*, or that our *sensations* are the same thing with their *objects*, which, being the thing in debate, is still begging the argument, by an equivocal question. So he might prove that, if a man in a dark night were groping out his way with a long pole in his hand, and felt something resist it which made him turn another way lest he should run his head against the wall, so he might prove, I say, that it were a contradiction for the man to say there was anything there, besides the pole itself, by *this same query*. For what, I pray you, says he, do you perceive, besides the pole in your own hand?

We may here again observe, as [earlier],[7] that this query of D. B.'s easily turns against himself. We say that which excites sensations in us is generally the objects of those sensations, existing from without, unless in the instances of dreams and frenzies, in which there still is a manifest difference from ordinary sensation. He says God, who is not the object of our sensations, is the immediate cause of them. How doth he disprove what we assert? Thus. You perceive *nothing* but your perceptions. The *cause* of your perceptions, which you assign, is not your perceptions themselves. Therefore you do not perceive this cause of your perceptions. Therefore *this cause of your perceptions is not at all*, or is but the same thing with those very perceptions. Here the fundamental reason of this inference is, because we perceive nothing but our own perceptions. But D. B. doth not perceive anything but his own perceptions, more than other men; and if his not perceiving the cause of his perception is a sufficient ground of *denying* such cause, or of making it the same thing with the very perceptions themselves, then God, not being perceived, either is not, or is but a very perception in the mind of man. *Absit blasphemia!* And thus his own argument will exterminate out of nature any other cause of perception he pleases to pitch upon. He says, matter, being once expelled out of nature, drags with it, &c. It is true, matter is but a contingent substance in nature; but, being once expelled out of nature, it drags more along with it, in his method of reasoning, than he is aware of; and it drags least of all our sceptical and impious notions with it, as he pretends. To suppose it absent multiplies these notions without end.

The last question in this demonstration, and which he designed should carry home the conviction of the whole, is, *And is it not plainly repugnant, that any of these [ideas], or any combination of them, should exist unperceived?* Here, you see, he presumes you have allowed him, according to his last query, that *sensations* and their *objects* are the same thing; and on this presumption his argument indeed is conclusive, but if you are not thus far complaisant, he is at a loss. And I answer: Our *ideas* surely cannot exist without the mind, but their *objects* may, and do. And they are still sensible objects, though they fall not under the senses at all times and in all places: i.e., though they are not *objected to the sense* in places where they are not, and at times when our senses are not directed to the places where they are. With respect to this it is observable that he hath another very short way of demonstrating his main point. He *supposes* that the term (to *exist*) hath the same import, when applied to corporeal things, as to be *perceived*, asserting (strongly indeed) that it is otherwise unintelligible. Whence it clearly follows, matter, which is *not perceived*, doth *not exist!* But the artificer seems to understand that his tools exist all the intermediate time after he lays them by at night till he takes them up again next morning. And, after this, it is unaccountable how this author could pretend (Sect. 82) that he doth not deny even corporeal substance in the *vulgar sense*, but only inert senseless matter; as if the artificer thought his tools were *artful, sensible* matter, or disappeared when he had them not in his hands, or even then were nothing but the *ideas* of instruments in the *ideas* of his hands. All this then ends in the following childish sophism: *Sensible things* are but the *objects* of *sense*. Whenever they are not the objects of sense, *they are no longer sensible things*. Therefore, when they are not the objects of sense, or not perceived, they *are not*. But would not D. B. allow his house to be a *combustible thing*, unless it were actually on fire? He might, with equal force of reason, prove that, unless it were in flame, it were no house at all.[8]

The considerable length of Baxter's examination of Berkeley has compelled us to omit some of it.[9] However, we should note that, because he takes the argument of *Principles* §4 to be central, Baxter has little more to say about Berkeley's other arguments, although he does note Berkeley's concession, in *Principles* §22, that if we can even conceive it *possible* for objects to exist without a mind, "I shall readily give up the cause." This becomes an occasion for Baxter to return to the point that the existence of matter must be at least *possible*, and then to argue for its *actual* existence. An interesting feature of his position is that something Berkeley took to be a great benefit of his system – the simplifying of the sciences, including mathematics – becomes in Baxter's eyes one of it fatal flaws. Berkeley, for example, thought it an advantage that problems about infinite divisibility (of the sort we met in Bayle) simply disappear once matter is rejected and it is accepted that ideas are composed of *sensible* minima. In the course of his argument Baxter stands this thinking on its head, arguing that the sciences positively require "matter". We include below a passage that comes immediately after Baxter's analysis of the argument of *Principles* §4, and follow it with other relevant material.

We may farther observe that it doth no great honour to this new scheme, nor those who pretend to admire it, that it forces the author to suspect that even mathematics may not be very sound knowledge at the bottom. In Sect. 118 he says, "To be plain, we suspect the mathematicians are no less deeply concerned than other men in the errors arising from abstract general ideas, and the existence of objects without the mind." And in Sect. 119 he says the theorems in arithmetic are *difficiles nugae*. A man ought to have a vast deal of merit, and to have obliged the world with surprising discoveries, to justify his attacking these sciences at this rate; or rather, no merit possible can warrant it. And it must give us but a bad opinion of the notions that necessitate a man to declare himself thus.[10]

[L]et us consider that whatever part of an idea is not perceived is *no part* of it; its *esse* is really *percipi*. (See D. B's *Principles*, Sect. 132, as also his *Opticks*.) A part of a perception not perceived is a contradiction indeed, being a part of it that is no part of it. Consequently a part less than the *minimum sensibile* (see again Sect. 127) is no part of it, or nothing. Therefore in the *idea* of a solid inch of matter, v.g., there is no part that might be expressed by this number 1,000,000,000,000 in the denominator, having unit for its numerator (or we may make the number greater, for those who have very good eyes), such a part being less than the *minimum sensibile*: or such a part is nothing at all. But if there be no such part, or if the million-millionth part is precisely nothing, the *whole idea* is made up of a million of million of *no ideas*: or the whole idea is no idea. For undoubtedly, a million or any number of nothings will never make something, nor will any number of *negations* of an idea ever make a *real idea*. Two, ten, a hundred, &c. negations of a thing will never amount to the thing itself. Thus unless a *real, solid, figured substance* were at least possible to exist without the mind, such a part of which would be a real part, of the same nature with the whole, our idea of the whole would be *impossible*, and *no idea*. This follows from asserting such a scheme as makes it necessary to maintain that *whatever we perceive not of matter is not*, which this author doth very explicitly. A little *abstraction of ideas*, to which he is such an enemy, would have been of use to him here. . . .

Again, *solidity, figure, divisibility*, &c. are either properties inhering in some substance, or substance itself (that thing, to wit, in which properties inhere, which we call, and must call, substance). If they are substance, *solidity* and *figure* will prove a *solid, figured* substance upon us. If they are only properties, they are either properties of our ideas, or not; if they are, then our ideas *are substance*, with respect to these properties, or the thing in which they inhere, and therefore solid, figured substances. A thing that hath solidity, figure, &c. as properties belonging to it, or predicable concerning it, must be *a solid, figured thing*. But that our ideas should be such, as upon this scheme they must be, is monstrous. At least, therefore, a substance must be possible, of which these are properties, for they are certainly properties of something. And if it be allowed that such properties exist now, or that the thing exists to which they belong, they will infer not only the *possibility*, but the *actual existence*, of matter.[11]

> Geometry, insists Baxter, has no point unless there is "*quantum* in nature" and "*extension* in rerum natura." "And if we allow *extension*, why not an *extended substance*?" Also, talk of such things as *centrifugal forces*, and fluids that are compressed or dilated, makes no sense in a world of "ideas". The upshot, in Baxter's eyes, is that Berkeley's overall scheme must lead to "unbounded scepticism" and "strike at the roots of all science." Nonetheless, Baxter anticipates an objection that might be made:

But, it will be said, could not *God Almighty* have excited all these ideas in separate spirits, and made them capable to investigate these properties of a solid, extended substance, which never actually existed? To this it is answered that indeed these truths concerning a solid extended substance were eternally in the Divine Intellect, before such substance existed. But then surely they were truths only with regard to that substance itself, and not with respect to *immaterial substance*, unless we should say that the real properties of matter were applicable to, and true concerning, a substance *not matter*. Thus, even Infinite Power could not prompt us with these ideas in respect of anything but what we believe to be the *objects* of them, not of our ideas themselves. *Which, by the way, realizes our knowledge and philosophy about material things more than it is of late fashionable to [allow]*.[12]

This being so, the next question is: Whether God Almighty (*a being of infinite veracity*) would have made it necessary for all those separate spirits (whom we call *men*) to pursue and attain a knowledge, less or more, or at least an experience, of the nature of a substance which no way existed, as fancying that a great part of their ease and comfort depended upon this, and have so constituted them that all of this species of beings in the world, not excepting one, are verily persuaded that they are continually conversant with this substance, and that it enters into their composition. The question is, I say, whether this being could have performed such a constant and universal piece of juggling. If it could answer a good and wise end that this substance should exist, *why doth it not exist?* If otherwise, why make us believe a thing exists, whose real existence could have answered no good and wise end? Can any supposition lay God under a necessity of constantly deceiving his creatures? And his rational creatures too? Will not such a supposition contradict his reason and his truth? This will have all the force of a just demonstration to sober men. Besides, since no man can be certain of the existence of other men upon this scheme, and since it is said that God excites in us all the ideas which we fancy are excited by bodies, we must say that when we think we are tempted by other men to commit an unjust or immoral action, God immediately tempts us: and this not only by exciting the ideas of the persuasives in the temptation (of the words and actions, to wit, which are nothing external), but in formally *contriving*, and *suggesting*, the obliquity of the sin we are tempted to. For, as hath been said, taking away the existence of their bodies, there is no kind of evidence left for the existence of the souls of men, who by the abuse of their freedom might tempt us. They who allow God to be a deceiver as to the first, can make no scruple of supposing him to impose on us in the last. I might mention the influence of this new refinement on the lives and practices of men. Though the obliquity of actions rises from the will, he who thinks theft, murder, or adultery nothing real beyond bare idea, and that, for aught he knows, he injures nobody, will be surely under less restraint to satisfy his inclinations of any kind. I might also mention the direct tendency of this improvement to atheism. Men will hardly allow the exciting illusory ideas in our minds of beauty and order, which nowhere really exist, such a proof of the power and wisdom of God, as an actually existing frame of material nature, where the grandeur, harmony, and proportion is permanent and real, existing from without, as well when we turn our thoughts from as to it.[13]

It is at this point that Baxter and Berkeley are most obviously divided. Baxter cannot get beyond the thought that a world of ideas would be "a dream and chimera," with the consequence that to suggest that God was responsible only for the order in *that* world would be to "convince God of a lie," and Baxter actually needs what he himself calls "unwieldy bulks of dead matter" for his own proofs of God's existence and power. Berkeley, of course, sees things very differently. We conclude with the following extract.

Now to return to where we began. Matter is *possible*, as hath been shown just before, but not *necessary*, as hath been also shown. What kind of evidence, or demonstration then, would we have for the existence of such a substance, which we have not? In reason and philosophy, its existence should be known from the *effects* it produces, or the *perceptions* it excites in us, and the perfections of that being who constituted it and our nature such that it should act, and we perceive it acting. To expect we should know it *without sensation* is to demand a proof of its existence inconsistent with the very idea we have of it. To insist that its existence should be investigable by abstract notions, though we get our ideas originally from sense, by which matter must first enter, is to show a great unskilfulness, or a fixed resolution to doubt; it is to suppose it a necessary and not a contingent being. Its existence hath no eternal necessary properties belonging to it; nor the existence of anything save the Deity. Therefore I conclude that the knowledge of the existence of external material objects, by sense, is *certain knowledge*, and the evidence as great as possibility and the nature of things can admit of, and, therefore, as great as the reasonable soul (as such) can desire.[14]

* * *

Whatever the strengths or weaknesses of Baxter's various criticisms of Berkeley, Berkeley's own judgment was that they did not merit a reply – that "to answer objections already answered, and repeat the same things, is a needless as well as disagreeable task."[15] Berkeley, we have seen, had long wanted the *Principles* to be taken seriously. He must have been disappointed both by the tone of Baxter's critique and by what he no doubt saw as a total misreading of his position, based as it was on a selective reading of his text, a tendency to ignore genuine difficulties in the concept of "matter", and an almost complete neglect of Berkeley's own attempts to anticipate and answer objections. For all that, one cannot help having some sympathy for Baxter. At one level, his reading of Berkeley as a skeptic, who adopted a position that could convince nobody, was a common one. Hume, we will see, took much the same view. At a deeper level, it has to be recognized that, without the benefit of any significant body of Berkeley scholarship to guide him, Baxter did make an earnest effort to grapple with some of Berkeley's actual arguments. He lacked, to be sure, the acuity of Samuel Johnson of Connecticut, who – as his letters to Berkeley show – had a far better understanding of Berkeley's position; but Baxter was a much abler critic than someone like Beattie, in whom, nearly thirty years later, we find the misunderstandings, but no careful attempt at argument.[16] Moreover, if Baxter does not tackle all issues as well as one might wish, some of his objections were arguably on the right track. Many more recent commentators would agree with him, for example, that the argument of *Principles* §4 is quite central for Berkeley and merits careful analysis, and a number would agree that Berkeley is particularly vulnerable when it comes to the problem of other minds. Equally, although all serious commentators now acknowledge that Berkeley *attempted* to reconcile his idealism with the beliefs of the "vulgar" about reality, far fewer see him as successful; while, in insisting that Berkeley failed to distinguish *sensations* from *objects* of sensation, Baxter anticipated an objection that subsequent critics from Thomas Reid to G. E. Moore would develop. Finally, we may say of Baxter that he expressed more fully than anyone before him the prevailing judgment on Berkeley's immaterialism in the two decades following the publication of the *Principles*.

Notes

1. Quoted in Bracken, *The Early Reception of Berkeley's Immaterialism*, p. 60.
2. Baxter, pp. 235–40. Baxter's book went through three editions (1733, 1737, and 1745), but with no changes of any substance. Our references are to the third edition (London, 1745), vol. 2.
3. Baxter, pp. 257–60.
4. J. M. Hone and M. M. Rossi, *Bishop Berkeley: His Life, Writings, and Philosophy* (London: Faber and Faber, 1931), p. 178n.
5. Baxter, pp. 261–62.
6. Bracken, p. 61. Bracken, Chapter 4, is on Chambers, and Appendix G gives extracts from the *Cyclopaedia*.
7. Baxter is referring to the passage in which he argued that, if the premise that

we perceive only our own perceptions leads to the conclusion that material substances do not exist, it will also prove the same of other spirits, "without excepting the Deity himself."

8. Baxter, pp. 264–75.

9. It is with some regret that we have omitted, for example, a long footnote in which Baxter ponders Berkeley's supposedly unaccountable claim that "to exist", in the case of corporeal objects, actually *means* the same as "to be perceived". We also omit the three closing parts of the section, which focus on Descartes, as well as a final note of about 4,000 words (which is in all three editions), in which Baxter replies to objections that he says have been made to his attempt to refute Berkeley. There is interesting material here and, if we suspected that any of the objections had come from Berkeley himself, we would certainly include them. It seems most unlikely that any did.

10. Baxter, pp. 275–76.

11. Baxter, pp. 278–80, 282–83.

12. The point of this italicized remark is made somewhat clearer by Baxter's endorsement in a footnote of an "axiom" proposed in Descartes' reply to the second set of *Objections* to the *Meditations*. Descartes writes: "[T]he objective reality of our ideas needs a cause which contains this reality not merely objectively but formally or eminently. It should be noted that this axiom is one which we must necessarily accept, since on it depends our knowledge of all things, whether they are perceivable through the senses or not."

13. Baxter, pp. 287–91.

14. Baxter, pp. 292–94.

15. From a 1734 letter to Johnson (*Works* VIII, p. 236), which contains Berkeley's only explicit mention of Baxter. Luce has suggested that Baxter's comments on Berkeley's treatment of mathematics may have played a role, however, in encouraging Berkeley to write the *Analyst*, which was published in the same year. See *Works* IV, p. 95 and note; cf. p. 56. Berkeley there refers to an unnamed person who had called upon him to "make good" what he had said on the topic in the *Principles*. If Baxter was that person, Berkeley's judgment of him was harsh indeed, for, said Berkeley, he "doth not appear to think maturely enough to understand either those metaphysics which he would refute, or mathematics which he would patronize." For a careful examination of Baxter's critique of Berkeley, see Bracken, Chapter 5.

16. James Beattie, *An Essay on the Nature and Immutability of Truth* (Edinburgh, 1770), Part 2, Chapter 2, Section 2.

SIXTEEN

David Hume

In 1737, at about the time he completed the manuscript of the *Treatise of Human Nature*, Hume wrote to his friend Michael Ramsay that to "easily comprehend the metaphysical parts of my reasoning," he should read Malebranche's *Search after Truth*, Berkeley's *Principles*, some of the "more metaphysical articles" in Bayle's *Dictionary*, and Descartes' *Meditations*.[1] This list is instructive both because it shows what works Hume thought would help a reader in understanding the *Treatise*, and because it should warn us against the hazards of two opposite tendencies in interpreting Hume. One is the tendency to which generations of students have been exposed in courses on "The Empiricists", where the impression may sometimes have been given that Locke, Berkeley, and Hume formed a self-contained philosophical movement, with Hume's views developing solely from the insight that Berkeley's criticisms of Locke could be pushed in an even more radical direction. The opposite tendency has been to hold that Berkeley was of only minor importance for Hume. A noted proponent of this latter view, Norman Kemp Smith, thought that Hume admired Berkeley's critique of abstraction, but that "in Berkeley's writings he does not seem otherwise to have been much interested."[2] The most extreme expression of it came when Richard Popkin (writing before the discovery of Hume's letter to Ramsay) said, "It is highly questionable, I believe, whether Hume ever read Berkeley, or derived any views from him."[3]

The letter to Ramsay suggests the need for a more balanced view. It shows, on the one hand, that Hume's views did not develop exclusively in the context of "British Empiricism"; on the other hand, it makes it unlikely that Hume had only a marginal interest in

Berkeley (still less that he had not read him).⁴ It would be surprising if Hume included, on a short list of works he thought would make his views more comprehensible, a book of little importance in the formation of those views.⁵ Nor is the fact that Berkeley is mentioned only once in the *Treatise* evidence that he played only a minor role in Hume's development. Hume rarely mentions other philosophers; in the *Treatise* Malebranche is mentioned twice, Bayle once, and Descartes not at all. Yet Hume urged Ramsay to read them all to better understand the *Treatise*, and the influence of Malebranche and Bayle can be discerned in it at a number of points. So, too, there is evidence of Berkeley's influence. To acknowledge that is neither to ignore the great differences between the two thinkers nor to suggest that a thinker of Hume's originality would merely take over somebody else's ideas without modification. It is not to be expected, therefore, that we will find Hume simply reproducing arguments from Berkeley. What we will find are certain parallels between the two thinkers that make it plausible to think that, at these junctures at any rate, Hume had learned lessons from Berkeley. We limit ourselves to the two topics where Hume himself spoke in praise of Berkeley's views.

1. Abstract Ideas

Hume proclaimed Berkeley's account of general ideas "one of the greatest and most valuable discoveries" of the day and sought to "confirm it" by arguments of his own. To this end, in the *Treatise*, Book 1, Part 1, §7, he first gives three arguments to prove that we cannot form ideas that are not fully determinate with respect to quantity and quality; then he gives an account of what general ideas are and how we come by them. Each of the three preliminary arguments invokes one of his own principles, but they also reflect a conviction Hume shares with Berkeley that an "idea", when not an actual sense impression, is a kind of image.⁶ In his first and third arguments there are further parallels with Berkeley. The first argument is that we cannot distinguish the precise degree of a quality from the quality, nor the precise length of a line, say, from the line itself; hence they are inseparable in our idea of them. Berkeley, too, firmly rejected the notion that we can form the idea of a quality or mode that has no determinate degree, denying, for example, that we can form an idea of motion "which is neither swift nor slow, curvilinear nor rectilinear" (*PHK*, Introduction §10). Hume's third argument is that what is impossible in fact must be impossible in idea. Berkeley would concur, and Hume's example of the absurdity of supposing "a triangle really existent, which has no precise proportion of sides and angles," and hence of supposing there is any such idea, can hardly fail to remind one of Berkeley's "killing blow" against Locke.

After arguing against the possibility of ideas that are *intrinsically* abstract, Hume describes the psychological mechanism whereby general ideas are formed, and in the process shows us "the nature of our abstract ideas and general terms." While he goes beyond Berkeley in his account of that mechanism, his view of the nature of those ideas and terms is close to Berkeley's. Here is Berkeley on what a general *word* is: "a word becomes general by being made the sign, not of an abstract general idea but, of several particular ideas, any one of which it indifferently suggests to the mind" (*PHK*, Introduction §11). Hume's view is the same: a term becomes general when it has "a customary conjunction" with many particular ideas. As for what a general *idea* is, Berkeley says: "an idea, which considered in it self is particular, becomes general, by being made to represent or stand for all other particular ideas of the same sort" (*PHK*, Introduction §12). Hume's view is similar, although the details of how one idea comes to represent other ideas – an account that involves his principle of the association of ideas – will not be found in Berkeley. That there should be originality here is hardly surprising – as Hume said of himself in the *Abstract* of the *Treatise*, "if any thing can intitle the author to so glorious a name as that of an *inventor*, 'tis the use he makes of the principle of the association of ideas, which enters into most of his philosophy".[7] It does not detract from the fact that the initial insight is one he attributes to Berkeley, and sees himself as confirming and developing. Hence the praise for Berkeley with which our extract begins.

A very material question has been started concerning *abstract* or *general* ideas, *whether they be general or particular in the mind's conception of them*. A great philosopher [in a footnote, Hume specifies: Dr. *Berkeley*] has disputed the receiv'd opinion in this particular, and has asserted, that all general ideas are nothing but particular ones, annexed to a certain term, which gives them a more extensive signification, and makes them recall upon occasion other individuals, which are similar to them. As I look upon this to be one of the greatest and most valuable discoveries that has been made of late years in the republic of letters, I shall here endeavour to confirm it by some arguments, which I hope will put it beyond all doubt and controversy. . . .

[O]ur abstract ideas have been suppos'd to represent no particular degree either of quantity or quality. But that this inference is erroneous, I shall endeavour to make appear, *first*, by proving, that 'tis utterly impossible to conceive any quantity or quality, without forming a precise notion of its degrees: And *secondly* by showing, that tho' the capacity of the mind be not infinite, yet we can at once form a notion of all possible degrees of quantity and quality, in such a manner at least, as, however imperfect, may serve all the purposes of reflexion and conversation.

To begin with the first proposition, *that the mind cannot form any notion of quantity or quality without forming a precise notion of the degrees of each*; we may prove this by the three following arguments. First, We have observ'd, that whatever objects are different are distinguishable, and that whatever objects are distinguishable are separable by the thought and imagination. And we may here add, that these propositions are equally true in the *inverse*, and that whatever objects are separable are also distinguishable, and that whatever objects are distinguishable are also different. For how is it possible we can separate what is not distinguishable, or distinguish what is not different? In order therefore to know, whether abstraction implies a separation, we need only consider it in this view, and examine, whether all the circumstances, which we abstract from in our general ideas, be such as are distinguishable and different from those, which we retain as essential parts of them. But 'tis evident at first sight, that the precise length of a line is not different nor distinguishable from the line itself; nor the precise degree of any quality from the quality. These ideas, therefore, admit no more of separation than they do of distinction and difference. They are consequently conjoined with each other in the conception; and the general idea of a line, notwithstanding all our abstractions and refinements, has in its appearance in the mind a precise degree of quantity and quality; however it may be made to represent others, which have different degrees of both.

We omit Hume's second argument, which turns on his principle that ideas are copies of impressions. Since impressions are fully determinate in respect of quality and quantity, Hume argues, ideas must be fully determinate, too.

Thirdly, 'tis a principle generally receiv'd in philosophy, that every thing in nature is individual, and that 'tis utterly absurd to suppose a triangle really existent, which has no precise proportion of sides and angles. If this therefore be absurd in *fact and reality*, it must also be absurd *in idea*; since nothing of which we can form a clear and distinct idea is absurd and impossible. But to form the idea of an object, and to form an idea simply is the same thing; the reference of the idea to an object being an extraneous denomination, of which in itself it bears no mark or character. Now as 'tis impossible to form an idea of an object, that is possest of quantity and quality, and yet is possest of no precise degree of either; it follows, that there is an equal impossibility of forming an idea, that is not limited and confin'd in both these particulars. Abstract ideas are therefore in themselves individual, however they may become general in their representation. The image in the mind is only that of a particular object, tho' the application of it in our reasoning be the same, as if it were universal.

Hume now proceeds to explain how certain ideas can be "particular in their nature," but at the same time "general in their representation."

This application of ideas beyond their nature proceeds from our collecting all their possible degrees of quantity and quality in such an imperfect manner as may serve the purposes of life, which is the second proposition I propos'd to explain. When we have found a resemblance among several objects, that often occur to us, we apply the same name to all of them, whatever differences we may observe in the degrees of their quantity and quality, and whatever other differences may appear among them. After we have acquired a custom of this kind, the hearing of that name revives the idea of one of these objects, and makes the imagination conceive it with all its particular circumstances and proportions. But as the same word is suppos'd to have been frequently applied to other individuals, that are different in many respects from that idea, which is immediately present to the mind; the word not being able to revive the idea of all these individuals, only touches the soul, if I may be allow'd so to speak, and revives that custom, which we have acquir'd by surveying them. They are not really and in fact present to the mind, but only in power; nor do we draw them all out distinctly in the imagination, but keep ourselves in a readiness to survey any of them, as we may be prompted by a present design or necessity. The word raises up an individual idea, along with a certain custom; and that custom produces any other individual one, for which we may have occasion. . . .

Nay so entire is the custom, that the very same idea may be annext to several different words, and may be employ'd in different reasonings, without any danger of mistake. Thus the idea of an equilateral triangle of an inch perpendicular may serve us in talking of a figure, of a rectilineal figure, of a regular figure, of a triangle, and of an equilateral triangle. All these terms, therefore, are in this case attended with the same idea; but as they are wont to be apply'd in a greater or lesser compass, they excite their particular habits, and thereby keep the mind in a readiness to observe, that no conclusion be form'd contrary to any ideas, which are usually compriz'd under them.

. . . ['T]is certain *that* we form the idea of individuals, whenever we use any general term; *that* we seldom or never can exhaust these individuals; and *that* those, which remain, are only represented by means of that habit, by which we recall them, whenever any present occasion requires it. This then is the nature of our abstract ideas and general terms; and 'tis after this manner we account for the foregoing paradox, *that some ideas are particular in their nature, but general in their representation*. A particular idea becomes general by being annex'd to a general term; that is, to a term, which from a customary conjunction has a relation to many other particular ideas, and readily recalls them in the imagination.[8]

2. The Existence of External Objects

Four sections of the *Treatise* deal with the topic of external objects (Book 1, Part 2, §6, and Part 4, §§2–4). This account, covering many pages, cannot be reproduced here. Instead, we shall give a sketch (omitting much important detail) of the position taken in the *Treatise*, followed by an extract from Hume's briefer presentation of his position in the *Enquiry concerning Human Understanding*. We do this because some of the similarities and differences between Hume and Berkeley on this matter can be more readily discerned in the *Treatise*, even though it is only in the discussion in the *Enquiry* that Berkeley is actually named.

The topic is introduced in Book 1, Part 2, §6 ("Of the idea of existence, and of external existence"), with Hume observing that "the idea of existence must either be deriv'd from a distinct impression, conjoin'd with every perception or object of our thought, or must be the very same with the idea of the perception or object." The first of these alternatives is rejected, thus leaving Hume committed to the second. Moreover (echoing *PHK* §1), " 'tis universally allow'd by philosophers, and is besides pretty obvious of itself, that nothing is ever really present with the mind but its perceptions or impressions and ideas." Hume's striking conclusion here, which is reminiscent of the one Berkeley draws in *PHK* §6, is: "Let us chace our imagination to the heavens, or to the utmost limits of the universe; we never really advance a step beyond ourselves, nor can conceive any kind of existence, but those perceptions, which have appear'd in that narrow compass."[9]

Hence the problem: what is the basis of our belief that objects have a continuing existence distinct from our transient perceptions? Hume addresses it in Book 1, Part 4, §2 ("Of scepticism with regard to the senses"). And what quickly emerges is that, for Hume, the belief is not one that can be simply dismissed, for, in practice, even the skeptic assents to the existence of body. The problem, therefore, is that of *accounting for* the belief, since according to Hume it is not susceptible to rational justification. Much of the discussion in the section is devoted to this, but this is not a matter we shall dwell on, for it owes little if anything to Berkeley. What is of interest is Hume's agreement with the skeptic that the belief is not one that can be *justified*. Indeed, under analysis, it would appear that the belief is actually false.

Ordinary people ("the vulgar"), Hume notes, make no distinction between *perceptions* and *objects*, and consequently attribute an independent and continuous existence to their perceptions, but the philosopher sees, correctly, that "every thing, which appears to the mind, is nothing but a perception, and is interrupted, and dependent on the mind." The vulgar form of the belief is "unreasonable" and, apparently, unsustainable. However, philosophers go wrong too. Because they, like the vulgar, are committed to the view that bodies have a continuous and independent existence, they take up the defense of an untenable "double existence of perceptions and objects." This analysis clearly has much in common with Berkeley's in *PHK* §56, where Berkeley also recognizes that "the vulgar" maintain that *ideas* have an existence independent of the mind "without ever dreaming that a contradiction [is] involved in those words," and then, like Hume, sees the philosophers as shifting to another position "which seems no less absurd, to wit, that there are certain objects really existing without the mind . . . of which our ideas are only images or resemblances, imprinted by those objects on the mind."

Certainly, for Hume, as for Berkeley, the philosophers' position here admits of no rational justification. The only reasoning that could establish it would be causal reasoning that began with our perceptions and inferred the existence of objects as their cause. "But as no beings are ever present to the mind but perceptions; it follows that we may observe a conjunction or a relation of cause and effect between different perceptions, but can never observe it between perceptions and objects. 'Tis impossible, therefore, that from the existence or any of the qualities of the former, we can ever form any conclusion concerning the existence of the latter, or ever satisfy our reason in this particular." Furthermore, even if the existence of "external continu'd objects" *could* be inferred, we would have to suppose them to be *like* our perceptions, for "we never can conceive any thing but perceptions, and therefore must make every thing resemble them." And yet, "we shou'd never have any reason to infer" that the supposed resemblance obtains. We are therefore left either with no conception of the supposed objects at all, or with the unjustifiable belief that they are like our perceptions. The claim that we "must make every thing resemble" our perceptions – or, as he put it in Book 1, Part 2, §6, that objects cannot be conceived of as "*specifically* different" from them – is Hume's version of the principle Berkeley expressed as "an idea can be like nothing but an idea" (*PHK* §8). Berkeley thinks it *refutes* the theory that ideas are "copies or resemblances" of things that are not ideas; Hume more cautiously says that, even *if* we allow that something that is not a perception could be like a perception, we could never justify belief in its existence.

In Book 1, Part 4, §4 ("Of the modern philosophy"), Hume argues against the "modern philosophers" who – viewing secondary qualities as mere perceptions – hold that bodies have only the primary qualities. The chief primary qualities, he says, are motion, extension, and solidity. Now the idea of motion *presupposes* that of a body *in* motion, and thus that of extension or solidity. However, the idea of extension itself presupposes that of color or solidity, for it is only colored or solid things that we can conceive of as extended. If, therefore, we exclude color from our idea of body, on the ground that it has no real existence, our idea of body must depend on that of solidity. But we can only form the idea of solidity by thinking of two bodies that do not penetrate each other; hence, to think of solidity, we must already have the idea of these bodies.

> Now what idea have we of these bodies? The ideas of colours, sounds, and other secondary qualities are excluded. The idea of motion depends on that of extension, and the idea of extension on that of solidity. 'Tis impossible, therefore, that the idea of solidity can depend on either of them. For that wou'd be to run in a circle, and make one idea depend on another, while at the same time the latter depends on the former. Our modern philosophy, therefore, leaves us no just nor satisfactory idea of solidity; nor consequently of matter.[10]

The conclusion Hume draws is that, if we allow that the secondary qualities have no existence independent of the mind, "there remains nothing in the universe, which has such an existence." Hume's point had already been made in the *Principles* (§§10–11), where Berkeley argued that "without extension solidity cannot be conceived" and that "extension, figure, and motion, abstracted from all other qualities, are inconceivable." And Hume's conclusion is much the same as the conclusion Berkeley reached in those sections.

The parallels between a number of Hume's arguments about "external existence" and some of Berkeley's suggest that Hume did learn useful lessons from Berkeley. Yet at no point did Hume slavishly follow him. In many ways the thinking of the two philosophers is clearly very different. To take one obvious case, even in the section "Of scepticism with regard to the senses," Hume alludes to a view he will defend in a later section that a mind is "nothing but a heap or collection of different perceptions, united together by certain relations." Hume could not have known, as we do, that the view that the mind is "a congeries of Perceptions" was one that Berkeley had himself toyed with in the *Philosophical Commentaries* (entries 577–81), but he must certainly have known that Berkeley's mature view was that the mind is a *substance*, and "entirely distinct" from its ideas.[11]

Moreover, even on the question of our belief in the continuous and independent existence of bodies there is very clear daylight between Berkeley and Hume. What is central for Hume is that reason and our natural beliefs are in *conflict* about whether "bodies" exist; so, against this background, he tries to explain why our natural beliefs inevitably triumph. As he says at the end of Part 4, §2, he takes it for granted that, even if the reader has seen that the arguments *against* the existence of bodies are indeed unanswerable, "an hour hence he will be persuaded there is both an external and internal world." Much of the section has been devoted to a psychological account of *how* we come by our ordinary beliefs concerning "bodies", and *why* those beliefs remain irresistible *despite* what reason would suggest. Berkeley's attitude to our ordinary beliefs may not be totally consistent, but, although he does sometimes write in a way that suggests that even the "vulgar" are mistaken in this area (e.g., *PHK* §§4 and 54–57),[12] his *preferred* line seems to be that *his* philosophical system actually *vindicates* our ordinary beliefs. If Hume was unimpressed by this claim, that is perhaps not surprising.

Here now is the extract from Hume's briefer statement of his position in the *Enquiry*.

It seems evident, that men are carried, by a natural instinct or prepossession, to repose faith in their senses; and that, without any reasoning, or even almost before the use of reason, we always suppose an external universe, which depends not on our perception, but would exist, though we and every sensible creature were absent or annihilated. Even the animal creation are governed by a like opinion, and preserve this belief of external objects, in all their thoughts, designs, and actions.

It seems also evident, that, when men follow this blind and powerful instinct of nature, they always suppose the very images, presented by the senses, to be the external objects, and never entertain any suspicion, that the one are nothing but representations of the other. This very table, which we see white, and which we feel hard, is believed to exist, independent of our perception, and to be something external to our mind, which perceives it. Our presence bestows not being on it: our absence does not annihilate it. It preserves its existence uniform and entire, independent of the situation of intelligent beings, who perceive or contemplate it.

But this universal and primary opinion of all men is soon destroyed by the slightest philosophy, which teaches us, that nothing can ever be present to the mind but an image or perception, and that the senses are only the inlets, through which these images are conveyed, without being able to produce any immediate intercourse between the mind and the object. The table, which we see, seems to diminish, as we remove farther from it: but the real table, which exists independent of us, suffers no alteration: it was, therefore, nothing but its image, which was present to the mind. These are the obvious dictates of reason; and no man, who reflects, ever doubted, that the existences, which we consider, when we say, *this house* and *that tree*, are nothing but perceptions in the mind, and fleeting copies or representations of other existences, which remain uniform and independent.

So far, then, are we necessitated by reasoning to contradict or depart from the primary instincts of nature, and to embrace a new system with regard to the evidence of our senses. But here philosophy finds herself extremely embarrassed, when she would justify this new system, and obviate the cavils and objections of the sceptics. She can no longer plead the infallible and irresistible instinct of nature: for that led us to a quite different system, which is acknowledged fallible and even erroneous. And to justify this pretended philosophical system, by a chain of clear and convincing argument, or even any appearance of argument, exceeds the power of all human capacity.

By what argument can it be proved, that the perceptions of the mind must be caused by external objects, entirely different from them, though resembling them (if that be possible) and could not arise either from the energy of the mind itself, or from the suggestion of some invisible and unknown spirit, or from some other cause still more unknown to us? It is acknowledged, that, in fact, many of these perceptions arise not from anything external, as in dreams, madness, and other diseases. And nothing can be more inexplicable than the manner, in which body should so operate upon mind as ever to convey an image of itself to a substance, supposed of so different, and even contrary a nature.

It is a question of fact, whether the perceptions of the senses be produced by external objects, resembling them: how shall this question be determined? By experience surely; as all other questions of a like nature. But here experience is, and must be entirely silent. The mind has never anything present to it but the perceptions, and cannot possibly reach any experience of their connexion with objects. The supposition of such a connexion is, therefore, without any foundation in reasoning.

To have recourse to the veracity of the supreme Being, in order to prove the veracity of our senses, is surely making a very unexpected circuit. If his veracity were at all concerned in this matter, our sense would be entirely infallible; because it is not possible that he can ever deceive. Not to mention, that, if the external world be once called in question, we shall be at a loss to find arguments, by which we may prove the existence of that Being or any of his attributes.

This is a topic, therefore, in which the profounder and more philosophical sceptics will always triumph, when they endeavour to introduce an universal doubt into all subjects of human knowledge and enquiry. Do you follow the instincts and propensities of nature, may they say, in assenting to the veracity of sense? But these lead you to believe that the very perception or sensible image is the external object. Do you disclaim this principle, in order to embrace a more rational opinion, that the perceptions are only representations of something external? You here depart from your natural propensities and more obvious sentiments; and yet are not able to satisfy your reason, which can never find any convincing argument from experience to prove, that the perceptions are connected with any external objects.

There is another sceptical topic of a like nature, derived from the most profound philosophy; which might merit our attention, were it requisite to dive so deep, in order to discover arguments and reasonings, which can so little serve to any serious purpose. It is universally allowed by modern enquirers, that all the sensible qualities of objects, such as hard, soft, hot, cold, white, black, &c. are merely secondary, and exist not in the objects themselves, but are perceptions of the mind, without any external archetype or model, which they represent. If this be allowed, with regard to secondary qualities, it must also follow, with regard to the supposed primary qualities of extension and solidity; nor can the latter be any more entitled to that denomination than the former. The idea of extension is entirely acquired from the senses of sight and feeling; and if all the qualities, perceived by the senses, be in the mind, not in the object, the same conclusion must reach the idea of extension, which is wholly dependent on the sensible ideas or the ideas of secondary qualities. Nothing can save us from this conclusion, but the asserting, that the ideas of those primary qualities are attained by *Abstraction*, an opinion, which, if we examine it accurately, we shall find to be unintelligible, and even absurd. An extension, that is neither tangible nor visible, cannot possibly be conceived: and a tangible or visible extension, which is neither hard nor soft, black nor white, is equally beyond the reach of human conception. Let any man try to conceive a triangle in general, which is neither *Isosceles* nor *Scalenum*, nor has any particular length or proportion of sides; and he will soon perceive the absurdity of all the scholastic notions with regard to abstraction and general ideas.

Hume here adds the following footnote:

This argument is drawn from Dr. Berkeley; and indeed most of the writings of that very ingenious author form the best lessons of scepticism, which are to be found either among the ancient or modern philosophers, Bayle not excepted. He professes, however, in his title-page (and undoubtedly with great truth) to have composed his book against the sceptics as well as against the atheists and free-thinkers. But that all his arguments, though otherwise intended, are, in reality, merely sceptical, appears from this, *that they admit of no answer and produce no conviction.* Their only effect is to cause that momentary amazement and irresolution and confusion, which is the result of scepticism.[13]

After the footnote, this part concludes:

Thus the first philosophical objection to the evidence of sense or to the opinion of external existence consists in this, that such an opinion, if rested on natural instinct, is contrary to reason, and if referred to reason, is contrary to natural instinct, and at the same time carries no rational evidence with it, to convince an impartial enquirer. The second objection goes farther, and represents this opinion as contrary to reason: at least, if it be a principle of reason, that all sensible qualities are in the mind, not in the object. Bereave matter of all its intelligible qualities, both primary and secondary, you in a manner annihilate it, and leave only a certain unknown, inexplicable *something*, as the cause of our perceptions; a notion so imperfect, that no sceptic will think it worth while to contend against it.[14]

* * *

The topics we have considered are not the only ones where there are parallels that suggest a probable influence of Berkeley on Hume. Others include the notion of substance as a collection of qualities (Hume's notion of substance and Berkeley's of "corporeal substance"); the notion of *minima sensibilia*; the reduction of space to an ordering of *minima sensibilia*, with the corresponding rejection of the doctrines of the infinite divisibility of space and of absolute or empty space; the notion of time as a succession of ideas, and the rejection of both absolute and infinitely divisible time.[15] We have dwelt only on two areas where Hume explicitly acknowledges Berkeley's contribution. Without detracting from Hume's indisputable originality, or taking the view that Berkeley was Hume's most important source, we should acknowledge that Berkeley was *one* among several thinkers who were important in the development of Hume's thought.

Notes

1. The letter can be found in R. H. Popkin, "So, Hume did Read Berkeley," *Journal of Philosophy* 61 (1964), pp. 774–75.
2. N. Kemp Smith, *The Philosophy of David Hume: A Critical Study of its Origins and Central Doctrines* (London: Macmillan, 1941), p. 257, note 1.
3. R. H. Popkin, in his review of George Boas, *Dominant Themes of Modern Philosophy*, *Journal of Philosophy* 56 (1959), p. 71.
4. In an earlier letter to Ramsay, dated 29th September 1734, Hume said it was a pleasure "to read over again today" Berkeley's *Principles*. The letter was first published in Michael Morrisroe, Jr, "Did Hume Read Berkeley? A Conclusive Answer," *Philological Quarterly* 52 (1973), pp. 310–15.
5. For a balanced estimate of Berkeley's influence on Hume, see Michael Ayers, "Berkeley and Hume: a question of influence," in *Philosophy in History: Essays on the Historiography of Philosophy*, ed. R. Rorty, J. B. Schneewind, and Q. Skinner (Cambridge: Cambridge University Press, 1984).
6. Berkeley uses "idea" for both sense impressions and images of the memory and imagination, whereas Hume calls the former "impressions" and only the latter "ideas". That distinction is not relevant here, for no one supposed that abstract ideas were sense impressions.
7. *A Treatise of Human Nature*, ed. L. A. Selby-Bigge. Second edition by P. H. Nidditch (Oxford: Clarendon Press, 1978), pp. 661–62.
8. *Treatise*, pp. 17–22.
9. In the Appendix to the *Treatise* Hume stresses that "we have no abstract idea of existence" (*Treatise*, p. 623), a claim that was central in Berkeley's thinking, too. Some years later, when defending the theological innocuousness of the claim that "we have no general idea of existence, distinct from every particular existence," Hume noted that in denying abstract ideas he was following "the present pious and learned Bishop of Cloyne." See *A Letter to a Gentleman from his Friend in Edinburgh* (first published in 1745), ed. E. C. Mossner and J. V. Price (Edinburgh: Edinburgh University Press, 1967), p. 26.
10. *Treatise*, p. 229.
11. It may be, however, that Berkeley's influence shows through even here. David Raynor, who argues that Hume had read the *Dialogues* as well as the *Principles*, suggests that Hume may have found the inspiration for his "bundle" theory of the self in Hylas's suggestion that Philonous (the Berkeleian) *should* regard the self as "a system of floating ideas." See David Raynor, "Hume and Berkeley's *Three Dialogues*," in *Studies in the Philosophy of the Scottish Enlightenment*, ed. M. A. Stewart (Oxford: Clarendon Press, 1990).
12. In *PHK* §§54–57, Berkeley is in effect tackling the same question that Hume puts to himself, though for Berkeley it comes in the form of an objection that

might be put to his own position – viz., that "the universal concurrent assent of mankind" is "an invincible argument in behalf of matter, or the existence of external things." What is interesting about these sections is that, after suggesting that *nobody* can hold this belief – "strictly speaking, to believe that which involves a contradiction, or has no meaning in it, is impossible" – Berkeley appears to concede that both the "vulgar" and the "philosophers" *do* (in their several ways) hold this belief, even though the belief is "absurd" and ought to be *corrected*. The contrast with Hume here is that Hume insists that the belief *must* be taken seriously, not, indeed, as one that can be *justified*, but as one that nobody – including Hume himself – can give up.

13. That this cannot be dismissed as a mere jibe against Berkeley, in the spirit of Andrew Baxter, or as merely "a chastisement of Berkeley for his skepticism," as Popkin once suggested, should be obvious. At this point in the *Enquiry* Hume is himself stressing that the arguments against external existence are unanswerable, even though he also holds that we are so constituted that we cannot accept them. Consequently, Ayers is surely right when he says of Hume's point about Berkeley's writings (they provide "the best lessons of scepticism, which are to be found either among the ancient or modern philosophers") that, coming from a skeptic, "even from a sceptic of a rather special sort, such comment would seem to be praise indeed." (Ayers [see note 5], p. 305.)

14. *An Enquiry concerning Human Understanding*, ed. L. A. Selby-Bigge. Third edition by P. H. Nidditch (Oxford: Clarendon Press, 1975), Section XII, Part I, pp. 151–55.

15. For discussion of some of these parallels, see David Raynor, " '*Minima Sensibilia*' in Berkeley and Hume," *Dialogue* 19 (1980), pp. 196–200; and Ayers, pp. 306–14.

SEVENTEEN

Samuel Johnson

No philosopher of the eighteenth century followed Berkeley more closely than the American thinker Samuel Johnson (1696–1772), the first president of King's College, New York (now Columbia University).[1] It is not surprising, perhaps, that Berkeley's writings found a sympathetic reader in New England, where the works of the Cambridge Platonist Ralph Cudworth and of Malebranche and John Norris had already found a receptive audience. The Puritan theology that dominated so much of New England's early thinking had, after all, itself stressed the total dependence of creatures on God and had taught that there is in the divine mind an archetypal idea of the whole of creation. Indeed, Jonathan Edwards, the leading colonial thinker of the early eighteenth century, taught a doctrine of occasionalism that was not unlike Malebranche's and of immaterialism that had some affinities with Berkeley's.[2] There was, therefore, fertile soil in New England for the seeds of Berkeley's immaterialism to take root in.

Johnson was reared a Congregationalist and educated at Yale in the Ramist philosophy favored by the Puritans, but as a young Yale tutor he became an avid reader and defender of the "new philosophers", studying the works of Locke, Newton, and Norris. He also read works of Anglican apologetics and converted to Anglicanism, becoming the first Anglican priest in Connecticut. Berkeley's arrival in Rhode Island, in 1729, was a notable event for the New England Anglican community, for Berkeley was both a noted Anglican thinker and, as Dean of Derry, the highest-ranking Anglican prelate thus far to visit New England. Johnson had recently read Berkeley's *Principles*, and he soon journeyed from Connecticut to Rhode Island to meet him. On that visit, and others, and in letters, they discussed

Berkeley's views at length. The upshot was that Johnson became an immaterialist, although not before he had raised some penetrating questions about Berkeley's system.[3]

In 1752, Johnson published his major work, *Elementa Philosophica*, the first textbook in philosophy printed in America. It is dedicated to Berkeley, and in it one meets many familiar Berkeleian themes: that bodies are combinations of passive ideas and exist only if perceived; that spirits are active, perceiving beings; that spirits alone are true causes; that God is the cause of our sense perceptions, and thus of the sensible world. But Johnson did not hesitate to join to Berkeley's doctrines others he had learned from Norris, Malebranche, Cudworth, Fénelon, and others. Thus, for example, he embraced the broadly Augustinian doctrine defended by several of these thinkers, according to which we possess – in addition to sense, imagination, and memory – a "pure intellect" that is illuminated by the light of the divine mind, whereby God enables us to perceive the "eternal truths" of logic, mathematics, metaphysics, and morality. This doctrine and Berkeley's seemed to him not just compatible but complementary: God is the cause of our perception of both the sensible and the intelligible worlds.

Johnson also seems to have thought that something like Malebranche's and Norris's theory of "infinite intelligible extension" (according to which the whole extended universe is a copy of an ideal and intelligible extension that exists in God's mind) could be used to clarify Berkeley's doctrine of archetypes. In the *Three Dialogues*, Berkeley had said that things have a twofold existence, as ectypes in our minds and archetypes in God's mind, but he gave no definite account of what we are to understand these archetypes to be.[4] In his letters to Berkeley, Johnson twice questioned him about his doctrine of archetypes. Did he not mean that our ideas are imperfect *copies* of God's ideas – the divine idea being "the original or archetype of ours, and ours a copy or image of His (our ideas images of His, in the same sense as our souls are images of Him)"?[5] If so, Johnson suggested, several objections that immaterialism might seem open to could be answered. To the objection that, for the immaterialist, things are impermanent and unstable, the reply must be that "the real original and permanent existence of things is archetypal, being ideas in *mente Divinâ*, and that our ideas are copies of them, and so far forth real things as they are correspondent to their archetypes." To the objection that space and time are purely subjective, it can be answered that they have an objective existence in God, for we can "conceive His immensity and eternity to be what in Him are correspondent to our space and duration." Further, the immaterialist need not deny that two people can be said to see "the same thing", for when you and I see a tree, although your idea of the tree will be distinct from mine, "our several trees must, I think be so many pictures (if I may so call them) of the one original, the tree in the infinite mind."[6]

Although Berkeley gave rather full answers to Johnson's other questions about his philosophy, his response to the questions about archetypes was short and unilluminating: "I have no objection against calling the ideas in the mind of God archetypes of ours."[7] When he gave his own account of archetypes, in *Elementa Philosophica*, Johnson continued to speak of our ideas as "faint copies" of God's, defending, in effect, a representative theory of perception, according to which our ideas are imperfect but representative copies of the archetypes in God's mind. Significantly, however, for a further account of archetypes, Johnson referred his readers not to Berkeley but to Norris's *Theory of the Ideal or Intelligible World*, where Norris defended Malebranche's doctrine that there is in God an eternal, uncreated, intelligible extension that is the archetype of the natural world. Johnson's immaterialism is, thus, an interesting hybrid: its core is Berkeleian, but to that core are added elements drawn from other philosophers. The following extracts are from *Elementa Philosophica*.[8]

ADVERTISEMENT

As I am of the opinion that little manuals of the sciences, if they could be well done, would be of good use to young beginners, what I aim at in this little tract is to be as useful to them as I can in the studies of metaphysics and logic, and this in order to the more particular studies of nature and morals, by giving as clear definitions as I am able in few words of the principal matters and terms whereof those studies consist; which I have endeavoured to do in an order of thoughts, gradually arising one after another, in a manner as instructive as could well be in so short a compass. I have also proposed to show how these studies, taking their rise from the first beginnings of sense, proceed on through the other studies, to raise the mind gradually to its highest perfection and happiness.

Though I would not be too much attached to any one author or system exclusive of any others, yet whoever is versed in the writings of Bishop Berkeley will be sensible that I am in a particular manner beholden to that excellent philosopher for several thoughts that occur in the following tract. And I cannot but recommend it to any one that would think with exactness on these subjects, to peruse all the works of that great and good gentleman (as well as those of Locke, Norris or Malebranche, and Cambrai[9]), if it were for no other reason, at least for this, that they will in the best manner lead him to think closely and to think for himself. And I was the rather willing to publish this logic because I think metaphysics a necessary part of that science, and that I apprehend it a great damage to the sciences that the old metaphysics are so much neglected, and that they might be rendered the more pleasant and useful by joining with them some improvements of the moderns. . . .

BOOK I: *NOETICA*

Chapter I

Of the Mind in general, its Objects and Operations

§2. *The definition of mind.* The word *mind* or *spirit*, in general, signifies any intelligent active being, which notion we take from what we are conscious of in ourselves, who know that we have within us a principle of conscious perception, intelligence, activity and self-exertion; or rather, that each of us is a conscious, perceptive, intelligent, active and self-exerting being. And by reasoning and analogy from ourselves, we apply it to all other minds or intelligences besides or superior to us, and (removing all limitations and imperfections) we apply it even to that Great Supreme Intelligence who is the universal Parent of all created spirits and (as far as our words and conceptions can go) may be defined, *an infinite Mind* or *Spirit*, or a *Being infinitely intelligent and active*. But by the *human mind*, we mean that principle of sense, intelligence and free activity which we feel within ourselves, or rather feel ourselves to be, furnished with those objects and powers, and under those confinements and limitations under which it hath pleased our great Creator to place us in this present state.

§5. *The original of our ideas*. Our minds may be said to be created mere *tabulae rasae*; i.e. they have no notices of any objects of any kind properly created in them, or concreated with them. Yet I apprehend, that in all the notices they have of any kind of objects, they have an immediate dependence upon the Deity, as really as they depend upon Him for their existence; i.e. they are no more authors to themselves of the objects of their perceptions, or the light by which they perceive them, than of the power of perceiving itself; but that they perceive them by a perceptual intercourse with that great Parent Mind, to whose incessant agency they are entirely passive, both in all the perceptions of sense, and in all that intellectual light by which they perceive the objects of the pure intellect. . . .

§6. *Of the senses*. By *sense* we mean those perceptions we have of objects *ab extra*, or by means of the several organs of our bodies. Thus, by feeling or touch we perceive an endless variety of tangible objects, resistance, extension, figure, motion, hard, soft, heat, cold, &c. By sight we perceive light and colours, with all their endlessly various modifications, red, blue, green, &c.; by hearing, we perceive sounds; by tasting, sapors; by smelling, odours, &c. These are called *simple ideas*. And of these, sorted out into a vast variety of fixed combinations, or *compound ideas*, distinct from each other, and in which they are always found to co-exist, consists every sort and individual body in nature, such as we call *man, horse, tree, stone, apple, cherry*, &c. And of all these various distinct combinations or compounds, connected together in such a manner as to constitute one most beautiful, useful and harmonious whole, consists what we call *universal nature*, or the entire *sensible* or *natural world*.

§7. *In which we are passive*. In the perception of these ideas or objects of sense, we find our minds are merely passive, it not being in our power (supposing our organs rightly disposed and situated) whether we will see light and colours, hear sounds, &c. We are not causes to ourselves of these perceptions, nor can they be produced in our minds without a cause, or (which is the same thing) by any imagined unintelligent, inert, or unactive cause (which indeed is a contradiction in terms), from whence it is demonstration that they must derive to us from an almighty, intelligent active cause, exhibiting them to us, impressing our minds with them, or producing them in us. And consequently (as I intimated), it must be by a perpetual intercourse of our minds with the Deity, the great Author of our beings, or by His perpetual influence or activity upon them, that they are possessed of all these objects of sense and the light by which we perceive them.

§8. *Ideas of sense not pictures but the real things.* These ideas or objects of sense are commonly supposed to be pictures or representations of things without us, and indeed external to any mind, even that of the Deity himself, and the truth or reality of them is conceived to consist in their being exact pictures of things or objects without us, which are supposed to be the real things. But as it is impossible for us to know what is without our minds and, consequently, what those supposed originals are, and whether these ideas of ours are just resemblances of them or not, I am afraid this notion of them will lead us into an inextricable scepticism. I am therefore apt to think that these ideas, or immediate objects of sense, are the real things, at least all that we are concerned with, I mean of the sensible kind, and that the reality of them consists in their stability and consistence, or their being in a stable manner exhibited to our minds, or produced in them, and in a steady connection with each other, conformable to certain fixed laws of nature which the great Father of Spirits hath established to Himself, according to which He constantly operates and affects our minds and from which He will not vary, unless upon extraordinary occasions, as in the case of miracles.[10]

§10. *Of archetypes.* Not that it is to be doubted but that there are archetypes of these sensible ideas, existing external to our minds; but then they must exist in some other mind and be ideas also as well as ours, because an idea can resemble nothing but an idea, and an idea ever implies, in the very nature of it, relation to a mind perceiving it or in which it exists. But then those archetypes or originals, and the manner of their existence in that eternal mind, must be entirely different from that of their existence in our minds – as different as the manner of His existence is from that of ours. In Him they must exist as in original intellect, in us only by way of sense and imagination; and in Him as originals, in us only as faint copies, such as he thinks fit to communicate to us according to such laws and limitations as he hath established, and such as are sufficient to all the purposes relating to our well-being, in which only we are concerned. Our ideas, therefore, can no otherwise be said to be images or copies of the archetypes in the eternal Mind than as our souls are said to be images of Him, or as we are said to be made after his image.[11]

§11. *Of consciousness, imagination and memory.* Thus much for sense. By *consciousness* is meant our perception of objects *ab intra*, or from reflecting or turning the eye of our mind inward and observing what passes within itself, whereby we know that we perceive all those sensible objects and their connections, and all the pleasures and pains attending them, and all the powers and faculties of our minds employed about them. . . .

§12. *Of the pure intellect and its acts.* But besides these powers of sense and imagination, we are conscious of what is called the *pure intellect*, or the power of conceiving of abstracted or spiritual objects, and the relations between our several ideas and conceptions, and the various dispositions, exertions and actions of our minds, and the complex notions resulting from all these; of all which we cannot be properly said to have *ideas*, they being entirely of a different kind from the objects of sense and imagination, on which account I would rather call them *notions* or *conceptions*. And they are either simple, such as perception, consciousness, volition, affection, action, &c., or complex, as spirit, soul, God, cause, effect, proportion, justice, charity, &c. And of all these, and what relates to them, consists the entire spiritual or moral world. . . .

§13. *Of intellectual light or intuitive evidence.* But before I proceed, I would, in order thereunto, first observe that no sooner does any object strike the senses, or is received in our imagination, or apprehended by our understanding, but we are immediately conscious of a kind of *intellectual light* within us (if I may so call it) whereby we not only know that we perceive the object, but directly apply ourselves to the consideration of it, both in itself, its properties and powers, and as it stands related to all other things. And we find that we are enabled by this intellectual light to perceive these objects and their various relations, in like manner as by sensible light we are enabled to perceive the objects of sense and their various situations.[12] So our minds are as passive to this intellectual light as they are to sensible light, and can no more withstand the evidence of it than they can withstand the evidence of sense. . . .

§14. *Whence it is derived.* Now if it be asked: Whence does this light derive, whereby all created minds at once perceive, as by a common standard, the same things alike to be true and right? – I answer, I have no other way to conceive how I come to be affected with this intuitive intellectual light, whereof I am conscious, than by deriving it from the universal presence and action of the Deity, or a perpetual communication with the great Father of Lights,[13] or rather his eternal Word and Spirit. For I know I am not the author of it to myself, being passive and not active with regard to it, though I am active in consequence of it. . . .

In the next extract we see Johnson fusing elements from heterogeneous sources: Descartes' *Cogito*, Malebranche's stress on our knowledge of "being in general", and Berkeley's identification of the existence of spirits with perceiving and acting, and of bodies with being perceived.

Chapter II

Of the Mind simply apprehending, and of its Objects more particularly

§2. *Of being in general.* As soon as the mind is possessed of any variety of objects, being assisted with that inward intellectual light abovementioned, deriving and, as it were, perpetually beaming forth from the great Fountain of all Light, both sensible and intellectual, it immediately falls to contemplating its ideas and conceptions and comparing them one with another. And here the first thing it is enlightened to know or be conscious of is its own existence, from the existence of its perceptions and exertions, and their objects, which it conceives of as real beings or things, whence it gets the notion of being in general. But even this first object of its knowledge it is made to know from that first principle of intellectual light, flowing from the Parent Mind, *that perception and action, and being perceived or acted upon, implies existence*, of which principle it has an inward intuitive sense and certainty. Hence it immediately infers, *I perceive and act, therefore I am; I perceive such an object, therefore it is*, &c. Not that its existence depends on my mind, but on that mind by whom I am enabled to perceive it. And as perceiving and acting, and being perceived and acted upon, implies existence or being, so *it is a contradiction for the same thing to be and not be at the same time*, for that would be to perceive and not perceive, to act and not to act, and to be perceived and not perceived, and acted upon and not acted upon, at one and the same time. And from these definitions arise the first great distinction of being into spirit and body, whereof the existence of the first consists in perceiving and acting, and that of the other in being passively perceived and acted. And here, to perceive or to act is called the *power*, and what is perceived or acted upon is called the *object*. So that by *being* is meant what really *is* or exists, in opposition to what is merely fictitious or imaginary, a creature of our own minds and not of him that made and enables us to perceive and act.

In our final extract, from Book II ("Ethica"), Chapter II, of the *Elementa Philosophica*, we find Johnson offering a proof of God's existence that clearly derives from Berkeley.

What I have thus argued [viz., that God exists][14] from my own existence, powers and faculties, and those of every other intelligent and active creature, and from the existence of eternal truth, may be also demonstrated from the existence of every sensible thing that I see, hear and feel from without me. I know that I am not the cause of any of those impressions that are made upon my senses – light, colours, sounds, tangible qualities, &c. I am sure they do not depend upon my will and activity, for I am entirely passive in the reception of them. Nor can they be without a cause, nor yet from any senseless, inert or unactive cause, for that is a contradiction in terms. They must therefore be the constant effects of an intelligent cause, intimately present with me and incessantly active upon me, who continually produces all these sensations in my mind, correspondent to the archetypes in his all-comprehending intellect, according to certain stable laws or fixed rules which He hath established to Himself, and which are commonly called the laws of nature. When, therefore, I consider the whole system of these sensible as well as the intelligible objects that surround me, and under the impression of which I continually live, I must conclude that *I live, and move, and have my being* in Him who is the perpetual and almighty Author of them.[15]

Notes

1. He is not to be confused with *the* Samuel Johnson who famously "refuted" Berkeley by kicking a stone.
2. Although Edwards was Johnson's pupil at Yale, he worked his views out before either he or Johnson had read Berkeley; Locke, however, and possibly Malebranche and Norris, played a role in the development of Edwards's thinking.
3. See the letters exchanged between them in Berkeley, *Works* II, pp. 265–94. On Johnson's visits to Berkeley, see Johnson's "Autobiography", in *Samuel Johnson, President of King's College: His Career and Writings*, ed. H. and C. Schneider (New York: Columbia University Press, 1929), vol. 1, pp. 24–27.
4. *Works* II, p. 254.

5. Ibid., p. 286.
6. Ibid., pp. 274–76, 285–87.
7. Ibid., p. 292.
8. *Elementa Philosophica* (Philadelphia, 1752), pp. vii-viii; Book I ("Noetica"), pp. 1–16; Book II ("Ethica"), pp. 28–29.
9. I.e., François Fénelon, Archbishop of Cambrai and author of *Démonstration de l'existence de Dieu* (1712), which was published in an English translation in 1713. Johnson refers to this work later, and there is some evidence that Berkeley admired it too: see David Berman, *George Berkeley: Idealism and the Man* (Oxford: Clarendon Press, 1994), p. 74.
10. In §9, which we have omitted, Johnson endorses Berkeley's account of the relationship between the objects of sight and touch, observing that the former are "signs" of the latter, depending on the "most wise and almighty will and fiat of the great Creator and Preserver of the world." In his note Johnson cites the *Principles* and *Dialogues* as well as the *Theory of Vision*.
11. See on this head Norris's *Ideal World*, Part I. [Johnson's note. The reference is to Norris's *Theory of the Ideal or Intelligible World*.]
12. This is Plato's doctrine in his *Epinomis*, &c. [Johnson's note.]
13. See the Archbishop of Cambrai [i.e., Fénelon] on this subject in his *Demonstration of the Existence of God*. And Norris or Malebranche. [Johnson's note.]
14. Earlier in this chapter, Johnson had given several arguments for the existence of God that owed much to ones given by Locke, Cudworth, Norris, and Fénelon.
15. *Vide* Bishop Berkeley's *Dialogues*, pp. 78, 79, &c. [Johnson's note. The passage in the *Dialogues* to which Johnson is referring his readers will be found in Berkeley, *Works* II, p. 214 (line 1) to p. 215 (line 19), which contains the observation that it is in God that "we live, and move, and have our being." On these words, taken from what was undoubtedly Berkeley's favorite text (Acts 17:28), which had also been cited by Malebranche (see above, p. 46), see Luce's note to *PHK* §66 in *Works* II, p. 70.

EIGHTEEN

French Reactions

Although some French journals did take note of Berkeley's works soon after their publication, Berkeley was destined to be counted a minor thinker by the French. Except for his theory of vision, which was embraced early by Voltaire and belatedly by Condillac, his views were rarely paid serious attention. One reason for this was that he continued often to be counted a "Malbranchiste de bonne foi" (as the *Mémoires de Trévoux* had put it). Thus, the great *Encyclopédie*, after setting out his views, declared: "Here we have, as you can see, pure Malebranchism, or something very near it. The author tried hard to prove that his views differ greatly from Father Male-branche's system, but the difference is so subtle that one must indeed be a determined metaphysician to be able to see it."[1] Now in the eyes of the Enlightenment *philosophes*, Descartes and Male-branche belonged to the past; the future was with Newton and Locke. D'Alembert typified this view when he wrote, in the *Encyclo-pédie's* "Preliminary Discourse", "Locke created authentic meta-physics much as Newton created physics" – a claim that Voltaire, Diderot, and Condillac could all endorse. If Berkeley was merely carrying the tradition of Malebranche further, he could be dismissed as passé. Another reason for not taking him seriously was that he was sometimes taken to teach "egoism" (solipsism) – a doctrine only a madman or a *poseur* could defend. Some, like Baron d'Holbach, found him guilty *both* of continuing the tradition of Malebranche *and* of egoism.[2] Only a few francophone writers – most notably the theologian D.-R. Boullier and the Swiss thinker Charles Bonnet – took Berkeley's philosophical views seriously, although they too rejected them. And only one important thinker of the French En-lightenment, Maupertuis, showed a positive affinity for Berkeley's immaterialism. To illustrate these attitudes, we first give extracts from the *Encyclopédie*, Diderot, and Voltaire that typify the view of Berkeley prevailing among the *philosophes*, then some passages from Boullier and Bonnet, and finally some from Maupertuis.

THE ENCYCLOPEDIA

Berkeley's views are cited in three articles – "Corps", "Égoïstes", and "Existence" – of that great compendium of Enlightenment learning and opinion, the *Encyclopédie*. We give here the article on the Egoists (written by d'Alembert), which – ignoring the fact that Berkeley never held that his mind was the only thing that exists – names him alone as an "egoist".

Egoists

One calls *egoists* that class of philosophers who recognize no truth other than that of their own existence – who do not believe that outside of us there is anything that is real or that resembles our sensations, who think bodies do not exist, etc. Egoism is Pyrrhonism pushed as far as it can go. Berkley [*sic*], among the moderns, has devoted all his energy to establishing it (see the article "Corps"). The *egoists* are at one and the same time the most extravagant of philosophers and the hardest to defeat: for how can the existence of objects be proved if not by our sensations? And how can this proof be used against those who believe that our sensations do not necessarily imply that there is something outside us? By what means will one go from the existence of the sensation to that of an object?[3]

DIDEROT

Diderot, chief architect of the *Encyclopédie*, wrote many of its articles, but not the article on "egoists". Nonetheless, from Diderot's most extended comment on Berkeley, found in his *Letter on the Blind*, we learn that Diderot too seems to have viewed Berkeley as an "egoist" (although the *term* he uses is "idealist"), and that he too saw Berkeley's position as the hardest to defeat.[4] However, while Diderot, like d'Alembert, certainly saw Berkeley's position as quite *absurd*, he also thought that, in one way, it was one that had to be taken seriously. This is because, as Diderot sees it, Berkeley's principles are "precisely the same" as those of Condillac – the foremost French defender of an empiricist theory of knowledge. Since Condillac claimed that his philosophy was built on Locke's, it is not surprising that an admirer of Locke, like Diderot, would ask Condillac how he avoided Berkeley's conclusions.

Philosophers are called *idealists* who, being aware only of their own existence and of the succession of sensations within themselves, do not admit anything else – a preposterous system that could be produced, it seems to me, only by somebody blind; a system that, to the disgrace of the human mind and of philosophy, is the hardest to combat, even though it is the most absurd of all. It is set out with as much candor as clarity in the *Three Dialogues* of Dr. Berkeley, the Bishop of Cloyne. The author of the *Essay* on our knowledge[5] really ought to examine this work; he would find in it matter for useful, pleasant, and subtle observations of the very sort he himself knows how to make. Idealism certainly deserves to be unmasked by him and there is in this hypothesis something to pique him, not so much because of its singularity as because of the difficulty of refuting it, given his own principles, for these are precisely the same as those of Berkeley. According to both of them, and according to reason, the terms *essence, matter, substance, support,* etc., bring hardly any light by themselves into our minds. Furthermore, the author of the *Essay on the Origin of Human Knowledge* [Condillac] judiciously notes that whether we soar into the heavens or plunge into the abyss, we never go out of ourselves, for all we perceive are our own thoughts.[6] Now this is the very conclusion reached in Berkeley's first dialogue and the foundation of his whole system. Wouldn't it be curious to see two foes grappling with each other whose weapons are so very much alike? If victory were to go to one of them, it could only be to him who knew best how to make use of those weapons. But certainly the author of the *Essay on the Origin of Human Knowledge* has just given, in his *Treatise on the Systems*, new proofs of the skill with which he can wield his, and has shown how formidable a foe he is of builders of systems.[7]

Condillac rose to Diderot's challenge in his *Traité des sensations* (1754), where he gave a subtle account of how the combination of kinesthetic and tactile sensations informs us that the cause of those sensations lies outside our minds. Unfortunately, since Berkeley, too, believed the cause of our sensations to be independent of our mind, Condillac did not thereby answer him. Ironically, in this work Condillac actually *embraced* Berkeley's theory of the relation of visual and tactile sensations – a theory he had rejected in the *Essay on the Origin of Human Knowledge*. (He probably knew the theory from Voltaire, although he noted that Berkeley had first proposed it.) In a further irony, Condillac had recently applauded Maupertuis's analysis of the meaning of "there is",[8] an analysis that, as we shall see, had affinities with Berkeley's immaterialism.

VOLTAIRE

Unlike some of Berkeley's early critics, Voltaire had actually read a number of Berkeley's works (it is clear from his writings that he had read at least the *Essay towards a New Theory of Vision*, the *Three Dialogues*, and *Alciphron*), and had met him and talked with him about his views. Furthermore, he enthusiastically embraced Berkeley's theory of vision, explaining and defending it in *Eléments de la philosophie de Newton* (1738).[9] He told Dortous de Mairan that, regarding our visual perception of size and distance, "the Bishop of Cloyne, an English scientist, is the only one I know of who has brought light to this little corner of darkness."[10] Not surprisingly, however, this enthusiasm did not extend to Berkeley's theological and metaphysical views. After reading *Alciphron*, Voltaire wrote to Andrew Pitt, "I will declare myself one of his admirers, but not one of his disciples," adding that *Alciphron* is "a party book rather than a religious book . . . more captious and acute than solid."[11] And of Berkeley's metaphysics Voltaire was as dismissive as Diderot had been. In the article "Body", in his *Philosophical Dictionary* (1764), Voltaire gives various arguments against Berkeley and repeats Locke's view that we cannot know what the substance of either mind or body is.

Body

Just as we don't know what a spirit is, so we are ignorant of what a body is: we see some of its properties; but what is the subject in which these properties reside? "There are only bodies," said Democritus and Epicurus; "There are no bodies," said the disciples of Zeno of Elea.

Bishop Berkeley of Cloyne is the last who claims, with a hundred sophisms, to have proved that bodies don't exist. They have, he says, neither color, nor odor, nor heat; these modalities are in your own sensations and not in the objects. He could have saved himself the trouble of proving this truth; it was known well enough. But from there he moves on to extension and solidity, which are the essence of a body; he thinks he can prove that there is no extension in a piece of green cloth, because the cloth is not really green; the sensation of green is in you alone, hence the sensation of extension also is in you alone. And, after he has thus destroyed extension, he concludes that solidity, which is attached to it, falls of its own weight – and thus there's nothing in the world but our ideas. So that, according to this scholar, ten thousand men killed by ten thousand cannon shots are fundamentally nothing but ten thousand apprehensions of our soul.

My lord, the bishop of Cloyne, had only himself to blame if he went to such ridiculous lengths. He believes he can show that there is no extension because a body seemed to him four times larger through his glasses than it was through his eyes, and four times smaller with the aid of another glass. From this he concludes that since a body cannot be at the same time four feet, sixteen feet, and a single foot in length, extension doesn't exist: hence there's nothing. All he needed to do was take a measure, and say: "Of whatever extension a body may appear to me, it is extended so many of these measures."

It would have been quite easy for him to see that extension and solidity are not like sounds, colors, tastes, odors, etc. Clearly, these are feelings excited in us by the configuration of parts; but extension is not a feeling. When this burning wood is extinguished, I am no longer warm; when the air no longer vibrates, I no longer hear anything; when this rose withers, I no longer smell it; but this wood, this air, and this rose have extension without any participation on my part. Berkeley's paradox isn't worth refuting.

It is useful to know how he was drawn into this paradox. A long time ago I had some conversations with him; he told me that he came to this opinion when he observed how men were unable to conceive what it is that receives extension. And in fact he triumphs in his book when he asks Hylas what that *substratum*, that substance, is. "It is the extended body," replies Hylas. Then the bishop (under the name of Philonous) laughs at him; and poor Hylas, seeing he has said that extension is subject to extension, and has therefore talked nonsense, is crestfallen, and admits that he doesn't understand it, that there is no body, the material world doesn't exist, there is nothing but a world of mind.

Hylas should merely have told Philonous: "We know nothing about the heart of this subject, this primal substance, extended, solid, divisible, mobile, shaped, etc.; I know it no better than I know the thinking, feeling, and willing subject; but still, that subject none the less exists, since it has essential properties of which it cannot be deprived."

We are all like most of the ladies of Paris: they live extremely well without knowing what goes into the stew; in the same way we enjoy bodies without knowing what they are composed of. What is the body made of? Of parts, and these parts resolve themselves into other parts. What are these last parts? Always bodies; you can go on dividing endlessly and never get any further. . . . [12]

DAVID-RENAUD BOULLIER

A French Protestant in the period after the Revocation of the Edict of Nantes, Boullier spent his life in Holland and England. He knew Berkeley it seems – perhaps they met during Boullier's years as pastor of London's French Reformed Church – and translated *Siris* into French.[13] T. E. Jessop rightly said of Boullier, "He was one of the very few who treated Berkeley's immaterialism seriously."[14] Where many showed only contempt for Berkeley (Jean Pierre de Crousaz said Berkeley's brains must be upside down[15] and Père Tournemine denounced his view as impious), Boullier called Berkeley one of the greatest philosophers of the century. In contrast to the *philosophes'* enthusiasm for Locke, Boullier rated Berkeley a more gifted metaphysician than Locke.[16] Boullier could not, however, embrace "the opinion of the illustrious Berkeley about the existence of bodies, despite the extreme veneration that I have for him and the singular friendship with which he has honored me."[17] Still, if Berkeley erred in this matter, "it was an error that could be made only by a very great genius."[18]

In his *Treatise on the True Principles that serve as the Foundation of Moral Certitude* (1737), Boullier set out the things he held one can be "morally certain" about, even though one cannot demonstrate their truth with "metaphysical certainty". These included well-attested facts of history, conclusions based on arguments from analogy, causal inferences from repeated observations, our belief that animals are conscious, that there is a world of spirits presided over by God, and that there is a material world. In the chapter in which he gave his reasons for being morally certain of a material world, Boullier explicitly declined to reply to Berkeley's view that it is not even *possible* that matter exists. He set the following footnote near the beginning of that chapter.

Mr. Berkeley, the present Bishop of Cloyne in Ireland, in his *Treatise concerning the Principles of Human Knowledge*, pushes this paradox [of calling the existence of bodies into question] infinitely farther than did Father Malebranche. Father Malebranche did not believe one can prove that bodies exist; Mr. Berkeley believes one can prove that bodies do not and cannot exist. He treats as absurd the supposition that there are, external to us, substances similar to what we call bodies or matter. His reasonings are drawn from the nature of our ideas, the insoluble difficulties that arise from the properties of the continuum, etc. I am not going to enter this debate, where the English author, who is indisputably one of the greatest philosophers as well as one of the finest minds of our century, fills one with admiration by the depth and subtlety of his metaphysics. I will here suppose, with Father Malebranche and everybody else, something that seems to me clear: that the idea of bodies, as well as the idea of minds, is representative of certain substances that at least *can* exist external to us, just as we perceive them to. Given this principle, that bodies are possible, I believe their actual existence can be demonstrated.[19]

The arguments that Boullier proceeded to give were not, thus, in reply to Berkeley. Nonetheless, his approach to the question of the existence of a material world differed markedly from that of most eighteenth-century French writers who had discussed the issue. The usual approach was either to dismiss doubts about the existence of matter out of hand (as doubts that could be taken seriously only by one whose brain was "upside down") or, when the question *was* taken at all seriously, to dismiss it fairly briskly (and in Cartesian fashion) by an appeal to God's veracity. Boullier, by contrast, set out at length several arguments for the existence of the material world, and it may be that it was the high regard he held Berkeley in that led him to treat the issue quite so seriously, even though he did not attempt to answer Berkeley directly. The line of argument he developed was that the supposition that matter exists best explains things that would otherwise be inexplicable: the agreement, order, and interconnection of the ideas each perceiver receives from his several senses; the perceptions we each have of a body to which we are at all times united; the fact that we feel bodily pain (which God would have no reason to allow us to experience if we had no material body that required our attention); and the agreement of the reports various perceivers give about what they perceive. To illustrate Boullier's approach to the question, we give the last of these arguments.

Consider further the agreement found among the perceptions of all intelligent beings. If matter does not exist, if the visible world is a mere phantom and not a collection of real beings or extended, movable, solid substances, if there is in all this no absolute reality, distinct from and independent of our minds, how does it come about that so many different minds agree in the reports they give about their perceptions? Why is the order among ideas and sensations the same for everyone, presenting the same universe to all? What accounts for that immutable order whereby the scene presented to one soul is infinitely varied as that soul successively occupies different circumstances and points of view, giving to all souls the same variety of scenes from different points of view? Surely if bodies are nothing but ideas put into our minds by God, those I perceive are not those perceived by another mind: why then do they agree with each other, if there is no common, identical object to which God applies both minds and which serves as their fixed model? Yet we find just such agreement. We all see the same world. The same universe is the object of our study and our investigations. Should another man occupy the same place I now occupy, I know he will see what I see, perceive what I perceive; such slight variation in sensations as may result from differences in our organs will not alter a basic uniformity in our perceptions.

For all men, the same effects will result from the same causes. And when, on the basis of my knowledge of nature's laws, I make and test certain experiments, I can be confident that anybody who wants to follow exactly the same procedure I have followed will get the same results as I got. If we work only from our own ideas when we study Nature, why do our ideas agree so precisely? But not even to speak of the procedures of scientists, the whole commerce of the life of men depends on this agreement in the perceptions that all have of one and the same world as their object and center. Without that, men would not be able to understand each other, or unite together, or communicate with one another in the course of their actions. If we consider society in relation to its moral state, it is the common principles of justice and reason that form the reciprocal bond between the men who compose it; if we consider it in relation to its natural state, that bond is formed by men's common ideas of a shared world that they take themselves to inhabit. When a Frenchman and a Japanese communicate their sensible perceptions to each other, you can see by the precise agreement of their ideas that these are representations of the same Whole. Without such agreement, it would be quite impossible for these two men to be enough of the same mind to communicate with each other.

Why would the Creator have applied all minds to the same object, by giving to all the same general idea and making them sense it as present, if that object didn't exist? Did he need to deceive them by a common illusion in order to unite them? Shouldn't one believe, instead, that it accorded with his wisdom to create such a world, which serves as the foundation of these concordant perceptions and of the union thereby established among all the members of human society? It seems to me that these considerations provide us with a true demonstration of the existence of bodies. It is, I grant, a demonstration that leads to certainty not of the metaphysical kind but of the moral kind; but that suffices to bring the matter to the highest degree of certainty.[20]

Boullier's arguments assume that ideas are representations of objects and so are best explained on the assumption that the world they represent exists. That he understood, however, Berkeley's very different view, according to which ideas are signs of other ideas, is suggested by his characterization of Berkeley's position in the preface to his translation of *Siris*. For Berkeley, he writes, "the corporeal world has no absolute existence but is a collection of appearances, a uniform course of phenomena connected together with admirable regularity and subject to a certain order that divine wisdom has established for the use and mutual communication of intelligent beings. . . . In the fixed laws of Nature he recognizes the sovereign liberty of the Creator. And rather than attribute to matter forces and faculties that it doesn't have, he sees in these diverse phenomena only so many signs and expressions of the power and eternal wisdom of a simple, immaterial, infinite Being."[21] While Boullier didn't accept this view, he at least had a better grasp on it than many others.

CHARLES BONNET

The Swiss philosopher and biologist, Charles Bonnet, author of several works widely read in the eighteenth century, was another who admired Berkeley while rejecting his views. In his autobiography, Bonnet said that he had been attracted to Berkeley's philosophy, but was unable to embrace it because its logical end was "le pur égoïsme".[22] He repeats this objection in the following extract from his *Essai de psychologie* (1754). For Bonnet, Berkeley cannot get beyond the conclusions of Descartes' first five *Meditations* – he can establish his own existence and God's, but nothing else. One might even think, from Bonnet's account, that Berkeley followed Descartes' order of proof, first establishing his own existence, then God's, but rejecting the conclusions of *Meditation Six*. In fact, of course, Berkeley's argument does not follow the Cartesian order (in his notebooks Berkeley even rejects the *Cogito*) and he would have denied Bonnet's claim that, on the Berkeleian view, "Bodies are but modifications of our souls."[23]

On the Philosophical Opinion that there are No Bodies

These are the difficulties [in explaining how body can act on mind, the topic of the preceding chapter] that have led an English theologian, as pious as he is bold, to claim that there are no bodies, and that the belief that bodies exist is the most fecund and dangerous source of error and impiety. If his book fails to persuade one, it at least proves how much even things we know most certainly can be made obscure and to what a degree the human mind is susceptible of doubt and delusion. Here is a summary of this subtle metaphysician's arguments.

We omit here Bonnet's lengthy summary of Berkeley's arguments, which concludes, "So according to this system, the Universe is purely ideal. Bodies are but modifications of our souls, having no more reality than colors, or the things we see in dreams." Then, before criticizing Berkeley, Bonnet rules out any attempt to answer him by appealing to God's veracity.

Let it not be objected that God deceives us by persuading us of the existence of things that do not exist. Does God deceive us when we dream, or in the judgments we make about colors, sizes, distances, etc.? Such is the nature of things, and such our present condition, that we see as outside us what is really in us, for we see extension and solidity though in fact there is nothing but perceptions and sensations. Is the universe, for all that, any less beautiful, less harmonious, less varied, less fit to promote the happiness of creatures? If an architect were to draw the plans for a splendid building and at the same time provide directions for how to build it, would he seem less skilled in his art just because he didn't execute these plans? The supreme architect has drawn the universe in so far as he has created spirits. For what a universe his hand has drawn in the mind of the cherubim! And what an Intelligence it is that can encompass, all at once, all these universes! For the rest, if divine revelation teaches us that bodies exist, it does so in the same way that it teaches us that the earth is at rest and that the sun revolves around it. For the end of revelation is to make us virtuous, not to make us subtle metaphysicians.

Now this system I have been describing is surely not intrinsically absurd, though it takes a metaphysical head to get a good grip on it. That we have no demonstrative proof of the existence of bodies is certain. The celebrated author of the theory of occasional causes[24] has already shown that, and the arguments given by the English theologian only set that proposition in a yet clearer light. But is it necessary, to be convinced of the existence of bodies, for somebody to present us with a rigorous demonstration? Do our senses not speak to us in a language clear enough, eloquent enough, forceful enough, to set this truth beyond doubt and to dissipate the clouds that a too subtle metaphysics gives rise to? Surely men will always be persuaded that bodies exist – and if this is a mistaken belief, never was a mistake so difficult to detect, never did a falsehood seem so much like the truth.

But let us attack our author's system more philosophically. Can we not detect a sophism in the following reasoning? It is evident that the things I perceive are nothing but my own ideas and that ideas cannot exist anywhere but in a mind: hence, they can be produced only by a mind; and so matter neither does nor can exist. Does our author not here confuse what the Schools wisely distinguished by the rather barbarous terms "formal" and "virtual"?[25] Hence, the cause of our ideas need not be the kind of thing in which ideas actually exist. It is indeed evident that the ideas we have of bodies cannot exist anywhere save in a mind, but does it necessarily follow that these ideas can be produced only by a mind? It is true that we do not know how the movement of a fibre can give rise to an idea in the soul; but can anyone rigorously prove such a thing impossible? Can anyone prove that God can create nothing but spirits? Surely one goes too far if one reduces the whole of creation to nothing but spiritual substances.

That's not all: our author grants that other men exist and that we communicate with them. Yet, given the terms of his system, I am assured only of my own existence and of God's existence: I think, therefore I am; I am; therefore there is an eternal cause of my existence. This is the whole chain of conclusions I am permitted to draw. I cannot draw from my own existence the conclusion that any other men exist, for everything in my experience that I would have supposed was caused by others depends solely on God's action on me. In which case the supposition that others exist is quite gratuitous. And how then will we converse with other spirits who are supposed to be our fellow creatures?[26]

MAUPERTUIS

Diderot wanted Condillac to show that his empiricism did not lead to Berkeley's conclusions. Another French empiricist, Pierre-Louis Maupertuis, actually embraced conclusions close to some of Berkeley's.[27] In *Philosophical Reflexions on the Origin of Languages and the Meaning of Words* (1748), from which our first selection comes, Maupertuis speculates on how language began and how words came to have meanings. At first, he thought, each particular word named some single perception, but because memory is limited, words quickly became general names applied to many perceptions that resembled each other. The first words thus were substantives like "tree" and "horse". When it was noticed that certain perceptions of both a tree and a horse had something in common, expressions like "I see" or "I touch" were invented and combined with "tree" or "horse" to produce sentences. Gradually, further distinctions were made as "I see" was distinguished from "I saw", "I will see", "I dream of", "I think of", all of which also can be combined with "a

tree" or "a horse". Finally, the repetition of many similar perceptions of a tree or a horse in similar circumstances led to the invention of the expression *there is* a tree or horse. Up to this point no
distinction had been made between perceptions and objects, Maupertuis thought, but the introduction of expressions like "there is"
gave rise to the notion that objects exist independently of our seeing
or touching them. But "there is a tree" is really just an abridgement
of a group of reports of perceptions such as "I saw a tree in this
place," "I see a tree in this place," and "Each time I return to this
place, I see the same tree." Hence, the belief in the existence of
bodies, external to our perceptions of them, has no foundation in
our perceptions themselves, but results only from carelessness about
what the words we use really mean. Once we get clear about the
meaning of expressions like "there is", we see the mistake in thinking that the tree can exist apart from any perception of it. The
following extract begins after Maupertuis has examined the beginnings of language and has arrived at the discussion of "there is".

XXIV. Now suppose I have a perception that I experience as a repetition of earlier perceptions and that is associated with certain circumstances that increase its force and seem to give it a great deal of reality:
e.g., I have the perception "I have seen a tree," joined to the perception
"I was in a certain place," and then I have the perception "I returned to
that place and I saw that tree," "I went yet again to that same place, and
saw the same tree," etc.; then this repetition of perceptions, plus the
accompanying circumstances, lead to the formation of a new perception:
"I will see a tree every time I go to that place," and finally to this: "*There
is* a tree."

XXV. This last perception confers, as it were, its reality on its object
and leads to a proposition about the existence of the tree as independent
of me. And yet it would be very hard to find in the proposition ["There
is a tree"] anything more than was in those preceding propositions that
were merely signs of my own perceptions. If I had had each of these
perceptions ("I see a tree," "I see a horse," etc.) just once, however vivid
each might have been, I think it doubtful I would have formed the
expression "there is". Had my memory been so large that I would not
have been disconcerted by the multiplication of signs for my perceptions
– big enough to contain a distinct sign for every single perception I have
ever had – I would perhaps never have formed the expression "there is",
even though I had had all the same perceptions that have led me to form

it. For isn't this expression just a way of abridging this whole collection of perceptions: "I see", "I saw", "I will see", etc.?

XXVI. In ordinary speech we say, "There are sounds." Most people think of these sounds as something that exists independently of them. Philosophers, however, have observed that the only existence sounds have independently of us is as a certain movement of the air, caused by vibrations of the sounding bodies and transmitted to our ears. Now what I perceive when I say "I hear a sound" – that is, my perception – certainly has no likeness to what is going on outside me, no likeness to the movement of a vibrating body. In effect, it is just a perception of the same sort as the perception "I see", and outside me there is no object that resembles it. Isn't the case the same with the perception "I see a tree"? While I may be able to trace what occurs in this perception further – while optical experiments may teach me that an image of a tree is traced on my retina – neither this image nor the tree resembles my perception.

XXVII. Perhaps it will be said that we get certain perceptions in several different ways: thus, "I see a tree," which comes from sight, is confirmed by my sense of touch. But while touch seems to agree with sight on various occasions, one can see that it is only by a kind of custom [*habitude*] that one of these senses can confirm the perceptions that one gets from another. If one had never touched the things one sees, and then touched one of them in the dark or with one's eyes closed, one would not recognize the object as the same thing that one had seen. The two perceptions "I see a tree" and "I touch a tree," which I can now represent by the signs CD and PD [C = "I touch", P = "I see", D = "a tree"], would then be represented by the signs CD and PQ, which would have no common element but would be completely different. The same could be said of perceptions that we take to be confirmed in a number of different ways.

XXVIII. I think almost all philosophers would agree with what I have said in the last two paragraphs, and would add, only, that there is always something external to me that causes these two perceptions, "I see a tree," "I hear a sound." But I invite them to re-read what I have said about the force of the expression "there is" and how we have come to form it. Furthermore, what is the point in saying that there is something that causes my perceptions when I say "I see", "I touch", "I hear", if what I see, touch, or hear, never resembles that cause? I will grant that our perceptions are dependent on some cause, because nothing happens without a reason. But what is that cause? I cannot penetrate it, since it resembles nothing that I perceive. Let us stay within the limits prescribed to an intellect like ours.[28]

> Like Berkeley, Maupertuis thus concluded that bodies do not have an existence independent of being perceived, though he differs sharply from Berkeley in holding that we cannot discover the cause of our perceptions. In this work, however, Maupertuis makes no mention of Berkeley, and one might suppose that he reached his views without knowing Berkeley's. That this was not so was shown when he replied to some criticisms Nicolas Boindin made of this work. Maupertuis's reply, from which the next extract is taken, shows he was aware that his view was close to Berkeley's. He here suggests, however, that Berkeley only attacked the error of believing that objects exist outside the mind in a "piecemeal" way, whereas he, Maupertuis, "undermined the structure's very foundations" by tracing it to "the abuse of words," or "a forgetfulness of their meaning." (Berkeley, too, of course, held that belief in the existence of things without the mind has roots in errors about language, but Maupertuis may not have recognized this if, as seems to be the case, he had read only the *Three Dialogues*.) Despite obvious differences in their positions, there seems no reason to suppose that reading Berkeley did not play a role in the development of Maupertuis's views.

If one follows the progress of my work down to paragraph *XXIX*, one sees that it not only explains in what sense bodies exist, but it also destroys any distinction one might like to make between two modes of existence, one in the mind, the other outside it. One can see what trouble a celebrated man, Mr. Berkeley, has taken, in a considerable work, *Dialogues between Hylas and Philonous*, to clear this matter up by divesting bodies of that reality independent of our perceptions that the vulgar attribute to them and that our negligence and prejudices endow them with. This philosopher attacks the system of our errors only piecemeal, demolishing the structure from the roof down; we have undermined the structure's very foundations – a structure quite different from that famous tower that the confusion of tongues prevented from being raised on the planes of Sennaar,[29] for this one is raised only on the abuse of words, or on a forgetfulness of their meaning. . . .

It seems that, despite his great sagacity, Mr. Boindin has not fully grasped the meaning of the expression "there is"; that he has stopped at the same point all other philosophers stop at, when – after agreeing that the objects we consider as existent may have no existence apart from that given them by our perception – they go on to distinguish this species of *intelligible* existence from another, viz., *material* existence, external to and independent of us: a distinction devoid of sense, which would not be made if what I have been saying were grasped.

No object external to us could resemble a perception: all philosophers, and even those who are not philosophers but who think a bit about it, agree with that. Some of them have already reduced bodies to simple phenomena and, to explain how these bodies come to be perceivable, have had recourse to the word "force"; but if these forces belong to objects themselves, one falls back into the impossibility of explaining how they act on us, while if they belong to the being who does the perceiving, then we say nothing more than that our perceptions have *an unknown cause*.

Finally, I must address the most important charge that Mr. Boindin has brought against me, which has to do with what I said about *duration*, and about the impossibility of our measuring it, or of discovering the cause of the connection and the succession of our ideas; what I have said about these matters raises the suspicion that I take our being to be necessary and eternal – a metaphysical view from which one could draw "some very shocking conclusions," the intimating of which, he thinks, was the true aim of my work, which the reflections on the origin of language served merely as a pretext for raising.

Any intellectual system, any system in which the revolutions of the stars, the movement of clocks, the books of chronicle and history are treated as mere phenomena will lead to these doubts that Mr. Boindin represents as so dangerous; and though our system goes perhaps further than others, it contains nothing that, if rightly understood, is a cause for more alarm, or for alarm at all. I can shield myself beneath the authority of writers who have reduced all that we see to phenomena without provoking any outcry from those who are the most orthodox – it is hardly fair that Mr. Boindin wants to accuse me of a crime that the pious have not reproached these others with.

But if anybody wants me to cite a still more direct and respectable authority, I will cite Mr. Berkeley, whose views are even closer to mine. Would one want my philosophy to be more timid than that of this bishop? I would not, then, be lacking in authorities, even if it were here a matter of justifying something very daring; and they would, I think, more than suffice in defense of a man whose state and manner of life permit an honest freedom of thought.

But I have no need here to cite authorities in my defense; I can show that my reflections about duration, about the impossibility of measuring it, or of discovering the cause of the connection and succession of our ideas, are far from inspiring any suspicion that our being is necessary and eternal. . . .

What Mr. Boindin means by "a necessary and eternal being" is, it seems, either what orthodox philosophers mean by *God*, conceived as *the necessary, eternal, infinite being, independent of all other things*, or what a different sect of philosophers has in mind when it ascribes these same attributes to the universe. Now is Mr. Boindin proposing that I think that man is either God or the universe? Is he suggesting that I think man is a necessary, eternal, infinite, independent being? Have I not attributed to man an existence so little necessary and so little eternal that I have said that between two perceptions that seem to him consecutive immense intervals might actually have passed during which he would not even have existed? Have I not regarded man as a being whose existence could be interrupted and then revived at any moment? What could be further from necessity and eternity than an existence that is perhaps not even continuous? . . .

I was content, a moment ago, to cite authorities, both because they sufficed to protect my opinions and because most of those with whom I deal are more convinced by authorities than capable of debating the doctrines they would like to censure. But let me say that the system that results from my reflexions about the origin of language solves or eliminates all the difficulties that swarm through other systems. Even in those systems that arrive at the point of granting that we cannot be certain that the objects we perceive have any existence other than in our souls, it can still be asked whether it is not possible for these objects to have, in addition to their intelligible existence, another existence that is real and independent of us; and then, if it is granted that objects are capable of this other existence, it is said that to doubt or deny that they have it is to go against what revelation teaches us when it speaks of these objects as existing. But once it is seen that the whole reality of these objects is, and can only be, what I have explained we mean when we arrive at the point of saying "there is", then no longer is there, nor can there be, a question of objects having different manners of existing: certainly it is indubitable that objects *exist* in the fullest sense of that word, and no longer can one find any opposition between their existence and what has been revealed to us.[30]

Although Maupertuis differs from Berkeley by insisting that we cannot determine the cause of our perceptions, there is a further affinity between their views that is not apparent in the above extracts. Maupertuis was an opponent of the materialists, like d'Holbach and La Mettrie, and saw in the views he defended a way of combatting materialism. Further, while he did not adopt the view that God is the immediate cause of our perceptions, he did hold that God must be the ultimate cause of the universe. Thus for Maupertuis, as for Berkeley, the denial of the material world had roots both in his empiricism and in a theologically motivated opposition to materialism.[31]

Notes

1. *Encyclopédie* (1751–80), s.v., "Corps", vol. 4, p. 262.
2. d'Holbach, *Système de la nature* (London, 1770), vol. 1, pp. 157–58 note.
3. *Encyclopédie*, s.v., "Égoïstes", vol. 5, p. 431.
4. Another who spoke of Berkeley as difficult to refute was Jean-Jacques Rousseau. Although he had no patience with the battles of the "idealists" and the "materialists" (see his *Profession de foi du vicaire savoyard*, I.4), Rousseau could say, "while all modern philosophy denies spirits, all of a sudden Bishop Berkeley rises up and maintains that there are no bodies. How is one ever to get the better of this fearsome logician? Take away the interior sentiment and I defy all modern logicians to prove to Berkeley that there are any bodies." (Letter to L. A. de Franquières, 15th January 1769.)
5. Condillac, whose *Essai sur l'origine des connaissances humaines* had been published in 1746.
6. These are the opening words of Condillac's *Essay*.
7. Diderot, *Lettre sur les aveugles* (London, 1749), pp. 96–100.
8. See his letter to Maupertuis, *Oeuvres philosophiques de Condillac*, ed. G. Le Roy (Paris: Presse Universitaire de France, 1948), vol. 2, p. 537.
9. Part 2, Chapters 6–7, and *Éclaircissement* §3.
10. Voltaire, *Complete Works*, ed. T. Besterman and others (Geneva: Institut et Musée Voltaire; Toronto: University of Toronto Press; Oxford: Voltaire Foundation, 1968–), vol. 88, p. 140.
11. Ibid., vol. 86, p. 274. Voltaire, however, rose to Berkeley's defense when the abbé Desfontaines (foolishly taking Alciphron for Berkeley's spokesman) charged that the work was "a tissue of libertine sophisms, wantonly contrived to destroy the principles of morality, politics, and religion." See Voltaire, *Oeuvres complètes* (Paris: Garnier Frères, 1877–85), vol. 22, p. 385.

12. Voltaire, *Philosophical Dictionary*, trans. P. Gay (New York: Harcourt, Brace, 1962), pp. 215–17.
13. As *Recherches sur les vertus de l'eau de goudron* (Amsterdam, 1745).
14. T. E. Jessop, *A Bibliography of George Berkeley* (The Hague: Martinus Nijhoff, 1973), p. 112.
15. Jean Pierre de Crousaz, *Examen du pyrrhonisme ancien et moderne* (The Hague, 1733), p. 97.
16. *Pièces philosophiques et littéraires* (1759), p. 100. Boullier also compared Berkeley favorably with Leibniz, asserting that "the system of Berkeley is infinitely more reasonable and rests on a foundation incomparably more plausible" than Leibniz's theory of monads (ibid., p. 66).
17. Ibid., p. 187n.
18. Ibid., p. 66.
19. *Traité sur des vrais principes qui servent de fondement à la certitude morale*, published together with the second edition of Boullier's *Essai philosophique sur l'âme des bêtes* (Amsterdam, 1737), vol. 1, p. 208n.
20. Ibid., pp. 214–17.
21. *Recherches sur les vertus de l'eau de goudron*, pp. xiv–xv, xviii.
22. Charles Bonnet, *Mémoires autobiographiques* (Paris: Vrin, 1948), p. 171.
23. On the *Cogito*, see *PC* 738; on ideas not being modes, see *PHK* §49.
24. Malebranche.
25. An allusion to the doctrine that a cause need not have the same nature as its effect, but only the power to produce it (whereby it contains the effect "virtually").
26. Chapter 33 of Bonnet's *Essai de psychologie* (Leyden, 1754).
27. For Maupertuis's empiricist views, see "Examen philosophique de la preuve de l'existence de Dieu," in *Histoire de l'Académie Royale des Sciences et Belles-Lettres* (Berlin, 1756).
28. From Maupertuis, *Réflexions philosophiques sur l'origine des langues et la signification des mots*, reprinted in *Sur l'origine du langage*, ed. R. Grimsley, Series: *Langue et cultures* 2 (Geneva: Librairie Droz, 1971), pp. 42–44.
29. The tower of Babel.
30. From Maupertuis's *Réponses* to Boindin (1756), reprinted in Grimsley, pp. 52–57.
31. See his "Essai de cosmologie," *Oeuvres* (Lyon, 1756), vol. 1, and *Lettres de M. de Maupertuis*, 2nd ed. (Berlin, 1753), pp. 20–24. On Maupertuis's opposition to materialism, see Aram Vartanian, *Diderot and Descartes* (Princeton: Princeton University Press, 1953), pp. 151–53, 271–72. See also L. Gossman, "Berkeley, Hume and Maupertuis," *French Studies* 14 (1960), pp. 304–24.

NINETEEN

German Reactions

The first German philosopher to set down his views about Berkeley seems to have been Leibniz, in his comments in his copy of the *Principles*.[1] The first published reactions to Berkeley in Germany, however, seem to have come in a passing mention of him in a note on Collier's *Clavis Universalis* in *Acta Eruditorum* (1717)[2] and in Christoph Matthaeus Pfaff's *Oratio de egoismo, nova philosophica haeresi* (*Oration on Egoism, a New Philosophical Heresy*), 1722. Pfaff, following Christian Wolff's system of classification, divided philosophers into skeptics and dogmatists, the dogmatists into monists and dualists, the monists into materialists and idealists, and the idealists into pluralists and egoists.[3] According to Pfaff, Descartes and Malebranche were idealism's chief precursors, Fardella, Collier, and Berkeley its chief representatives. Berkeley's views – whatever his intentions – lead, Pfaff thinks, to solipsism.[4] Wolff himself later classified Berkeley as an idealist,[5] and the classification stuck. According to Wolfgang Breidert, German writers at first merely mentioned Berkeley as an example of an idealist, "but in consequence of the increasing discussion of so-called idealism during the 18th century the attention on Berkeley increased, too."[6] In 1756, J. C. Eschenbach published a translation, in a single volume, of Berkeley's *Three Dialogues* and Collier's *Clavis Universalis*, and in an appendix sought to refute the idealism of both thinkers.[7] But by far the best-known attack on Berkeley in eighteenth-century Germany was made by Kant, who was eager to distinguish his own "critical idealism" from "the mystical and visionary idealism of Berkeley."

KANT

The first review of the *Critique of Pure Reason* construed Kant's idealism as a revival of Berkeley's.[8] The review deeply provoked Kant, who said it exuded "the breath of pure animosity."[9] Fearful that readers would confound his views with Berkeley's, Kant sought, in passages in the *Prolegomena to any Future Metaphysics* (1783) and in two additions to the second edition (1787) of the *Critique*, to show how fundamental were the differences between other forms of idealism and his own "critical idealism".[10] The chief way in which Kant thinks he differs from an idealist like Berkeley is that the latter, he maintains, embraces the following doctrines, which he, Kant, rejects: (1) there are no "things in themselves" lying behind the "appearances" we perceive; (2) "outer objects" (bodies in space) are "sheer illusion" (the difference between this claim and the first is that, for Kant, "things in themselves" belong to the noumenal realm, "outer objects" to the phenomenal); and (3) only minds exist. Our first extract comes from the *Prolegomena*.

Idealism consists in the assertion that there are none but thinking beings; all other things which we believe are perceived in intuition are nothing but representations in the thinking beings, to which no object external to them in fact corresponds. On the contrary, I say that things as objects of our senses existing outside us are given, but we know nothing of what they may be in themselves, knowing only their appearances, i.e., the representations which they cause in us by affecting our senses. Consequently, I grant by all means that there are bodies without us, that is, things which, though quite unknown to us as to what they are in themselves, we yet know by the representations which their influence on our sensibility procures us, and which we call bodies. This word merely means the appearance of the thing, which is unknown to us but is not therefore less real. Can this be termed idealism? It is the very contrary.

Long before Locke's time, but assuredly since him, it has been generally assumed and granted without detriment to the actual existence of external things that many of their predicates may be said to belong, not to the things in themselves, but to their appearances, and to have no proper existence outside our representation. Heat, color, and taste, for instance, are of this kind. Now, if I go further and, for weighty reasons, rank as mere appearances also the remaining qualities of bodies, which are called primary – such as extension, place, and, in general, space, with all that which belongs to it (impenetrability or materiality, shape, etc.) – no one in the least can adduce the reason of its being inadmissible. As little as the man who admits colors not to be properties of the object in itself but only to be modifications of the sense of sight should on that account be called an idealist, so little can my doctrine be named idealistic merely because I find that more, nay, *all the properties which constitute the intuition of a body belong merely to its appearance.* The existence of the thing that appears is thereby not destroyed, as in genuine idealism, but it is only shown that we cannot possibly know it by the senses as it is in itself. . . .

I have myself given this my theory the name of transcendental idealism, but that cannot authorize anyone to confound it either with the empirical idealism of Descartes (indeed, his was only an insoluble problem, owing to which he thought every one at liberty to deny the existence of the corporeal world because it could never be proved satisfactorily), or with the mystical and visionary idealism of Berkeley (against which and other similar phantasms, our *Critique* contains the proper antidote). My idealism concerns not the existence of things (the doubting of which, however, constitutes idealism in the ordinary sense), since it never came into my head to doubt it; but it concerns the sensuous representation of things, to which space and time especially belong. Regarding space and time and, consequently, regarding all appearances in general, I have only shown that they are neither things (but are mere modes of representation) nor are they determinations belonging to things in themselves. But the word "transcendental," which for me never means a reference of our cognition to things, but only to our faculty of cognition, was meant to obviate this misconception. Yet rather than give further occasion to it by this word, I now retract it and desire this idealism of mine to be called "critical." But if it be really an objectionable idealism to convert actual things (not appearances) into mere representations, by what name shall we call that which, conversely, changes mere representations into things? It may, I think, be called *dreaming* idealism, in contradistinction to the former, which may be called *visionary* idealism, both of which are to be refuted by my transcendental, or better, *critical* idealism.[11]

Philosophers, Kant thinks, have hitherto supposed that we must choose between "transcendental realism", the doctrine that things in themselves are in space and time, and "dogmatic idealism", the doctrine that spatio-temporal objects are illusions. Given that dichotomy, we cannot blame "the good Berkeley" for choosing the latter, since the former gives rise to insoluble paradoxes (viz., the "antinomies of pure reason"). But the dichotomy is a false one – there is a third choice: transcendental or critical idealism. According to it, the mind's own structure conditions how things appear to it. In particular, the mind's structure necessitates that things distinct from it appear to be in space (and that all things, including the mind's appearance to itself, appear to be in time). Hence, although the spatially located bodies we perceive by "outer sense" are not things in themselves, as the "transcendental realist" supposes, neither are they mere illusion (i.e., something – a dream or hallucination – that *seems* to be outside empirical consciousness but is not). Rather, the spatio-temporal world is *how* things in themselves *appear* to minds like ours. Kant added the following passage to the second edition of the *Critique*, almost certainly in part to distinguish his own view, that the bodies perceived by outer sense are appearance (*Erscheinung*), from what he takes to be Berkeley's view, that they are illusion (*Schein*).

When I say that the intuition of outer objects and the self-intuition of the mind alike represent the objects and the mind, in space and in time, as they affect our senses, that is, as they appear, I do not mean to say that these objects are a mere *illusion*. For in an appearance the objects, nay even the properties that we ascribe to them, are always regarded as something actually given. Since, however, in the relation of the given object to the subject, such properties depend upon the mode of intuition of the subject, this object as *appearance* is to be distinguished from itself as object *in itself*. Thus when I maintain that the quality of space and of time, in conformity with which, as a condition of their existence, I posit both bodies and my own soul, lies in my mode of intuition and not in those objects in themselves, I am not saying that bodies merely *seem* to be outside me, or that my soul only *seems* to be given in my self-consciousness. It would be my own fault, if out of that which I ought to reckon as appearance, I made mere illusion.[12] That does not follow as a consequence of our principle of the ideality of all our sensible intuitions – quite the contrary. It is only if we ascribe *objective reality* to these forms of representation, that it becomes impossible for us to prevent everything being thereby transformed into mere *illusion*. For if we regard space and time as properties which, if they are to be possible at all, must be found in things in themselves, and if we reflect on the absurdities in which we are then involved, in that two infinite things, which are not substances, nor anything actually inhering in substances, must yet have existence, nay, must be the necessary condition of the existence of all things, and moreover must continue to exist, even although all existing things be removed, – we cannot blame the good Berkeley for degrading bodies to mere illusion. Nay, even our own existence, in being made thus dependent upon the self-subsistent reality of a non-entity, such as time, would necessarily be changed with it into sheer illusion – an absurdity of which no one has yet been guilty.[13]

> Thus both objects in space that we perceive by "outer sense" and the empirical self that we know by "inner sense" should be recognized as *appearances*, not things in themselves. Therefore, as Kant tells us in the following extract from the first edition of the *Critique*, we can embrace a sort of *empirical* dualism, since both matter and the thinking self belong to the world as we experience it. What must be rejected is any theory that purports to tell us the nature of things in themselves – not only *metaphysical* dualism (some things in themselves are minds, others are bodies), but also its "two counteralternatives", materialism (all are bodies) and "pneumatism" (all are minds). Berkeley is not mentioned here, but Kant clearly regarded him as a representative of "pneumatism".

If then we ask, whether it follows that in the doctrine of the soul dualism alone is tenable, we must answer: 'Yes, certainly; but dualism only in the empirical sense'. That is to say, in the connection of experience matter, as substance in the [field of] appearance, is really given to outer sense, just as the thinking 'I', also as substance in the [field of] appearance, is given to inner sense. Further, appearances in both fields must be connected with each other according to the rules which this category introduces into that connection of our outer as well as of our inner perceptions whereby they constitute one experience. If, however, as commonly happens, we seek to extend the concept of dualism, and take it in the transcendental sense, neither it nor the two counteralternatives – *pneumatism* on the one hand, *materialism* on the other – would have any sort of basis, since we should then have misapplied our concepts, taking the difference in the mode of representing objects, which, as regards what they are in themselves, still remain unknown to us, as a difference in the things themselves. Though the 'I', as represented through inner sense in time, and objects in space outside me, are specifically quite distinct appearances, they are not for that reason thought as being different things. Neither the *transcendental object* which underlies outer appearances nor that which underlies inner intuition, is in itself either matter or a thinking being, but a ground (to us unknown) of the appearances which supply to us the empirical concept of the former as well as of the latter mode of existence.[14]

If the "ground" of appearances is "to us unknown", what prevents me from doubting, as Descartes did, whether anything exists other than my mind, or from positively asserting, as Berkeley did, that minds are the only substances? Kant gave his definitive answer in the "Refutation of Idealism" (added in the second edition of the *Critique*). He deals here only briefly with Berkeley, whose argument he takes, in effect, to be this: space and everything in it are either things in themselves or illusions; but they cannot be things in themselves; therefore they are illusions. Since he has already argued in the Transcendental Aesthetic that this is a false dichotomy, he merely refers the reader to that. He here takes as his main target Descartes, who supposed that the "I" can be certain that it exists even while doubting the existence of external objects. Kant undertakes to prove that I can determine my own existence in time only because I am immediately aware of objects in space. My "inner experience" (empirical self-consciousness) is always successive – nothing in it represents to me something permanent. Were I conscious of nothing but these successive states of inner experience, "I should have as many-coloured and diverse a self as I have representations of which I am conscious to myself."[15] It is my "outer experience" of permanent substances in space (not things in themselves but phenomenal substances that are different from my empirical self-consciousness) that enables me to perceive something permanent; without this outer criterion of the permanent, I could have no empirical consciousness of myself as a subject enduring through successive moments of time. Hence, Descartes could only be conscious of his own mind if he were also conscious of enduring objects different from his mind. Although Descartes' "problematic idealism", not Berkeley's "dogmatic idealism", is the official target of the "Refutation", we give the statement of its "proof", for it seems to apply to Berkeley, certainly as Kant construes him, just as much as it would to Descartes. This is because Berkeley holds that (1) minds exist and (2) there are no objects external to them – the very claims that Kant here professes to prove incompatible.

The Refutation of Idealism

Idealism – meaning thereby *material* idealism – is the theory which declares the existence of objects in space outside us either to be merely doubtful and indemonstrable or to be false and impossible. The former is the *problematic* idealism of Descartes, which holds that there is only one empirical assertion that is indubitably certain, namely, that 'I am'. The latter is the *dogmatic* idealism of Berkeley. He maintains that space, with all the things of which it is the inseparable condition, is something which is in itself impossible; and he therefore regards the things in space as merely imaginary entities. Dogmatic idealism is unavoidable, if space be interpreted as a property that must belong to things in themselves. For in that case space, and everything to which it serves as condition, is a non-entity. The ground on which this idealism rests has already been undermined by us in the Transcendental Aesthetic. Problematic ideal-ism, which makes no such assertion, but merely pleads incapacity to prove, through immediate experience, any existence except our own, is, in so far as it allows of no decisive judgment until sufficient proof has been found, reasonable and in accordance with a thorough and philo-sophical mode of thought. The required proof must, therefore, show that we have *experience*, and not merely imagination of outer things; and this, it would seem, cannot be achieved save by proof that even our inner experience, which for Descartes is indubitable, is possible only on the assumption of outer experience.

Thesis

The mere, but empirically determined, consciousness of my own existence proves the existence of objects in space outside me.

Proof

I am conscious of my own existence as determined in time. All determi-nation of time presupposes something *permanent* in perception. This permanent cannot, however, be something in me, since it is only through this permanent that my existence in time can itself be deter-mined. Thus perception of this permanent is possible only through a *thing* outside me and not through the mere *representation* of a thing outside me; and consequently the determination of my existence in time is possible only through the existence of actual things which I perceive outside me. Now consciousness [of my existence] in time is necessarily bound up with consciousness of the [condition of the] possibility of this time-determination; and it is therefore necessarily bound up with the existence of things outside me, as the condition of the time-determination. In other words, the consciousness of my existence is at the same time an immediate consciousness of the existence of other things outside me.

Note 1. It will be observed that in the foregoing proof the game played by idealism has been turned against itself, and with greater justice. Idealism assumed that the only immediate experience is inner experience, and that from it we can only *infer* outer things – and this, moreover, only in an untrustworthy manner, as in all cases where we are inferring from given effects to determinate causes. In this particular case, the cause of the representations, which we ascribe, perhaps falsely, to outer things, may lie in ourselves. But in the above proof it has been shown that outer experience is really immediate,[16] and that only by means of it is inner experience – not indeed the consciousness of my own existence, but the determination of it in time – possible. Certainly, the representation 'I am', which expresses the consciousness that can accompany all thought, immediately includes in itself the existence of a subject; but it does not so include any *knowledge* of that subject, and therefore also no empirical knowledge, that is, no experience of it. For this we require, in addition to the thought of something existing, also intuition, and in this case inner intuition, in respect of which, that is, of time, the subject must be determined. But in order so to determine it, outer objects are quite indispensable; and it therefore follows that inner experience is itself possible only mediately, and only through outer experience.[17]

Berkeley would certainly have rejected Kant's interpretation of his philosophy. According to Kant, Berkeley degrades bodies to "mere illusion", but Berkeley explicitly denies that such is his view (*PHK* §§34–40). Kant also takes Berkeley to hold that only minds exist, whereas Berkeley insists "That the things I see with mine eyes and touch with my hands do exist, really exist, I make not the least question" (*PHK* §35). Berkeley *does* deny that there are "things in themselves", if by that we mean material substances; but Kant himself did not hold that things in themselves were material substances, while Berkeley, on his side, allows for "an external archetype" of our ideas, although "it must be supposed to exist in that mind which comprehends all things."[18] Indeed, a plausible case can be made for the claim, defended by some, that Berkeley and Kant conceive the "phenomenal world" in similar ways. The question of the relation of their views has given rise to a large literature (even the question of whether Kant had read the German translation of the *Dialogues* or knew Berkeley's views only at second hand has been given different answers). We can here do no more than note that opinions about the relation of their "idealisms" have ranged from the view that they verge on being indistinguishable to the view that they are profoundly different.[19] However *that* may be, it remains the case that Kant's *desire* to distinguish his own "critical idealism" from the "idealisms" of Descartes and Berkeley led him to make some notable additions to the *Critique*'s second edition. Indeed, in the view of some – though by no means all – of Kant's commentators, these additions signal very significant changes in Kant's position, changes that one noted commentator, Norman Kemp Smith, has characterized as marking a transition from Kant's initial "subjectivism" to his mature "phenomenalism".[20]

HERDER

There were perhaps no greater admirers of Berkeley among important eighteenth-century German philosophers than Johann Georg Hamann and Johann Gottfried Herder. Both men had personal ties to Kant, but were opponents of his philosophy. Hamann wrote a "metacritique" of Kant's *Critique of Pure Reason* in which he objected that, in his preoccupation with the "pure forms of thought" and the "antinomies of pure reason", Kant had overlooked the central role of language, for "not only does the whole ability to think rest upon language . . . but language is also the central point of reason's misunderstanding of itself."[21] Language is our helpmeet, said Hamann, but also our seducer, especially when it betrays us into empty abstractions. Not surprisingly, it was for his critique of abstraction and the abuse of language that Berkeley was especially valued by Hamann. But he also prized what he took to be Berkeley's influence on Hume. Hamann, mystical and hostile to rationalism, admired Hume for showing the vanity of reason's pretensions, but he believed Hume here followed Berkeley's lead. Thus, after noting Hume's praise for Berkeley's critique of abstract ideas, Hamann declared that it should be acknowledged "that the new scepticism owes more to the older idealism than this casual, single occasion would incidentally give us to understand, and that without Berkeley Hume would scarcely have become the great philosopher which criticism, in unanimous gratitude, makes him out to be."[22]

Like his friend Hamann, Herder was a keen admirer of Berkeley. "I regard his system as being, like the systems of Spinoza, Fénelon, Leibniz, and Descartes, *fictions*, as being poetry – what system is anything else or should be regarded as anything else? – and in Berkeley the poetry is great, keen, and thoroughly well sustained."[23] Inspired by Hamann's example, Herder, too, wrote a "metacritique" of Kant's *Critique*. In it, he rose, in a qualified way, to Berkeley's defense. To classify Berkeley simply as an "idealist" fails to do justice to his system, Herder thinks, for that system is not opposed to realism. Where Kant took Berkeley to look upon things other than the mind as illusions, Herder stresses that Berkeleian ideas are *real* things, existing in God. Herder does not examine Berkeley's views in any detail. His is a more sweeping appreciation and critique, mixed together with his own enthusiasms and slams at Kant. (It is Kant, not Berkeley, who is the main target of the harsh words Herder has for "idealists".) However, that he recognized a sense in which Berkeley can be viewed as a realist suggests that Herder appreciated aspects of Berkeley's thought that were ignored not only by Kant but by many others in the eighteenth century.[24]

On Berkeley's Idealism

The language of every philosophical system shows what world of ideas it was formed in; this can be shown true of the Ancients as well as of Cartesianism, Spinozism, Leibniz's philosophy, and finally even of Berkeley's idealism.

We do an injustice to this serious and subtle thinker if we take his system for mere bantering, or as opposed to realism. The ideas he represented as existing in the everlasting Spirit were, for him, the most real ideas, and he repeatedly contrasted them, with the greatest force and truth, to the empty figments and abstractions of language. The only thing he was a foe of was a non-entity: dead matter – a thing that, though dead, is supposed to produce effects and that, though devoid of concepts, is supposed to give rise to concepts. This is the matter that he banished from Philosophy, because it is a contradiction, and from Creation, because it is a non-entity.[25]

Immaterialism, therefore, is what Berkeley's system should be called (if one wants to give it a name), as his followers in England were originally called Immaterialists.[26] Yet so far was it from being Berkeley's intention to found a sect that what he wanted, instead, was to put an end to philosophical sects, by stripping away the excesses of abstraction and calling men back to the concrete detail of experience. It was to this end, for example, that he wrote his *Essay towards a New Theory of Vision*, in which he traced with subtlety and care the origin of, and differences between, our ideas of sight, touch, and understanding, though his account was not without some flaws.[27]

When we represent Berkeley's system aright, we show how consistent Berkeley is. He accepts – indeed expressly reiterates – that real ideas do not spring from the depth of our own souls and that we do not have power over them; rather, it is by another Spirit, i.e., by the Powers of Nature (with dead matter wholly forgotten), that ideas are caused in, or impressed on, or implanted in us, or (in some such way) come to us. And he thereby embraced, without qualification, the whole sensible world. "Why, therefore," we may say to this humane thinker,[28] "did you make language so unhelpful to yourself? Why did you erect your true observations and distinctions on a contrived paradox? We willingly grant you that ideas and sensations are only in us and can only be in us; we grant, for example, that the tableau of objects of sight will, to a newborn infant, or to a man born blind who has just got his sight, appear as a colored plane of light lying directly against his eye: experiments have confirmed this. But after infancy we leave this flat visual world behind and, with the help of our various senses, we enlarge the world that surrounds us. We create for ourselves the concepts and measures of space, size, shape, motion, distance – whose origins and relations you have yourself so diligently sought to discover. In this way did that surface that at first lay directly upon our eyes come to be a picture that is felt as well as seen – an orderly, measurable picture, the signs for which, as expressed in our language, though not always precise, are nonetheless intelligible and suggestive. Language is the storehouse of thousands of experiences, as you yourself appreciate in recognizing that every idea we call an object is really a whole congeries of ideas, replete with qualities and perceivable characteristics. Why then do you want to throw us back to the very first moment of our inexperienced infancy, reducing the whole luminous Creation to a flat surface of light in us? Surely you don't want to do that. Make use, therefore, of the riches experience has won for us. Improve upon the signs our language uses, but don't destroy them. With your first tenet, that all these ideas come to us unbidden (however they may come and from wherever), you have posited and acknowledged the whole world external to yourself."

It is this principle, too, that undermines the very foundation of idealism (if any such dream of doubt ever really entered into any human soul). What awakens the dreamer is not the concept of a measure of time, but rather the concept of cause and effect that resides in his self-consciousness. The idealist cannot fail to know, from his own self-awareness, that not all his ideas spring from the depths of his own mind, but that some come to him in a succession and an order that are governed by laws, in accordance with analogies of permanence and change, and that his power over such ideas extends no farther than a power to elaborate, retain, recall, separate, or combine them. Very well then! These ideas or sensations that are not created by us, that come to us in law-governed ways, are what we call the world of our senses, the external world. Even the idealist calls them that when he distinguishes them from the ideas of imagination he creates within himself. His paradox is thus nothing but an abuse of language, a useless idiom and solecism. We can leave this way of talking to him who fancies it, provided he'll be obliging and leave us our way of expressing ourselves. "If I am a representation in you, then you must grant that you are a representation in me too; let each of us invite the other in, as a guest, to his world. When you come into mine, be a gracious guest, not a churlish one, and I'll be content to let you use the language of your tribe."

But if, as in Swift's tale, brother Peter is determined rudely to force his language on others, proclaiming it the one true philosophical language in the world – if, turning his idealism into a crude, exclusive egoism, he asserts, "I create the world, for I make human understanding, and through it all sensibility. Behold the forms! Without me there would be no nature, for it is I who give law and order to nature!" – if he goes on like this, then one had better quietly get out of the way of this Father-God. His madness does not deserve the name *Idealism*, for it neither provides true ideas nor permits a critique of them. All he offers are empty intuitions, contentless forms and schemata – in short, literary phantasms [*Letternphantasmen*]; so his delusion, if it must have a name, can only be called a literary phantasm [*Letternphantasmus*].[29]

There was a man in our century who spoke with angels and spirits and, by making use of his organs, angels saw and spirits felt and talked: that was Swedenborg.[30] What we learned, however, from his heavenly secrets (*arcana coelestia*) – from all his conversations with the spirits – was really only what Swedenborg needed to say to himself, for how he imagined this or that spirit conformed to his own concepts and prejudices. So too, we learn nothing from Critical Idealism[31] that is not the result of the most ordinary experience expressed in the most intricately abstract language. Matter, extension, form, space, time, synthesis, schema: all of these lie there, in a matted ball of careless language that is either left in a tangle or is worked up into some a priori fantasy.

The word *Idea* meant much to the ancients; the word *idealism* signified the domain of the purest ideas. In this sense idealism is certainly not opposed to reality but is itself the richest and strictest realism.

We conclude this chapter by taking brief note of a nineteenth-century thinker who held Berkeley in higher regard than did perhaps any other great German philosopher. Schopenhauer's *World as Will and Representation* (1818) opens with a battle cry, "The world is my representation," and proceeds to declare: "This truth is by no means new. It was to be found already in the sceptical reflections from which Descartes started. But Berkeley was the first to enunciate it positively, and he has thus rendered an immortal service to philosophy, although the remainder of his doctrines cannot endure."[32] Berkeley established the general truth that objects exist only in relation to subjects, but it was Kant who showed the specific ways in which the existence of objects in space, time, and causal interconnection depend upon the subject.[33] Schopenhauer dismisses Kant's claim that his idealism and Berkeley's are antithetical, seeing in that merely Kant's fear of appearing too idealistic. At places in the *Critique*'s first edition, "Kant expounds his decided idealism with great beauty and clarity," but in his eagerness to repulse the charge that he was an idealist, Kant distinguished, in the second edition, the (phenomenal) object from our representation of it, a distinction that Schopenhauer rejects. "The distinction between the representation and the object of the representation is, however, unfounded. Berkeley had already demonstrated this, and . . . in fact it follows from Kant's own wholly idealistic point of view in the first edition."[34] The upshot of this flight from idealism in the second edition, according to Schopenhauer, is that the *Critique* "became disfigured and spoilt; it was a self-contradictory book, whose sense therefore could not be thoroughly clear and comprehensible to anyone."[35] The change that Schopenhauer here deplores is the very one that Kemp Smith sees as marking Kant's advance over his own earlier subjectivism – but they both see it as a change born, in part, of Kant's struggle to distinguish his idealism from Berkeley's.

Notes

1. See Chapter XIV. On Berkeley's relation to German philosophy, see Wolfgang Breidert, "On the Early Reception of Berkeley in Germany," in *Essays on the Philosophy of George Berkeley*, ed. E. Sosa (Dordrecht: Reidel, 1987); for a fuller account, see W. Breidert, "Die Rezeption Berkeleys in Deutschland im 18. Jahrhundert," *Revue internationale de philosophie*, no. 154 (1985), pp. 223–41, and Eugen Stäbler, *George Berkeley's Auffassung und Wirkung in der deutschen Philosophie bis Hegel* (Zeulenroda, 1935). Also A.-L. Leroy, "Influence de la philosophie berkeleyenne sur la pensée continentale," *Hermathena*, no. 82 (1953), pp. 27–48.
2. In 1727, *Acta Eruditorum* reviewed the second edition of the *Three Dialogues* and pronounced it "a mingling of the philosophies of *Descartes, Malebranche,* and *Spinoza.*" (Quoted in H. M. Bracken, *The Early Reception of Berkeley's Immaterialism*, p. 1.)
3. Wolff proposed this division in the Preface to the second edition of his *Vernünftige Gedanken von Gott, der Welt und der Seele des Menschen* (Halle, 1722).
4. *Oratio de egoismo* (Tübingen, 1722), pp. 17–18.
5. In *De differentia nexus rerum sapientis et fatalis necessitatis* (Halae Magdeburgensis, 1724), p. 75 (Wolff here links Berkeley with Collier), and in *Psychologia rationalis* (Frankfurt, 1734), p. 25.
6. Breidert, "On the Early Reception of Berkeley in Germany," p. 233.
7. J. C. Eschenbach, *Samlung der vornehmsten Schriftsteller die die Würcklichkeit ihres eignen Körpers und der ganzen Körperwelt läugnen* (Rostock, 1756).
8. The review appeared in the *Zugabe zu den Göttingischen Anzeigen von gelehrten Sachen* for January 19, 1782; it is translated in *The Real and the Ideal: Berkeley's Relation to Kant*, ed. R. C. S. Walker (New York: Garland, 1989), pp. xv–xxii.
9. *Kant: Philosophical Correspondence 1759–99*, ed. and trans. A. Zweig (Chicago: University of Chicago Press, 1967), p. 99.
10. *Prolegomena*, §13, Remarks 2 and 3, and Appendix (which replies to the review); *Critique of Pure Reason*, 2nd ed., B67–71, B274–79.
11. Kant, *Prolegomena to Any Future Metaphysics*, trans. P. Carus, revised by J. W. Ellington (Indianapolis: Hackett, 1977), §13, Remarks 2 and 3, pp. 32–33, 37. Reprinted by permission of Hackett Publishing Company, Inc. All rights reserved. In the last sentence, "dreaming idealism" refers to Descartes' view, "visionary idealism" to Berkeley's.
12. We omit a footnote that Kant adds here.

13. *Critique of Pure Reason*, trans. N. Kemp Smith (London: Macmillan, 1929), pp. 88–89 (B69–71).
14. *Critique*, pp. 351–52 (A379–380).
15. *Critique*, p. 154 (B134).
16. We omit a footnote that Kant adds here.
17. *Critique*, pp. 244–46 (B274–77).
18. *Works* II, p. 248.
19. This range of opinion is represented in the articles on the relation of Berkeley's and Kant's philosophies collected in the volume edited by Walker (see note 8).
20. N. Kemp Smith, *A Commentary to Kant's "Critique of Pure Reason"* (2nd ed., London: Macmillan, 1923), pp. 270–84, 298–321. Even H. J. Paton, a vigorous critic of Kemp Smith's views about Kant's development, granted that Kant's desire to distinguish his position from Berkeley's was a source of important changes of emphasis in the *Critique*'s second edition. See Paton's *Kant's Metaphysic of Experience: A Commentary on the First Half of the "Kritik der reinen Vernunft"* (London: Allen & Unwin, 1936), vol. 2, pp. 375–76.
21. J. G. Hamann, "Metacritique of the Purism of Reason," translated in R. G. Smith, *J. G. Hamann, 1730–1788: A Study in Christian Existence, with Selections from his Writings* (New York: Harper, 1960), p. 216.
22. Ibid., p. 213.
23. Quoted in Robert T. Clark, Jr., *Herder: His Life and Thought* (Berkeley: University of California Press, 1955), p. 178.
24. The following extract is translated from Herder's *Eine Metakritik zur Kritik der reinen Vernunft* (1799), in *Herders Sämtliche Werke*, ed. Bernhard Suphan (Berlin, 1881), vol. 21, pp. 163–67.
25. It is, therefore, a quite false notion of the Berkeleian system when, in the Critical Philosophy, it is said: "The latter is the *dogmatic* idealism of Berkeley. He maintains that space, with all the things of which it is the inseparable condition, is something which is in itself impossible; and he therefore regards things in space as merely imaginary entities." *Critique of Pure Reason*, [B] 274. How foreign to Berkeley's system are these words and imputations! [Herder's note.]
26. "He became the founder of a sect, called the Immaterialists, by the force of a very curious book on that subject; Dr. Smalridge and many other eminent persons were his proselytes." Swift. [Herder's note. Berkeley talks in warm terms of Smalridge, who became Bishop of Bristol, in letters written to Percival in 1713, noting that they have had agreeable conversations, but he does not go so far as to describe Smalridge as a convert (see *Works* VIII, pp. 67–69).]
27. *An Essay towards a New Theory of Vision*. This work, along with his *Treatise concerning the Principles of Human Knowledge*, deserves translation and discussion, although when he rails against mathematics, he goes quite astray, demanding of mathematics something it is not its office to provide. [Herder's note.]
28. "To Berkeley every virtue under heav'n." Pope. [Herder's note.]
29. The object of Herder's scorn here is Kant's doctrine that space and time arise

from the mind's "forms" of intuition, and nature's laws from "schemata" produced by the understanding. This paragraph is thus aimed *directly* at Kant.

30. Emanuel Swedenborg (1688–1772), Swedish scientist and mystic, who, in his eight-volume *Arcana Coelestia*, gave vivid depictions of his experiences in the spirit world.

31. Kant's idealism.

32. *The World as Will and Representation*, trans. E. F. J. Payne (New York: Dover, 1966), vol. 1, p. 3.

33. Vol. 2, p. 8.

34. Vol. 1, p. 444.

35. Vol. 1, p. 435.

TWENTY

Thomas Reid

Thomas Reid was born in 1710, the year in which Berkeley's *Principles* was published, but his philosophical writings date from well after the publication of Hume's *Treatise of Human Nature* and reflect the influence of both men. Indeed, it was Reid's reading of Hume that dictated his attitude to Berkeley, whom he had read and thought about very carefully. Thus in 1763, the year before the publication of his own *Inquiry into the Human Mind, on the Principles of Common Sense*, Reid was able to write to Hume that "Your system appears to me not only coherent in all its parts, but likewise justly deduced from principles commonly received among philosophers; principles which I never thought of calling in question, until the conclusions you draw from them in the Treatise of Human Nature made me suspect them."[1] Reid had, we learn, not only once accepted what he refers to elsewhere as "the doctrine of ideas," but had even embraced Berkeley's denial of matter as a consequence, until Hume taught him that the consequences of accepting the underlying doctrine were even *more* radical than Berkeley had supposed. We thus find in Reid an interpretation of Berkeley's position that, in our day, will strike many as familiar. Berkeley, in Reid's view, took over principles from others and pressed from them conclusions that soon led to the philosophy of David Hume, who, by denying spirits as well as matter, "drowned all in one universal deluge."[2]

These words are from the *Inquiry*, but the selections that follow are from two chapters in Essay II of Reid's *Essays on the Intellectual Powers of Man* (1785). Both chapters are devoted to Berkeley, and in them we meet Reid's account of the route that led Berkeley to immaterialism. We shall also find, in our extract from the second of the chapters, some of the considerations that led to Reid's rejection of a principle that Berkeley took to be "evident", that is, that the objects of human knowledge are "ideas", together with a brief summary of Reid's alternative to the "doctrine of ideas." Reid's own positive teachings are not, however, our chief concern here, although they are of considerable historical importance, forming, as they did, the basis for what came to be known as the Scottish "common-sense" school of philosophy.

The first of the two chapters (Chapter 10) is entitled "Of the sentiments of Bishop Berkeley."

GEORGE BERKELEY, afterwards Bishop of Cloyne, published his "New Theory of Vision," in 1709; his "Treatise concerning the Principles of Human Knowledge," in 1710; and his "Dialogues between Hylas and Philonous," in 1713; being then a Fellow of Trinity College, Dublin. He is acknowledged universally to have great merit, as an excellent writer, and a very acute and clear reasoner on the most abstract subjects, not to speak of his virtues as a man, which were very conspicuous; yet the doctrine chiefly held forth in the treatises above mentioned, especially in the two last, has generally been thought so very absurd, that few can be brought to think that he either believed it himself, or that he seriously meant to persuade others of its truth.

He maintains, and thinks he has demonstrated, by a variety of arguments, grounded on principles of philosophy universally received, that there is no such thing as matter in the universe; that sun and moon, earth and sea, our own bodies, and those of our friends, are nothing but ideas in the minds of those who think of them, and that they have no existence when they are not the objects of thought; that all that is in the universe may be reduced to two categories – to wit, *minds*, and *ideas in the mind*.

But, however absurd this doctrine might appear to the unlearned, who consider the existence of the objects of sense as the most evident of all truths, and what no man in his senses can doubt, the philosophers who had been accustomed to consider ideas as the immediate objects of all thought, had no title to view this doctrine of Berkeley in so unfavourable a light.

They were taught by Des Cartes, and by all that came after him, that the existence of the objects of sense is not self-evident, but requires to be proved by arguments; and, although Des Cartes, and many others, had laboured to find arguments for this purpose, there did not appear to be that force and clearness in them which might have been expected in a matter of such importance. Mr Norris had declared that, after all the arguments that had been offered, the existence of an external world is only probable, but by no means certain. Malebranche thought it rested upon the authority of revelation, and that the arguments drawn from reason were not perfectly conclusive. Others thought that the argument from revelation was a mere sophism, because revelation comes to us by our senses, and must rest upon their authority.

Thus we see that the new philosophy had been making gradual approaches towards Berkeley's opinion; and, whatever others might do, the philosophers had no title to look upon it as absurd, or unworthy of a fair examination. . . .

Like Voltaire and a number of others, Reid viewed Berkeley's *New Theory of Vision* very favorably, holding that, "taken by itself, and without relation to the main branch of his system, [it] contains very important discoveries, and marks of great genius," but after a relatively brief discussion of its chief theses and merits, Reid returns to Berkeley's main system.

In the new philosophy, the pillars by which the existence of a material world was supported, were so feeble that it did not require the force of a Samson to bring them down; and in this we have not so much reason to admire the strength of Berkeley's genius, as his boldness in publishing to the world an opinion which the unlearned would be apt to interpret as the sign of a crazy intellect. A man who was firmly persuaded of the doctrine universally received by philosophers concerning ideas, if he could but take courage to call in question the existence of a material world, would easily find unanswerable arguments in that doctrine. . . .

Reid's analysis of Berkeley's position is thus simple. Berkeley follows his philosophical predecessors in supposing it "evident" that all the objects of human knowledge are ideas in our own minds. And once that is accepted, "then, indeed, the existence of a material world must be a dream that has imposed upon all mankind from the beginning of the world." However, while Berkeley draws the logical conclusion from the doctrine that we perceive only ideas, he fails to give any justification for that doctrine.

The foundation on which such a fabric rests ought to be very solid and well established; yet Berkeley says nothing more for it than that it is evident. If he means that it is self-evident, this indeed might be a good reason for not offering any direct argument in proof of it. But I apprehend this cannot justly be said. Self-evident propositions are those which appear evident to every man of sound understanding who apprehends the meaning of them distinctly, and attends to them without prejudice. Can this be said of this proposition, That all the objects of our knowledge are ideas in our own minds? I believe that, to any man uninstructed in philosophy, this proposition will appear very improbable, if not absurd. However scanty his knowledge may be, he considers the sun and moon, the earth and sea, as objects of it; and it will be difficult to persuade him that those objects of his knowledge are ideas in his own mind, and have no existence when he does not think of them. If I may presume to speak my own sentiments, I once believed this doctrine of ideas so firmly as to embrace the whole of Berkeley's system in consequence of it; till, finding other consequences to follow from it, which gave me more uneasiness than the want of a material world, it came into my mind, more than forty years ago, to put the question, What evidence have I for this doctrine, that all the objects of my knowledge are ideas in my own mind? From that time to the present I have been candidly and impartially, as I think, seeking for the evidence of this principle, but can find none, excepting the authority of philosophers.

We shall have occasion to examine its evidence afterwards. I would at present only observe, that all the arguments brought by Berkeley against the existence of a material world are grounded upon it; and that he has not attempted to give any evidence for it, but takes it for granted, as other philosophers had done before him.

But, supposing this principle to be true, Berkeley's system is impregnable. No demonstration can be more evident than his reasoning from it. . . .

Reid is well aware that Berkeley himself claims, in Reid's words, "to take part with the vulgar against the philosophers, and to vindicate common sense against their innovations," and he gives a faithful account of the considerations that led Berkeley to make this claim, though he concludes, as many others have concluded, that Berkeley fails in his attempt to reconcile his opinions with those of the vulgar. It is unfortunate, says Reid, that "he did not carry this suspicion of the doctrine of philosophers so far as to doubt of that philosophical tenet on which his whole system is built – to wit, that the things immediately perceived by the senses are ideas which exist only in the mind!" Like Mill later, Reid is unconvinced by Philonous's attempt to answer Hylas's charge that, on his principles, no two people can perceive the same thing; unlike Mill, however, Reid apparently sees some merit in Berkeley's case against atheism. We rejoin Reid as he makes this point, and follow him as he goes on to what was by now a familiar objection to Berkeley, and to a further analysis of the historical roots of his immaterialism.

The evidence of an all-governing mind, so far from being weakened, seems to appear even in a more striking light upon his hypothesis, than upon the common one. The powers which inanimate matter is supposed to possess, have always been the stronghold of atheists, to which they had recourse in defence of their system. This fortress of atheism must be most effectually overturned, if there is no such thing as matter in the universe. In all this the Bishop reasons justly and acutely. But there is one uncomfortable consequence of his system, which he seems not to have attended to, and from which it will be found difficult, if at all possible, to guard it.

The consequence I mean is this – that, although it leaves us sufficient evidence of a supreme intelligent mind, it seems to take away all the evidence we have of other intelligent beings like ourselves. What I call a father, a brother, or a friend, is only a parcel of ideas in my own mind; and, being ideas in my mind, they cannot possibly have that relation to another mind which they have to mine, any more than the pain felt by me can be the individual pain felt by another. I can find no principle in Berkeley's system, which affords me even probable ground to conclude that there are other intelligent beings, like myself, in the relations of father, brother, friend, or fellow-citizen. I am left alone, as the only creature of God in the universe, in that forlorn state of *egoism* into which it is said some of the disciples of Des Cartes were brought by his philosophy.

Of all the opinions that have ever been advanced by philosophers, this of Bishop Berkeley, that there is no material world, seems the strangest, and the most apt to bring philosophy into ridicule with plain men who are guided by the dictates of nature and common sense. And, it will not, I apprehend, be improper to trace this progeny of the doctrine of ideas from its origin, and to observe its gradual progress, till it acquired such strength that a pious and learned bishop had the boldness to usher it into the world, as demonstrable from the principles of philosophy universally received, and as an admirable expedient for the advancement of knowledge and for the defence of religion.

During the reign of the Peripatetic philosophy, men were little disposed to doubt, and much to dogmatize. The existence of the objects of sense was held as a first principle; and the received doctrine was, that the sensible species or idea is the very form of the external object, just separated from the matter of it, and sent into the mind that perceives it; so that we find no appearance of scepticism about the existence of matter under that philosophy.

Des Cartes taught men to doubt even of those things that had been taken for first principles. He rejected the doctrine of species or ideas coming from objects; but still maintained that what we immediately perceive, is not the external object, but an idea or image of it in our mind. This led some of his disciples into Egoism, and to disbelieve the existence of every creature in the universe but themselves and their own ideas.

But Des Cartes himself – either from dread of the censure of the church, which he took great care not to provoke; or to shun the ridicule of the world, which might have crushed his system at once, as it did that of the Egoists; or, perhaps, from inward conviction – was resolved to support the existence of matter. To do this consistently with his principles, he found himself obliged to have recourse to arguments that are far-fetched, and not very cogent. Sometimes he argues that our senses are given us by God, who is no deceiver; and, therefore, we ought to believe their testimony. But this argument is weak; because, according to his principles, our senses testify no more but that we have certain ideas: and, if we draw conclusions from this testimony, which the premises will not support, we deceive ourselves. To give more force to this weak argument, he sometimes adds, that we have by nature a strong propensity to believe that there is an external world corresponding to our ideas.

Malebranche thought that this strong propensity is not a sufficient reason for believing the existence of matter; and that it is to be received as an article of faith, not certainly discoverable by reason. He is aware that faith comes by hearing; and that it may be said that prophets, apostles, and miracles are only ideas in our minds. But to this he answers, that, though these things are only ideas, yet faith turns them into realities; and this answer, he hopes, will satisfy those who are not too morose.

It may perhaps seem strange that Locke, who wrote so much about ideas, should not see those consequences which Berkeley thought so obviously deducible from that doctrine. Mr Locke surely was not willing that the doctrine of ideas should be thought to be loaded with such consequences. He acknowledges that the existence of a material world is not to be received as a first principle – nor is it demonstrable; but he offers the best arguments for it he can; and supplies the weakness of his arguments by this observation – that we have such evidence as is sufficient to direct us in pursuing the good and avoiding the ill we may receive from external things, beyond which we have no concern. . . .[3]

Mr Norris, in his "Essay towards the Theory of the Ideal or Intelligible World," published in 1701, observes, that the material world is not an object of sense; because sensation is within us, and has no object. Its existence, therefore, he says, is a collection of reason, and not a very evident one.

From this detail we may learn that the doctrine of ideas, as it was new-modelled by Des Cartes, looked with an unfriendly aspect upon the material world; and, although philosophers were very unwilling to give up either, they found it very difficult to reconcile them to each other. In this state of things, Berkeley, I think, is reputed the first who had the daring resolution to give up the material world altogether, as a sacrifice to the received philosophy of ideas.

Our next selection comes from Chapter 11, which is entitled "Bishop Berkeley's sentiments of the nature of Ideas." In this chapter Reid reveals that he has been struck by Berkeley's distinctions between "ideas" and "notions" and between ideas of *sense* and ideas of *imagination*, but he is highly critical of Berkeley's treatment of both these distinctions, arguing that Berkeley fails to do justice to "notions", and rejecting his view that the supposed ideas of imagination differ from those of sensation only by being less vivid, regular, and constant.[4] We omit this material, however, and focus on Reid's fundamental claim, which is that, while "sensations" may *accompany* "perceptions", the sensation must not be confused with either the perception or its object. The distinction between *sensation* and *perception* is central to Reid's epistemology. With Berkeley, he held that a sensation can resemble nothing but another sensation.[5] Further, he acknowledged that *sensations* do not have objects that are distinct from them (for example, in a feeling of pain – a paradigm of sensation for him – we do not find two things, a feeling and a pain). But *perceptions*, on Reid's view, do and must have objects – objects that are distinct from them. By a "perception" Reid understands a mental operation that is typically joined to a sensation but that includes both a conception of the object perceived *and* an irresistible belief in the present existence of that object.[6] Reid writes:

As there can be no notion or thought but in a thinking being; so there can be no sensation but in a sentient being. It is the act or feeling of a sentient being; its very essence consists in its being felt. Nothing can resemble a sensation, but a similar sensation in the same or in some other mind. To think that any quality in a thing that is inanimate can resemble a sensation, is a great absurdity. In all this, I cannot but agree perfectly with Bishop Berkeley; and I think his notions of sensation much more distinct and accurate than Locke's, who thought that the primary qualities of body are resemblances of our sensations, but that the secondary are not.

That we have many sensations by means of our external senses, there can be no doubt; and, if he is pleased to call those ideas, there ought to be no dispute about the meaning of a word. But, says Bishop Berkeley, by our senses, we have the knowledge *only* of our sensations or ideas, call them which you will. I allow him to call them which he will; but I would have the word *only* in this sentence to be well weighed, because a great deal depends upon it.

For, if it be true that, by our senses, we have the knowledge of our sensations only, then his system must be admitted, and the existence of a material world must be given up as a dream. No demonstration can be more invincible than this. If we have any knowledge of a material world, it must be by the senses: but, by the senses, we have no knowledge but of our sensations only; and our sensations have no resemblance of anything that can be in a material world. The only proposition in this demonstration which admits of doubt is, that, by our senses, we have the knowledge of our sensations only, and of nothing else. If there are objects of the senses which are not sensations, his arguments do not touch them: they may be things which do not exist in the mind, as all sensations do; they may be things of which, by our senses, we have notions, though no ideas; just as, by consciousness and reflection, we have notions of spirits and of their operations, without ideas or sensations.

Shall we say, then, that, by our senses, we have the knowledge of our sensations only; and that they give us no notion of anything but of our sensations? Perhaps this has been the doctrine of philosophers, and not of Bishop Berkeley alone, otherwise he would have supported it by arguments. Mr Locke calls all the notions we have by our senses, ideas of sensation; and in this has been very generally followed. Hence it seems a very natural inference, that ideas of sensation are sensations. But philosophers may err: let us hear the dictates of common sense upon this point.

Suppose I am pricked with a pin, I ask, Is the pain I feel, a sensation? Undoubtedly it is. There can be nothing that resembles pain in any inanimate being. But I ask again, Is the pin a sensation? To this question I find myself under a necessity of answering, that the pin is not a sensation, nor can have the least resemblance to any sensation. The pin has length and thickness, and figure and weight. A sensation can have none of those qualities. I am not more certain that the pain I feel is a sensation, than that the pin is not a sensation; yet the pin is an object of sense; and I am as certain that I perceive its figure and hardness by my senses, as that I feel pain when pricked by it. . . .

In sensation, properly so called, I can distinguish two things – the mind, or sentient being, and the sensation. Whether the last is to be called a feeling or an operation, I dispute not; but it has no object distinct from the sensation itself. If in sensation there be a third thing, called an idea, I know not what it is.

In perception, in remembrance, and in conception, or imagination, I distinguish three things – the mind that operates, the operation of the mind, and the object of that operation. That the object perceived is one thing, and the perception of that object another, I am as certain as I can be of anything. The same may be said of conception, of remembrance, of love and hatred, of desire and aversion. In all these, the act of mind about its object is one thing, the object is another thing. There must be an object, real or imaginary, distinct from the operation of the mind about it. Now, if in these operations the idea be a fourth thing different from the three I have mentioned, I know not what it is, nor have been able to learn from all that has been written about ideas. And if the doctrine of philosophers about ideas confounds any two of these things which I have mentioned as distinct – if, for example, it confounds the object perceived with the perception of that object, and represents them as one and the same thing – such doctrine is altogether repugnant to all that I am able to discover of the operations of my own mind; and it is repugnant to the common sense of mankind, expressed in the structure of all languages.

* * *

In the course of a summing up of his picture of the then recent developments in philosophy, Reid observed: "Mr Locke had taught us, that all the immediate objects of human knowledge are ideas in the mind. Bishop Berkeley, proceeding upon this foundation, demonstrated, very easily, that there is no material world. . . . But the Bishop, as became his order, was unwilling to give up the world of spirits. . . . Mr Hume shews no such partiality in favour of the world of spirits. He adopts the theory of ideas in its full extent; and, in consequence, shews that there is neither matter nor mind in the universe; nothing but impressions and ideas."[7] Reid's writings were very influential, first in Scotland, later in America and even in France and Germany, and clearly played a role in establishing the traditional picture of the "triumvirate" of British Empiricists, moving ineluctably from Locke through Berkeley to Hume's skepticism. That story has been challenged by a number of recent scholars, but it is probably the one still told in many a philosophy classroom.

Notes

1. *The Works of Thomas Reid* (hereafter "*RW*"), ed. Sir William Hamilton (Edinburgh, 1863), vol. 1, p. 91.
2. *RW*, vol. 1, p. 103. It should be stressed here that, although Reid certainly saw *Locke* as a very prominent exponent of the "doctrine of ideas", and therefore held that there was a natural route from Locke to Berkeley, and from Berkeley to Hume, he did not hold that the principles concerned derived *solely* from Locke. The principles, he says, were "commonly received among philosophers." (Like many of Berkeley's earlier critics, Reid was conscious of a strong affinity between Berkeley's view and Malebranche's. See *RW*, vol. 1, pp. 103, 266, 464.)
3. We omit here a passage in which Reid conjectures, on the strength of a rather obscure remark of Locke's in *Essay* 4.10.18 regarding the creation of matter, that Locke himself may have "had a glimpse" of a system such as Berkeley's, but "left it to those who should come after him to carry his principles their full length, when they should by time be better established, and able to bear the shock of their opposition to vulgar notions." This conjecture would be very interesting were it correct; in fact it is almost certainly false – see Hamilton's note (*RW*, vol. 2, p. 924); cf. Michael Ayers, *Locke* (London: Routledge, 1991), vol. 2, pp. 59–60. That Reid makes it, on the basis of scant evidence, can really only be explained by his conviction that, given that "Berkeley's system follows from Mr Locke's, by very obvious consequence," one might have *expected* Locke to have seen that this was so.

4. Later, Reid examines Berkeley's treatment of abstract ideas, agreeing with Berkeley that there can be no abstract *ideas* in what he takes to be Locke's sense, but insisting that there are "abstract and general conceptions." *RW*, vol. 1, pp. 406–9.

5. Commenting on this point, which Reid had already made in the *Inquiry*, Joseph Priestley went so far as to suggest that, in embracing even this doctrine – that sensations can resemble only sensations – Reid was unwittingly playing into Berkeley's hands and cutting the mind off from the external world. See Joseph Priestley, *An Examination of Dr. Reid's Inquiry into the Human Mind* [etc.] (London, 1774), pp. 60–61.

6. See *RW*, vol. 1, pp. 229–30, 258–60, 310–13; cf. pp. 182–86.

7. *RW*, vol. 1, p. 293.

TWENTY-ONE

John Stuart Mill

We give the last word in this volume to J. S. Mill, the foremost British empiricist of the nineteenth century. Mill's standing as a philosopher gives us one good reason for looking at some of his comments on Berkeley, but so too does the fact that they come from his review of A. C. Fraser's *Works of George Berkeley, D.D., formerly Bishop of Cloyne*, the first complete edition of Berkeley's works. Fraser's edition, which included (in a deeply flawed form) the then newly discovered notebooks that we now know as the *Philosophical Commentaries*, ushered in a new era of Berkeley scholarship and of interest in Berkeley's philosophy. Thus Mill, who was well into his sixties and coming toward the end of his life when he reviewed this edition, can be said to stand at the end of one era and at the threshold of a new one. He was, as we shall see, very enthusiastic about Berkeley. That enthusiasm provides a further reason for including Mill in our volume. Mill is extravagant in his praise of Berkeley. The list he gives of great names in philosophy includes Plato, Hobbes, Locke, Hume, Descartes, Spinoza, Leibniz, and Kant, and yet it is Berkeley he accounts "the one of greatest philosophic genius."

Such lavish praise would have found few echoes, then or even since. Yet Mill's enthusiasm is not hard to account for. For, while it is certainly true that Berkeley's merits as a philosopher are indeed considerable (albeit not so stupendous as Mill thinks), what Mill admires Berkeley for most are those doctrines that have some clear parallel in Mill's own philosophy. Thus, each of what Mill describes as Berkeley's "three first-rate philosophical discoveries" stands in close relation to one of Mill's own doctrines. The first, Berkeley's theory of how we come habitually to associate tangible distance and magnitude with various sensations that attend *vision*, Mill sees as an important contribution to the associationist theory he was himself a leading proponent of; the second, Berkeley's attack on abstract ideas, and his account of general thought and reasoning, accords with Mill's own anti-abstractionism; and the third, Berkeley's account of the bodies we suppose external, Mill sees as foreshadowing (in so far as it is correct) his own *phenomenalist* account of physical reality. Mill's phenomenalism has been described as "Berkeley without God,"[1] but, more generally, it is not unfair to say that, in what follows, Mill praises Berkeley in so far as Berkeley anticipates Mill, and criticizes him only where their views are discrepant. As one writer has rather unkindly but not implausibly put it, "Berkeley made the Mills, father and son, possible, and it is only because this seems a lesser feat to us than it did to Mill that we esteem him less."[2]

Professor Fraser, and the University of Oxford, have done a good service to philosophy, in recalling the attention of students to the writings of a great man, by the publication of a new, and the first complete, edition of his works. Every tiro in metaphysics is familiar with the name of Berkeley, and thinks himself perfectly well acquainted with the Berkeleian doctrines: but they are known, in most cases, so far as known at all, not from what their author, but from what other people, have said of them, and are consequently, by the majority of those who think they know them, crudely conceived, and their most characteristic features misunderstood. Though he was excelled by none who ever wrote on philosophy in the clear expression of his meaning, and discrimination of it from what he did not mean, scarcely any thinker has been more perseveringly misapprehended, or has been the victim of such persistent *ignoratio elenchi*; his numerous adversaries having generally occupied themselves in proving what he never denied, and denying what he never asserted. If the facilities afforded by Professor Fraser's labours induce those who are interested in philosophy or in the history of philosophy to study Berkeley's speculations as they issued from his own mind, we think it will be recognised that of all who, from the earliest times, have applied the powers of their minds to metaphysical inquiries, he is the one of greatest philosophic genius: though among these are included Plato, Hobbes, Locke, Hartley, and Hume; Descartes, Spinoza, Leibnitz, and Kant. For, greatly as all these have helped the progress of philosophy, and important as are the contributions of several of them to its positive truths, of no one of them can it be said as of Berkeley, that we owe to him three first-rate philosophical discoveries, each sufficient to have constituted a revolution in psychology, and which by their combination have determined the whole course of subsequent philosophical speculation; discoveries, too, which were not, like the achievements of many other distinguished thinkers, merely refutations of error, and removal of obstacles to sound thinking, but were this and much more also, being all of them entitled to a permanent place among positive truths. These discoveries are –

1. The doctrine of the acquired perceptions of sight: that the most important part of what our eyes inform us of, and in particular externality, distance, and magnitude, are not direct perceptions of the sense of sight, but judgments or inferences, arrived at by a rapid interpretation of natural signs; the signification of which signs is taught to us neither by instinct nor reason, but by experience.
2. The non-existence of abstract ideas; and the fact that all the general or class notions by means of which we think or reason, are really, whether we know it or not, concrete ideas of individual objects.
3. The true nature and meaning of the externality which we attribute to the objects of our senses: that it does not consist in a substratum supporting a set of sensible qualities, or an unknown somewhat, which, not being itself a sensation, gives us our sensations, but consists in the fact that our sensations occur in groups, held together by a permanent law, and which come and go independently of our volitions or mental processes.

The first-mentioned of these three speculations was the earliest great triumph of analytic psychology over first appearances (dignified in some systems by the name of Natural Beliefs); and at once afforded a model and set an example to subsequent analysts.

The second corrected a misconception which darkened the whole theory of the higher operations of intellect, making impossible any real progress in the analysis of those operations until the error had been got rid of. The Conceptualists stopped the way in philosophy, as at an earlier period the Realists had done. Berkeley refuted them, and, while adopting what was true in the doctrines of Nominalism, laid the foundation of a theory of the action of the mind in general reasoning, far ahead of anything which the Nominalists had arrived at.

Thirdly and lastly, the speculations of Berkeley concerning our notion of the external world, besides their psychological importance as an analysis of perception, were the most memorable lesson ever given to mankind in the great intellectual attainment of not believing without evidence. From that time a new canon of belief, and standard of proof, were given to thinkers, on all the abstruser subjects of philosophical inquiry.

The three together have made Berkeley the turning-point of the higher philosophy in modern times. As a matter of historical fact, this admits of no dispute. Psychology and metaphysics before and after Berkeley differ almost like ancient and modern history, or ancient and modern physics. His first two discoveries have been the starting-point of the true analytic method of studying the human mind, of which they alone have rendered possible the subsequent developments; while his reasonings on Matter have confessedly decided the direction of all succeeding metaphysical thought, alike in those who accepted, wholly or partially, the doctrine of Berkeley, and in those who fought against it.

When to all this it is added that, in mere literary style, he can take rank among the best writers of an age not unjustly regarded as in that respect the great age of English prose literature, there is reason enough that a knowledge of his doctrines should be sought in his own works, and that the present edition of them should not rest idly on library shelves, but should be part of the familiar reading of all serious students of the philosophy or history of the human mind.

In reading Berkeley's writings as a connected whole, one is forcibly struck with the completeness with which all his characteristic doctrines had been wrought out in his mind, before he gave publicity to any of them. In the very interesting common-place book (or rather note-book) kept by Berkeley when a student at the University of Dublin, and which Professor Fraser has had the good fortune and merit of bringing to light, every opinion distinctive of Berkeley is already found, even down to his points of dispute with the mathematicians; and found, not in germ merely, but almost as complete in point of mere thought, as in any of his subsequent writings. What is called his idealism, or disbelief in Matter, had not only been reached by him, but had become a fixed habit of thought at that early age. This fact is not without psychological interest, as explaining the sincere astonishment manifested in many passages of his writings, that his interpretation of sensible phenomena should not, as soon as understood, be seen to be the self-evident and common-sense view of them. Such examples of the mental law – that a mode of representing things to ourselves with which we have grown familiar, however opposed it may be to common opinion, tends to become, in our own minds, apparently self-evident – should not, when they come before us, be dismissed as the eccentricities of an individual, but should make us reflect how much more likely it is that the common opinion itself may also be indebted for its apparent self-evidence to its still greater degree of familiarity, often unbroken by the suggestion, even to fancy, of anything contradictory to it.

The doctrine of Berkeley's first psychological work, the *Essay towards a New Theory of Vision*, seems, and indeed is, quite independent of immaterialism; and has been accepted by the great majority of subsequent psychologists, most of whom have adopted a hostile attitude towards his idealism. But, though he published the theory of the acquired perceptions of sight before his main doctrine (which it only preceded by a year), in his own mind there was an intimate connection between them. For, the form in which he liked to represent to himself those visual appearances of linear and aërial perspective, and those muscular sensations attending movements of the globes of the eyes, which, being interpreted, inform us of tangible distance and magnitude, was that of a language in which God speaks to us, and the meaning of which, derived solely from his will, is taught to us, not by direct instruction, but by experience. Now, Berkeley's idealism was an extension of this notion to the whole of our bodily sensations. As considered by him, all these are the direct act of God, who by his divine power impresses them on our minds without the intervention of any passive external substance, and who has established among them those constant relations of co-existence and successions required for our guidance in life, which suggest to us the unfounded idea of objects external to us, other than minds or spirits. The doctrine of the *Essay on Vision* might be conceived as a first step towards this system, and derived, no doubt, an additional recommendation to Berkeley from fitting so well into it; but in itself it rests on evidence strictly its own, and is equally compatible with either opinion as to the externality and substantiality of physical nature. Accordingly, it received almost unanimous assent from philosophers of both opinions, until, in our time, some unsuccessful attempts have been made to overthrow it.

Mill here clearly has in mind, in particular, Samuel Bailey's *A Review of Berkeley's Theory of Vision* (London, 1842), which Mill had quickly replied to in the *Westminster Review*, and T. K. Abbott's *Sight and Touch* (London, 1864). As A. A. Luce observes in his introduction to *Works*, vol. I, these hostile treatments challenged the by then widespread enthusiasm for Berkeley's *New Theory of Vision*, an enthusiasm Mill shared. We omit the rest of what Mill has to say about this, the first of Berkeley's "first-rate philosophical discoveries," for it concerns the *New Theory of Vision* rather than the *Principles* or *Dialogues*. We merely note that Berkeley's originality here, according to Mill, lies in this: "The power of the law of association in giving to artificial combinations the appearance of ultimate facts was then for the first time made manifest." Although Mill recognizes that *for Berkeley* God plays an important role in the story, Mill himself does not, as we shall see, warm to that aspect of Berkeley's philosophy.

The second of Berkeley's great contributions to philosophy – his theory of general thought – is, that it is carried on, not, as even Locke imagined, by means of general or abstract ideas, but by ideas of individuals, serving as representatives of classes. All ideas, it was maintained by Berkeley, are concrete and individual, which yet is no hindrance to our arriving, by means of them, at truths which are general. When, for example, we prove the properties of triangles, the idea in our mind is not, as Locke supposed, the abstract idea of a triangle which is nothing but a triangle – which is neither equilateral, isosceles, nor scalene – but the concrete idea of some particular triangle, from which, nevertheless, we may conclude to all other triangles, if we have taken care to use no premises but such as are true of any triangle whatever. This doctrine, which is now generally received, though perhaps not always thoroughly comprehended, was undoubtedly, like that of the acquired perceptions of sight, intimately connected in Berkeley's mind with his ideal theory; for he regarded the notion of matter, apart from sensations in a mind, as the supreme instance of that absurdity, an abstract idea. As in the theory of vision, so in this, Berkeley broke the neck of the problem. He for the first time saw to the bottom of the Nominalist and Realist controversy, and established the fact that all our ideas are of individuals; though he left it to his successors to point out the exact nature of the psychological machinery (if the expression may be allowed) by which general names do their work without the help of general ideas. The solution of this, as of so many other difficulties, lies in the connotation of general names.[3] A name, though common to an indefinite multitude of individual objects, is not, like a proper name, devoid of meaning; it is a mark for the properties, or for some of the properties, which belong alike to all these objects, and with these common properties it is associated in a peculiarly close and intimate manner. Now – though the name calls up, and cannot help calling up, in addition to these properties, others in greater or smaller number which do not belong to the whole class, but to the one or more individual members of it which, for the time being, are serving as mental types of the class – these other ingredients are accidental and changeable; so that the idea actually called up by the class name, though always that of some individual, is an idea in which the properties that the name is a mark of are made artificially prominent, while the others, varying from time to time, and not being attended to, are thrown into the shade. What had been mistaken for an abstract idea, was a concrete image, with certain parts of it fluctuating (within given limits) and others fixed, these last forming the signification of the general name; and the name, by concentrating attention on the class-attributes, prevents the intrusion into our reasoning of anything special to the individual object which in the particular case is pictured in the mind.

The third of Berkeley's distinctive doctrines, and that by which his name is best known, is his denial of Matter, or rather of Matter as defined by philosophers; for he always maintained that his opinion is nearer to the common belief of mankind than the doctrine of philosophers is. Philosophers, he says, consider matter to be one thing, and our sensible impressions, called ideas of sense, another: they believe that what we perceive are only our ideas, while the Matter which lies under them and impresses them upon us is the real thing. The vulgar, on the contrary, believe that the things they perceive are the real things, and do not believe in any hidden thing lying underneath them. And in this I, Berkeley, differ with the philosophers, and agree with the vulgar, for I believe that the things we perceive are the real things, and the only things, except minds, that are real. But then he held with the philosophers, and not with the vulgar, that what we directly perceive are not external objects, but our own ideas; a notion which the generality of mankind never dreamed of. Accordingly, at the conclusion of his fullest and clearest exposition of his own doctrine (the *Dialogues between Hylas and Philonous*), Berkeley says that the truth is at present "shared between the vulgar and philosophers: the former being of opinion that those things they immediately perceive are the real things; and the latter, that the things immediately perceived are ideas which exist only in the mind."

It was enough for Berkeley to say, and this he was fully justified in saying, that he did not deny the validity of perception, nor of conscious-

ness; that he affirmed the reality of all that either the vulgar or philosophers really perceive by their senses, and denied only what was not a
perception, but a rapid and unconscious inference, like the inference
which is mistaken for perception when we judge of externality and
distance by the eye; with the difference, however, that in this last case
the inference is legitimate, having experience to rest upon, while in the
case of matter there is no ground in experience or in anything else for
regarding the sensations we are conscious of as signs of the presence of
anything, except potentialities of other sensations. Berkeley might say
with truth, and in his own language he did say, that he agreed with the
common opinion of mankind in all that they distinctly realise to themselves under the notion of matter. For he agreed in recognising in the
impressions of sense a permanent element, which does not cease to exist
in the intervals between our sensations, and which is entirely independent of our own individual mind (though not of all mind). And he was
quite right in maintaining that this is all that goes to make up the
positive notion which mankind have of material objects. The point at
which he diverged from them was where they add to this positive notion
a negative one – viz., that these objects are not mental, or such as can
only exist in a mind. Without including this, it is impossible to give a
correct account of the common notion of matter; and on this point an
unmistakeable difference existed between Berkeley and the common
mind. It was competent to Berkeley to maintain that this part of the
common notion is an illusion; and he did maintain this, in our opinion
successfully. He was not equally successful in showing how the illusion
is produced, and in what manner it grows into a *de*lusion. He gives as a
sufficient explanation "that men knowing they perceived several ideas,
whereof they themselves were not the authors – as not being excited
from within, nor depending on the operation of their wills – this made
them maintain those ideas or objects of perception had an existence
independent of and without the mind, without ever dreaming that a
contradiction was involved in those words." It is not surprising that this
explanation should not be accepted as sufficient. For our thoughts, also,
do not always depend on our own will; and therefore, on this theory,
our thoughts, as well as our sense-perceptions, should sometimes be
considered to be external to us. Berkeley escapes from this difficulty by
greatly exaggerating the dependence of the thoughts upon the will. He
also adds, as another distinction between sensations and thoughts, that
the former are "not excited from within." But the very notions of
without and within, in reference to our mind, involve belief in extern-

ality, and cannot, therefore, serve to account for the belief. Berkeley left this part of his theory to be completed by his successors. It remained for them to show how easily and naturally, when a single sensation of sight or sound indicates the potential presence, at our option, of all the other sensations of a complex group, this latent though present possibility of a host of sensations not felt, but guaranteed by experience, comes to be mistaken for a latent cause of the sensations we actually feel; especially when the possibilities, unlike the actual sensations, are found to be common to us with other minds. This has been shown, perhaps more fully and explicitly than ever before, in the present generation. That it could not be so distinctly pointed out by Berkeley, was partly because he had not thoroughly realised the fact, that the permanent element in our perceptions is only a potentiality of sensations not actually felt. He saw indeed, quite clearly, that *to us* the external object is nothing but such a potentiality. "The table I write on," he says in the *Principles of Human Knowledge*, "I say exists, that is, I see and feel it; and if I were out of my study I should say it existed – meaning thereby that if I was in my study I might perceive it, or that some other spirit does perceive it." But in itself the object was, in his theory, not merely a present potentiality, but a present actual existence, only its existence was in a mind – in the Divine Mind. This is the positive side of his theory, not so generally known or attended to as the negative side, and which involves, we think, some serious logical errors.

It must here be observed, that Berkeley was not content with maintaining that the existence of a material substratum is neither perceived by the senses, nor proved by reason, nor necessary to account for the phenomena, and is therefore, by the rules of sound logic, to be rejected. He thought that it could be disproved. He considered the notion of matter to involve a contradiction: and it was true that the notion as defined by many philosophers did so. For their definition of matter affirmed it to be purely passive and inert; yet they regarded material objects as the exciting causes of our sensations. There was no refuting Berkeley when he said that what is passive and inert cannot cause or excite anything. To the notion of philosophers that the causes of our sensations might be "the configuration, number, motion, and size of corpuscles," he replied by an appeal to consciousness. Extension, figure, and motion, he said, are ideas, existing only in the mind; "but whoever shall attend to his ideas, whether of sense or reflection, will not perceive in them any power or activity; there is, therefore, no such thing contained in them. A little attention will discover to us that the very being of an idea implies passiveness and inertness in it, insomuch that it is impossible for an idea to do anything, or, strictly speaking, to be the cause of anything. Whence it plainly follows that extension, figure, and motion cannot be the cause of our sensations." From this he deduces that as our sensations must have a cause, and as this cannot be other sensations (or ideas), and as there exists no physical thing except sensations (or ideas), the cause of our sensations must be a spirit. He thus anticipates the doctrine of which so much use has been made by later philosophers of a school opposed to his own; that nothing can be a cause, or exert power, but a mind.

It would have been well if the thinker who was almost the founder and creator of the Experience philosophy of mind, had contented himself with (in the language of Kant) a *criticism* of experience – with distinguishing what is and what is not a subject of it: instead of, as we find him here, dispensing with experience, by an *à priori* argument from intuitive consciousness. For it is in vain to consult consciousness about the existence of a power. Powers are not objects of consciousness. A power is not a concrete entity, which we can perceive or feel, but an abstract name for a possibility; and can only be ascertained by seeing the possibility realised. Intuitive perception tells us the colour, texture, &c., of gunpowder, but what intuition have we that it can blow up a house? True it is that all we can observe of physical phenomena is their constancies of co-existence, succession, and similitude. Berkeley had the merit of clearly discerning this fundamental truth, and handing down to his successors the true conception of that which alone the study of physical nature can consist in. He saw that the causation we think we see in nature is but uniformity of sequence. But this is not what he considers real causation to be. No physical phenomenon, he says, can be an efficient cause; but our daily experience proves to us that minds, by their volitions, can be, and are, efficient causes. Let us be thankful to Berkeley for the half of the truth which he saw, though the remainder was hidden from him by that mist of natural prejudice from which he had cleared so many other mental phenomena. No one, before Hume, ventured to think that this supposed experience of efficient causality by volitions is as mere an illusion as any of those which Berkeley exploded, and that what we really know of the power of our own volitions is only that certain facts (reducible, when analysed, to muscular movements) immediately follow them. Berkeley proceeded to argue, that since our sensations must be caused by a mind, they must be given to us by the direct action of the Divine Mind, without the employment of an unintelligible inert substance as an intermediate link. Having no efficacy as a means, this passive substance could only intervene, if at all, not as a cause, but as an occasion, determining the Divine Being to give us the sensations: a doctrine actually held by Malebranche and other Cartesians, but to Berkeley inadmissible, since what need can the Deity have of such a reminder? Indeed, Malebranche admitted that on his theory there would be no necessity for believing in this superfluous wheel in the machinery, if its existence had not been, as he supposed it to be, expressly affirmed in Scripture. Therefore, thought Berkeley, all that is termed perception of material objects is the direct action of God upon our minds, and no substance but spirit has any concern in it.

But Berkeley did not stop here. That which is the immediate object of perception according to previous philosophers, and the sole object according to Berkeley, was our ideas – a much-abused term, never more unhappily applied than when it was given as a name to sensations and possibilities of sensation. These ideas (argued Berkeley) are admitted to have a permanent existence, contrasted with the intermittence of actual sensations; and an idea can have no existence except in a mind. They exist in our own minds only while we perceive them, and in the minds of other men only while those other men perceive them; how then is their existence sustained when no man perceives them? By their permanently existing in the mind of God. This appeared to Berkeley so conclusive an argument for the existence of a Supreme Mind, that it might well take the place of all the other evidences of natural theology. There must be a Deity, because, if there were not, there would be no permanent lodging-place for physical nature; since it has no existence out of a mind, and does not constantly and continuously exist in any finite mind. And he sincerely believed that this argument put a final extinguisher upon "atheism and scepticism." All that we perceive must be in a mind, and when no finite being is perceiving it, there is only the Divine Mind for it to abide in. This quaint theory presents a distant and superficial resemblance to Plato's doctrine of ideas; and in *Siris*, which in its metaphysical part contains the latest of Berkeley's statements of his opinion, he presses Plato and the Platonists (who, as Coleridge says, should rather be called the Plotinists) into the service of his theory; leading Professor Fraser to believe that the theory itself had undergone modifications, and had been developed in his later years into something more nearly akin to Realism. To our mind the passages in *Siris* do not convey this impression. There is a wide chasm between Berkeley's doctrine and Plato's, and we do not believe that Berkeley ever stepped over it. The Platonic

Ideas were self-existent and immaterial, but were as much external to the Divine Mind as to the human. The gods, in their celestial circuits, so imaginatively depicted in the *Phaedrus*, lived in the perpetual contemplation of these Ideas, but were neither the authors, nor were their minds the seat and habitation of them; their sole privilege above mankind was that of never losing sight of them. Moreover Plato's Ideas were not, like Berkeley's, identified with the common objects of sense, but were studiously and most broadly distinguished from them, as being the imperishable prototypes of those great and glorious attributes – beauty, justice, knowledge, &c. – of which some distant and faint likeness may be perceived in the noblest only of terrestrial things. We see no signs that Berkeley ever drew nearer to these opinions; and it seems to us that his citations of the Platonists were not an adoption of their doctrines, but an attempt to show that they had, in a certain sense, made an approximation to his, at least to the extent of throwing off the vulgar opinions.

The part of Berkeley's theory on which he grounded what he deemed the most cogent argument for a Deity, is obviously the weak and illogical part of it. While showing that our sensations, equally with our thoughts, are but phenomena of our own mind, he recognised, with the rest of the world, a permanent element in the sensations which does not exist in the thoughts; but he had an imperfect apprehension of what that permanent element is. He supposed that the actual object of a sensible perception, though, on his own showing, only a group of sensations, and suspended so far as we are concerned when we cease to perceive it, comes back literally the same the next time it is perceived by us; and, being the same, must have been kept in existence in another mind. He did not see clearly that the sensations I have to-day are not the same as those I had yesterday, which are gone, never to return; but are only exactly similar; and that what has been kept in continuous existence is but a potentiality of having such sensations, or, to express it in other words, a law of uniformity in nature, by virtue of which similar sensations might and would have recurred, at any intermediate time, under similar conditions.[4] These sensations, which I did not have, but which experience teaches me that I might have had at any time during the intermission of my actual sensations, are not a positive entity subsisting through that time: they did not exist as sensations, but as a guaranteed belief; implying constancy in the order of phenomena, but not a spiritual substance for the phenomena to dwell in when not present to my own mind. Professor Fraser, in several of his annotations, expresses the opinion that Berkeley did not mean, when a sensation comes back after an interval, that it is numerically the same, but only that it is the same in kind. But if the same only in kind, how can it require to be kept individually in existence during the interval? When the momentary sensation has passed away, the occurrence, after a time, of another and exactly similar sensation, does not imply any permanent object, mental any more than material, to keep up an identity which does not really exist. If Berkeley thought that what we feel is retained in actual, as distinguished from potential, existence, when we are no longer feeling it, he cannot have thought that it is nothing more than a sensation. And in truth, by giving it the ambiguous and misleading name Idea, he does leave an opening for supposing it to be more than a sensation. His Ideas, which he supposes to be what we perceive by our senses, are nothing different, and are not represented by him as anything different, from our sensations: he frequently uses the words as synonymous: yet he doubtless would have seen the absurdity of maintaining that the sensation of to-day can be really the same as the sensation of yesterday, but he saw no absurdity in affirming this of the idea. By means of this word he gives a kind of double existence to the objects of sense: they are, according to him, sensations, and contingencies, or permanent possibilities, of sensation, and yet they are also something else; they are our purely mental perceptions, and yet they are independent objects of perception as well; though immaterial, they exist detached from the individual mind which perceives them, and are laid up in the Divine Mind as a kind of repository, from which it almost seems that God must be supposed to detach them when it is his will to impress them on us, since Berkeley rejects the doctrine of Malebranche, that we actually contemplate them in the Divine Mind. This illogical side of Berkeley's theory was the part of it to which he himself attached the greatest value; and he would have been much grieved if he had foreseen the utter neglect of his favourite argument for Theism. For it was for this, above all, that he prized his immaterial theory. Indeed, the war against freethinkers was the leading purpose of Berkeley's career as a philosopher.

In the rest of the review, Mill focuses on other works included in the Fraser edition. He praises Berkeley's mastery of the dialogue form in *Alciphron*, calls *A Defence of Free-thinking in Mathematics* "one of the finest pieces of philosophic style in the English language," and has qualified praise for the *Querist*. When it comes to *Passive Obedience*, however, Mill, foremost of the classical (or, as is now said, "Act") Utilitarians, has harsh criticism for Berkeley's "exaggerated application of that cardinal doctrine of morality, the importance of general rules." He views Berkeley, to be sure, as "distinctly and absolutely an utilitarian," but a utilitarian "of Paley's sort, who believed that God's revealed Word is the safest guide to utility" – and, as other of his writings show, Mill had little liking for Paley. Nor does Mill share Fraser's enthusiasm for *Siris*. We will here say no more of Mill's views about these works, which fall outside the province of this volume, except to note that, for all his high regard for Berkeley, Mill does not fail to observe that Berkeley is sometimes unfair to those he opposes, especially to Mandeville, Shaftesbury, and the "free-thinkers", who are under attack in *Alciphron*, as well as to Hobbes and Spinoza. Berkeley, Mill believes, attacked " 'sceptics and atheists' without any authentic knowledge of their arguments; for few, if any, writers in his time avowed either scepticism or atheism."

* * *

Fraser's edition of Berkeley's works marked the beginning of a period, which continues to the present, that has seen a great proliferation of serious studies of every aspect of Berkeley's philosophy. It has also been a period in which admiration for Berkeley reached new heights, and in which it has not just been the idealists who have claimed him as an illustrious ancestor. When William James called Charles Sanders Peirce the founder of pragmatism, Peirce himself replied, "Berkeley on the whole has more right to be considered the introducer of pragmatism into philosophy than any other one man, though I was more explicit in enunciating it."[5] William James, too, counted Berkeley a progenitor of pragmatism: "Berkeley's criticism of 'matter' was . . . absolutely pragmatistic. Matter is known as our sensations of colour, figure, hardness and the like. They are the cash-value of the term."[6] Positivists also have seen in Berkeley a forerunner. Thus what is probably the best-known defense of logical positivism opened with the declaration, "The views which are put forward in this treatise derive from the doctrines of Bertrand Russell and Wittgenstein, which are themselves the logical outcome of the empiricism of Berkeley and David Hume."[7] It is yet a different Berkeley – Berkeley the common-sense realist – who emerges in the works of two of the leading Berkeley scholars of the twentieth century, A. A. Luce and T. E. Jessop, who also produced the magnificent edition of Berkeley's works that superseded Fraser's.[8] In the course of three centuries, therefore, Berkeley has been viewed as a Malebranchean, an egoist, a skeptic, an empiricist, an idealist, a pragmatist, a proto-positivist, and a common-sense realist. That he could be seen in such diverse lights suggests how rich and many-faceted his philosophy is.

Notes

1. See G. J. Warnock, *Berkeley* (Harmondsworth: Penguin Books, 1953), pp. 236–37. For a clear statement of Mill's position on "matter", see J. S. Mill, *An Examination of Sir William Hamilton's Philosophy* (New York: Henry Holt, 1873), vol. 1, chap. 11.
2. F. E. Sparshott, in *Collected Works of John Stuart Mill*, general editor J. M. Robson (Toronto: University of Toronto Press, 1963–91), vol. 11, p. xlvi. Mill's review, which first appeared in the *Fortnightly Review* (November 1871), is reprinted in the same volume, pp. 451–71. We have followed that text.
3. That Mill, for all his *indebtedness* to Berkeley, in this as in other areas, sees himself as having advanced well *beyond* Berkeley is indicated both here and by a footnote at the end of this paragraph: "This subject is more fully elucidated in Chap. xvii of [Mill's own] *An Examination of Sir William Hamilton's Philosophy* [London, 1865], and in the notes to the new edition of Mr. James Mill's *Analysis of the Human Mind* [2nd ed., edited by Mill, London, 1869.]"
4. In a similar spirit, Mill, in a footnote, criticizes Philonous's answer in the *Dialogues* (*Works* II, pp. 247–48) to the charge that, on Berkeley's principles, no two people can see the *same* thing. "Berkeley's usual acuteness has here deserted him; for it is evident that he misses the real double meaning of 'same' – that which is numerically identical, and that which is only exactly similar."
5. Peirce's letter to James of 23rd January 1903, in R. B. Perry, *The Thought and Character of William James* (Boston: Little, Brown, 1935), vol. 2, p. 425. Like Mill, Peirce wrote a long review of Fraser's edition of Berkeley's works; it appeared in *The North American Review*, October 1871, and is reprinted in *Collected Papers of Charles Sanders Peirce*, ed. C. Hartshorne, P. Weiss, and A. Burks (Cambridge: Harvard University Press, 1931–58), vol. 8, pp. 9–38.
6. William James, *Pragmatism, A New Name for Some Old Ways of Thinking* (London: Longmans, Green, 1907), pp. 89–90. (James dedicated this work to Mill, "our leader were he alive today.")
7. A. J. Ayer, *Language, Truth and Logic* (London: Victor Gollancz, 1936), p. 11. On Berkeley's anticipations of positivism, see Karl Popper, "A Note on Berkeley as Precursor of Mach and Einstein," in *Locke and Berkeley: A Collection of Critical Essays*, ed. C. B. Martin and D. M. Armstrong (Garden City: Anchor Books, 1968); John Myhill, "Berkeley's 'De Motu': An Anticipation of Mach," in *George Berkeley: Lectures delivered before the Philosophical Union of the University*

of California, ed. S. C. Pepper, K. Aschenbrenner, and B. Mates (Berkeley: University of California Press, 1957).

8. For an account and evaluation of the realist interpretation of Berkeley argued for by Luce and Jessop, see Harry M. Bracken, *The Early Reception of Berkeley's Immaterialism: 1710–1733*, revised edition (The Hague: Martinus Nijhoff, 1965), Appendix A: "Berkeley's Realisms". Since them, A. C. Grayling has argued that Berkeley is committed to a *form* of "realism", and that, "So far as the basic intuitions of common sense go, Berkeley would appear less an affronter of them than his competitors, and this remains true even at the level of theory, where Berkeley's results are no more *strange* than those arrived at by, say, contemporary physics." See A. C. Grayling, *Berkeley: The Central Arguments* (London: Duckworth, 1986), p. 22 and *passim*.

Index of Names

Index of Subjects